THE HERITAGE OF CHRISTIAN THOUGHT

ROBERT LOWRY CALHOUN

THE HERITAGE OF CHRISTIAN THOUGHT

ESSAYS IN HONOR OF ROBERT LOWRY CALHOUN

EDITED BY

Robert E. Cushman and Egil Grislis

HARPER & ROW, PUBLISHERS
NEW YORK, EVANSTON, AND LONDON

Grateful acknowledgment is made to the Duquesne University Press for permission to reprint "The Sense of Tradition in the Ante-Nicene Church," by Albert C. Outler, from *Journal of Ecumenical Studies,* Vol. I, No. 3, pp. 460–484.

FIRST EDITION

LIBRARY OF CONGRESS CATALOG CARD NUMBER: 65-15390

D-P

Contents

Preface

Robert Lowry Calhoun, Sterling Professor of Historical Theology in Yale University and Fellow of Saybrook College, retires at the end of the academic year 1965 after forty-one years of brilliant and influential teaching founded upon the highest standards of exacting scholarship and intellectual self-discipline. While for a quarter century or more Professor Calhoun annually taught a course in the history of philosophy with exciting verve and unfailing competence in Yale College, thereby contributing to the humane learning of undergraduates, his principal role was that of teacher of historical theology in Yale Divinity School from 1923 until now.

As a student and later a colleague of Douglas Clyde Macintosh, Professor Calhoun's theological rearing came in the period of the ascendancy of philosophy of religion in American theological studies, when the prevailing viewpoint was heavily weighted on the side of the sciences of religion and post-Kantian philosophy and theology. Professor Calhoun's distinctive contribution must be seen—and against this background—as a decision to re-explore older deposits of philosophical and Christian wisdom lying well beyond and behind the eighteenth- and nineteenth-century Kantian philosophical settlement.

In philosophy he returned to Greek wisdom, and in the history of doctrine, to the early Church fathers, the doctors of medieval Christianity, and the Reformation theologians. I express the judgment that, in this way, he made a quite distinctive contribution to the twentieth-century recovery of classical Christian thought in American Protestantism and at the same time enabled his students to see this theological inheritance against the background of the wisdom of the Greeks.

It does not in consequence suffice to say, however truly, that Professor Calhoun's stance tended to be that of Christian humanism in an authentic form—an inheritance of the best in Greek and Christian wisdom; it is more important to note that in the nineteen-thirties he opened a way for sympathetic rediscovery of classical Christian positions, both Catholic and Protestant. This not only prepared the ground for informed intellectual commerce with the then emergent neo-orthodox theology—which in those days liberal American religious thought was truly ill-prepared to receive or to measure—but provided norms for critical assessment of the new Continental theology as it broke in waves over the American theological scene.

On the strength of this rediscovery of the obscured deposit of historic Christian truth, Professor Calhoun was not only himself among the best equipped of American theologians to enter, as he did, the international ecumenical dialogue of the forties and fifties; he had at the same time afforded to his students the perspective, the tools, and the substance of learning needful to enter into responsible discussion with their counterparts in the world ecumenical movement. And this for many of them, both scholars and pastors, has been a most timely provision in fulfillment of the role that Providence has enforced as their theological and ecclesiastical vocation at mid-twentieth century and, seemingly, for the foreseeable future.

It is in deserved recognition of this timely and distinctive contribution which Professor Calhoun made to the intellectual vision of his students in a surpassingly effectual way, that the writers of this volume offer it in fitting tribute, affection, and enduring gratitude to him, their teacher.

With rigorous fidelity to the canons of sound historical scholarship, Professor Calhoun mightily helped doctrinally illiterate children of liberal American Christianity in the thirties and forties to recover a critical comprehension of the well-nigh unsearchable riches of inherited Christian wisdom. He demonstrates that the past is not only preface but preface indispensable to responsible existence in the present.

Professor Calhoun will continue to do this. In his more recent attention to the work of systematic theology, he has sought to illuminate contemporary dogmatic problems in the light of historic faith. Intellectual honesty he personifies. With him the canons of Aristotelian logic came, as it were, "built-in." As for historical evidences, they are assessed with scrupulous sobriety that often makes him the despair of his most aspiring students. Yet with all of this he mingles compassion for persons and unaffected concern for their largest well-being; and in his time he is known to have championed neglected issues and embattled causes.

We thank him; we thank him for a lifetime of unflagging and disciplined commitment, first of all, to God and the common life, then to the one Holy Catholic Church, to his students through forty-four years of teaching, and last of all, as the rubric has it, to Yale.

ROBERT E. CUSHMAN

Duke University Divinity School
February 1, 1965

A Biographical Sketch

Robert Lowry Calhoun, Sterling Professor of Historical Theology at Yale University, was born in 1896 in St. Cloud, Minnesota. He graduated from Carleton College in 1915, studied in 1919–20 at Oxford University, and at Yale University took a B.D. degree in 1918, an M.A. in 1919, and a Ph.D. in 1923. He received the D.D. degree from the University of Chicago in 1941, and from Oberlin in 1944, the LL.D. from Carleton in 1946, and the D.D. from Princeton in 1957.

He taught philosophy and education at Carleton College from 1921 to 1923, and in the fall of that year became a member of the faculty at the Yale Divinity School, where in 1942 he was appointed Pitkin Professor of Historical Theology. He was an exchange professor at the University of Amsterdam in 1952–53.

He has been special lecturer at Yale in 1934, Ohio Wesleyan University in 1935, Colgate Rochester Theological Seminary in 1937 and 1958, Princeton in 1938 and 1943, the Theological Seminary of the Reformed Churches in the United States and the Jewish Theological Seminary in 1940, the University of Virginia in 1941, the Pacific School of Religion in 1942, Harvard in 1943, Vanderbilt in 1944, the University of Chicago in 1947, the Columbia University Bi-Centennial Celebration in 1954, and Cornell University in 1958–59.

He is married to Ella Wakeman Calhoun, and they have four children, David, Edward, Robert Maurice, and Harriet Wrenn.

V. C.

THE HERITAGE OF CHRISTIAN THOUGHT

To Recall in Gratitude Robert Lowry Calhoun

VIRGINIA CORWIN
Charles N. Clark Professor of Religion and Biblical Literature
Smith College
Northampton, Massachusetts

Robert Lowry Calhoun to a rare degree has spoken to and for his generation. The unique quality of a human being eludes definition, and this is especially true of a man creative and strong enough to have exerted so wide an influence. But on an occasion when friends and former students have set themselves to celebrate his achievement and to hail the years ahead it is appropriate to recall in gratitude what so many have shared. The outward marks of distinction are apparent; the inward sources of strength must be intuited.

His most unfailing and appreciative audiences, made up year after year of the students of theology or philosophy at the Divinity School or at Yale College, know him as one of the great teachers. No student of his will forget the lucid lectures on the history of philosophy or of Christian doctrine that pour forth apparently without effort, unsupported by a single visible note. No student who has himself become a teacher can remember them without a stab of envy, unworthy but perhaps natural enough, for virtuosity of that sort is not achieved by many. But the response of the listener can only be one of keen pleasure. The thought of a man gone centuries ago—St. Augustine, for example, or Origen—takes shape before the mind, every essential detail in place if one looks for it carefully, but the line and structure of the whole dominate, and the part is held in true proportion. One can believe that meaning stands out with a clarity not known even by its original creator, hindered as he was by the circumstances of life from seeing his work from a distance, or seeing it completed.

This extraordinary effect of clarity is not achieved by sacrificing a man or his conceptions to a scheme of one's own. The hope of scholars, perhaps always elusive, must be, as Calhoun has said, "to watch the light illuminate the past as it has been, and not force on the past a pattern of their own choosing." Students know that they are watching a master teacher who is also an austerely honest historian, testing the theses of other scholars by reading the sources in their original language, by controlling the less well-known writings and personal letters, and making his independent report. He protests that he knows but little of the domain he traverses, yet the listener is not deceived. There are ranges beyond the ranges, to be sure, and no one can have trodden them all, but Calhoun has tracked over an amazing area and the profound learning is offered with disarming modesty.

In the lectures the dialogue of earlier generations can be heard; Aristotle takes issue with Plato, and the Nicene formulas are defended and argued down; or a whole age impelled by new interests or assumptions forces thought out into untraveled country. The unrelenting teacher asks similar excellence of understanding of his students, and by that outrageous expectation surprises them into doing better than their best. The pages of a formidable bibliography point out the way the scholar must go; in the student beginning the history of philosophy or the fledgling theologian the ruggedness of the road may evoke despair rather than determination, but, however haltingly, he sets forth. He will not lightly disappoint the expectations of a teacher of such faith. It is said that a Yale College class in the history of philosophy was once faced by the same examination that Calhoun had devised for the doctoral candidates. The results were no doubt to be judged by different standards, but that examination must have given the undergraduates a fearful jolt. Even if the story be legend its core is true; and the continuing popularity of a course making such awesome demands tells much about its teacher.

His students are grateful for more than the excellence of the lectures, and the masterly re-creation of the heritage of the past—of Plato, or the Church Fathers. An ill-defined question thrust into a lecture is treated with kindness beyond its deserts, rephrased and presented at its best before it is answered respectfully. The inquirer and the critic are welcomed and encouraged. In Calhoun's office, piled high with the evidence of reading for lectures just completed, or articles promised for the oppressively near future, a chair is cleared with a hospitable gesture, and time set aside for other uses is emptied with no shadow of hesitation. Ashes are knocked from the pipe, a match flares up, and an air of leisure settles into the room. The students across the years whose doctoral dissertations he has directed, and his friends and colleagues, have there availed themselves of his critical judgment and, perched uneasily beside piles of the sources, have entered into exploration of a complex problem of the past, or an urgent present concern. That generous and costly gift of time and friendship can never be forgotten.

An equally large audience has known him as teacher under less formal academic circumstances. For perhaps twenty-five summers he gave short courses at Hazen conferences or church gatherings, or at ministers' summer sessions, often at Union Theological Seminary. In the thirties the discussion of religion was apt to be dominated either by a bias for the contemporary and the scientific, or by denominational concerns. Calhoun's lectures on Christian doctrine were a thrust against both kinds of parochialism. The possession of an ampler sense of history made the present more significant and open. The men and women who heard him during those summers were helped "to find freedom in and from the past, freedom towards the still undiscovered future." Or he discussed the existence and nature of God—perennial questions sharpened by the humanist temper of those years. It was a job that not many could do, for it called for a fresh evaluation of imperfectly understood assumptions. Calhoun met the challenges honestly and sympathetically, for his interest in the truths discovered by scientists made him fully aware of their importance, but his critical mind refused to allow that the presuppositions of a narrow scientism or humanism were adequate. His own thought expressed a richer humanism, open not only to contemporary experience but to the insights of other ages, in philosophy and the long dialogue of Christianity. The title of his book *God and the Common Life* suggests precisely that humanism and in it one finds his conviction that knowledge of God is not a matter of rational proof alone, but must be grounded in the every day relations of person with person, and deep engagement with values that have a claim upon men.

By 1940 the issues were set by the evidences of dissolution in the western world, and the need to counter it. Calhoun entered fully into the new problems, and he played an active part in the work of the wider church that was coming into existence. Churchman, as well as teacher, he had already been speaking to the church beyond denominational lines, and also working wherever a denominational group such as the Social Action Committee of the Congregational Churches was wrestling with problems of justice in society. Then, and later in the fifties when he worked on the Commission on the Bases of Christian Social Action, he served both his denomination and the wider church. His ministry in the Congregational Churches has always been exercised for a congregation that could not be gathered together within four walls.

War destroyed peacetime ambiguities and forced Christians, like all men, to face the question of ultimate loyalty. Calhoun's answer was a strong pacifist protest—and this not because the pacifist way would guarantee peace, as some held, but because he saw war as absolutely antithetic to the love which must be the norm for life. Such a protest is doomed to be a minor note in the turmoil of a nation at war, but Calhoun turned to implement his belief in whatever ways were open. He worked for the conscientious objectors, and helped to devise ways in which they could offer service to the nation without violating the limits of conscience. They were painfully isolated in a country committed to war; but the fundamental problem was not a dispute between state and church, but a gnawing uncertainty within the church. The Federal Council of Churches called together a commission on the Relation of the Church to the War, made up both of Christian pacifists and of those who believed that the Christian might have to participate in war to oppose yet greater evil in society. Calhoun was chairman of it, and wrote its important statement on the Problem of War; later he served on a Commission of Christian Scholars to study the moral implications of atomic war. Neither report presents a decisive answer to the questions troubling the church, but each is notable for its honesty, and for the spirit of charity and respect which bound together men who disagreed on crucial issues. They express the growing Protestant conviction that when religion is true to its calling it must judge as well as sanction; neither pacifist nor nonpacifist accepted war as inevitable.

From 1937, when he joined the commission preparing for the Oxford Conference on Life and Work, Calhoun has been one of the most influential American theologians of the ecumenical movement. Within the emerging World Council of Churches he has participated in one after another of the groups that met for study of the practices and faith of the churches. In the thirties he was repeatedly invited to represent the American theological position that seemed to European theologians dangerously empirical and contemptuous of tradition. But his command of history and his innate catholicity of mind earned him a place that had little to do with his American origin. And he has rare talent for acting as catalyst in discussion. Anyone who has sat with him in the group, quaintly known decade after decade as the "Younger Theologians," knows his genius for bringing discussion out of an impasse by suggesting an aspect of thought somehow forgotten, or for cutting through semantic tangles by learned reference to history. Moreover, he has a disarming way of summarizing an argument so that while opposing views are fully recognized the clutter of the unessential is swept aside and fresh areas of common understanding emerge. The groups bringing into being the World Council of

Churches, effected at Amsterdam in 1948, were fortunate in being able to draw upon these skills.

As chairman of the North American section of the Theological Commission on the Church following the Lund Conference on Faith and Order of 1952, he helped to draft preliminary documents for the delegates to the Second Assembly at Evanston in 1954. He was significantly involved in hammering out the final form of the report, *Christ—the Hope of the World.* He has at once patient tolerance for opposing views, and unshakable trust that men will learn even from an alien truth when it is honestly unfolded. His own comment on Evanston is illuminating: "I should find an assembly as large and diverse as this, in which controversial affirmations were avoided, or in which they brought only acquiescence, a very depressing sort of gathering." His extraordinary powers of leadership were fully exercised at the Oberlin conference on Faith and Order in 1957 in developing the theme, "The Unity We Seek."

Although his gifts as philosopher and theologian have been so much in demand by his contemporaries that they have often competed with more narrowly academic pursuits, as well as practical Christian ethical concerns, Calhoun surrendered neither. His work for the conscientious objectors during the War was an example, and we should place with this his service as national vice-president of the American Association of University Professors during the critical years of the McCarthy controversy. It is characteristic of him to protest sharply when he senses injustice or believes that men who hold unpopular truths are being silenced or endangered. Again and again he has raised his voice in defense of a democratic and just society.

In the middle of the century the view has become widely influential that for modern men Christianity can rest only on faith; all else is a construct of the human mind, ideology, and subject to the fashions of cultural change. Calhoun has been deeply critical of this tendency, and, whatever that much maligned word may mean, he continues to be the exponent of a "liberal" theology, though if his kind of liberalism had been more widely understood the word might have had a different history in our time. His position has altered, but not its main substance or underlying temper. For him radical fideism is an oversimplification—a one-sided statement of truth; he sees no ultimate contradiction between faith and reason. Plato's thought is congenial to him, and reason, seen as the exercise of disciplined thought, still commends itself as the best tool man has. It may not be as pure as the Greeks would have it, but neither is it identical with the assumptions of a culture. Not all insights can be fitted neatly together; stubbornly individualistic facts proclaim truth not yet domesticated. But he will not enthrone paradox as final. Though he cannot deny its existence, he treats it not as an ultimate discontinuity, but a sign that a new and more inclusive approach is needed.

As a critic of the antirational tendencies of our day Calhoun has an influential place as an interpreter of Christianity and religious philosophy for the many who stand uneasily on the edges of religious faith and for whom the exclusive claims of faith seem dangerously obscurantist. He has lectured widely in university circles on religion among the humanities, on religion and natural law, and on several aspects of religious knowledge, always diligently exploring the language of religion or the complementary work of reason and revelation. He holds that critical reason and profound faith are both necessary to the man who would try to understand the world and live responsibly in it. It may yet be that, when the extremes of fideism and of positivism that are perhaps overpersuasive in our day, have somewhat spent their force, the searching and tempered rationalism of Calhoun's critical religious realism will be seen to speak a deeper wisdom.

These are rare qualities of heart and mind that we have recalled, yet they suggest only the part of life that is at least half open to the discerning view. Behind it a rich personal life has supported intellectual and religious endeavor. Much of this lies locked in reticence, but one source of strength and delight is shared generously. Friends scattered across the world remember the good conversation, or the voices of great music, while afternoon sunlight floods the old house in Bethany. Not all philosophers have found so frank a pleasure in the earthy side of life: the savor of good food, the absolute promises of seed catalogues, minor experiments in chicken farming, or the joy of picking Red Astrakhans in a hot August noon. Sometimes these interests, or the frustrations incident to building a phonograph speaker, have contrived stealthy competition with the lectures and articles that waited to be written, but that is not their final importance. They have always provided a necessary link with the common life—the satisfaction of skillful work which can be recognized and respected by all men. The intellectual who does not know the compensation of working with his hands is the poorer. The philosopher must envision the general and the universal, but he may not ignore the stubborn and absorbing particulars of life. The theologian must keep his perspective in a world which is at once God's creation and the place where men estranged by egotism are still drawn to live with each other in justice and compassion. As both theologian and philosopher, Calhoun can speak to his generation of ultimate concerns, because he knows the elemental experiences common to men. His essay on Eliot's *Four Quartets* reveals a personal knowledge of the strange interrelations of suffering and faith. They are words of honesty and reassurance: "Only by finding ourselves taken up into the suffering of all mankind are we made able to look beyond the suffering, and to sense meaning in this common fate and terror—a meaning which only a saint who lives in the timeless moment . . . can really apprehend. But even we 'Who are only undefeated Because we have gone on trying' can at least from time to time be led to glimpse it."

The Sense of Tradition in the Ante-Nicene Church

ALBERT C. OUTLER
Professor of Theology
Perkins School of Theology
Southern Methodist University
Dallas, Texas

The Christian Church originated in an act of divine traditioning (*actus tradendi*) at Pentecost—when the apostolic memories were finally transformed into the apostolic kerygma and the loyalties of the disciples of Jesus of Nazareth were transmuted into their faith "that God has made this Jesus . . . both Lord and Messiah."[1] Since that day, the survival of the Church has depended, always at least in part, on the traditionary process by which its time in the world has been prolonged. Tradition, both as act and process, constitutes both the source and the method by which Christians, since Pentecost, have been enabled to know and to respond to the revelation of God in Christ.

It was altogether natural that, in the beginning, this traditionary process was oral. It shaped up and took form in a society where memory served largely in the place of manuscript, where the Old Testament was the only "Scripture" in the Church, and where the occasions which called forth the earliest Christian writings were chiefly pastoral and propaedeutic. They were, in effect, the written word in the stead of the apostolic presence. Acts 6 reflects an early crisis in which it was determined that the chief business of the leaders in the Christian community was "prayer and the service of the Word" (6:4). This *diakonia tou logou* implies a continuing effort of rehearsing and fixing the meaning of the oral tradition in the absence of an authoritative text or canon.[2]

[1] Acts 2:36.
[2] Cf. Birger Gerhardsson, *Memory and Manuscript: Oral Tradition and Written Transmission in Rabbinic Judaism and Early Christianity* (Uppsala, 1961), 231–261.

Thus the traditionary process is coeval with the historical origins of the Christian community. Even when the Christian Scriptures were produced, and finally recognized as such, there was still an urgent need in the Church for an authoritative *magisterium,* by which the apostolic message in the Scriptures might find vital expression in the spoken word and in Christian nurture. Tradition was the dynamic medium of the kerygma; the kerygma was the veritable essence of the tradition; and it seems to have occurred to no one except the heretics to conceive of a radical discrepancy between the two. Indeed, one may define a heretic as one who failed to recognize the consilience between the written and oral tradition of the Church. More than any other single factor, it was the staying power of tradition that sustained the Church in her long agony and anomaly in the Graeco-Roman world—and especially in her experience as *religio illicita.*

One can hardly exaggerate the tensions thrust upon the Church in the course of her transplantation from her original setting into her Gentile environment in the second century. Seceded from its Jewish matrix, with its early eschatological expectations knocked askew—lacking a creed, a canon, a fixed liturgy, or even a developed leadership—the Christianity of the second century had still to attempt the business of traditioning both the message and the *koinonia* of an upstart religion which still bore the marks of its Jewish background—and all of this in a most unlikely atmosphere. The wonder is not that they did not do it as well as a modern Protestant might demand[3] but that they managed it as well as they did. There was no time in the second century when the odds were not better than even that Christianity would simply disintegrate under the twin pressures of doctrinal confusion and social disfavor.

Yet in the small budget of Christian writing that has survived from this period, there is a strange sense of solid confidence in the Church's survival in history, and its authority to deal with a ceaseless round of crises and tumults. The Petrine images of "a chosen race, a royal priesthood, a dedicated nation, and a people claimed by God for his own, to proclaim the triumph of him who has called [them] out of darkness into his marvelous light"[4] were vividly held before the Christian mind. Their leaders were traditioners—trust officers of the Christian treasure of truth, qualified judges of "right teaching." They had a sense of tradition—an intuition of the active presence of the Holy Spirit as resident governor in the community, as celebrant of its holy mysteries, as guarantor of its destiny. As a consequence, they felt capable of

[3] Cf. doctrinaire judgments on this point in Thomas F. Torrance, *The Doctrine of Grace in the Apostolic Fathers* (Edinburgh: Oliver & Boyd, 1948), and Samuel Laeuchli, *The Language of Faith* (New York and Nashville: Abingdon, 1962).

[4] I Pet. 2:9.

dealing with the challenges of heresy and schism long before there were fixed *dogmata* which defined heresy precisely. This was possible because they believed they could identify the Christian tradition, in either its oral or written form, and also differentiate it from all aberrations of it.[5] This gave them a sense of freedom in the Spirit to interpret the Christ-Event in new circumstances and contexts, as these unfolded in a history that kept on happening. When, finally, the Church was more fully furnished with canon, creeds, and polity, many Christians realized that it was tradition that had ministered to them in their survival—and that one of its chief ministrations had been the depositing of the apostolic tradition in the New Testament and the binding of the Church to this as touchstone.

In the so-called "Apostolic Fathers," the sense of tradition is omnipresent but nowhere explicated as a formal theory. These men assume the traditionary process rather than argue for it. Their norms of authority regularly rest upon the apostolic teachings and also some sort of traditional interpretation of those teachings. The kerygma proclaimed the saving power of God in the history of Jesus of Nazareth. Both history and kerygma were perpetuated in history by tradition and, together, are to be traditioned to others, always in faithful obedience to the original *traditum*—i.e., God's own self-giving in Christ, in which he did "not withhold his own Son but *traditioned* Him for us all. . . ."[6]

The Christian writers of this transitional period find it easy to think of God's revelation as manifested, in equal validity, in the written Old Testament, in the Christian oral tradition, and in those Christian writings which had already begun to be identified as decisive traditioners of the apostolic tradition.[7]

---

[5] Cf. Dionysius of Alexandria in Eusebius, *The Ecclesiastical History,* VII, 7 (trans. by Hugh H. Lawlor and John E. D. Oulton, London: S.P.C.K., 1927), I, 221: "And in the third of those on baptism, which the same Dionysius wrote to Philemon the Roman presbyter, he related the following: 'But as for me, I read both the compositions and the traditions of the heretics, polluting my soul for a little with their abominable thoughts, yet all the while deriving this advantage from them, that I could refute them for myself and loathed them far more. And indeed a certain brother, one of the presbyters, attempted to dissuade and frighten me from becoming involved in the mire of their wickedness, for he said that I should injure my own soul; and said truly, as I perceived. But a vision sent by God came and strengthened me, and a word of command was given me, saying expressly: "Read all things that may come to thy hand. For thou art able to sift and *prove* each matter; which thing was originally the cause of thy faith." I accepted the vision, as agreeing with the apostolic saying addressed to the stronger: "Be approved money-changers." ' "

[6] Cf. Rom. 8:32. See also Rom. 4:25, I Cor. 11:23, Gal. 2:20, Eph. 5:2, all instances of the use of *paradidonai* to denote God's original traditioning of Jesus Christ for the redemption of mankind.

[7] Cf. E. Flesseman-Van Leer, *Tradition and Scripture in the Early Church* (Assen: Van Gorcum, 1954), 66 f.

Ignatius is an interesting instance of this pastoral understanding of tradition. Journeying from Antioch to Rome, he is rejoiced to discover that the Christians of Smyrna, Ephesus, and Philadelphia hold to the same basic faith as his own Antiochene tradition.[8] This consensus in tradition was not surprising (he says) since the bishops, who are the chief agents of the tradition, obtained their ministerial office in the *koinonia* "not by nor for themselves, nor through men, nor through vanity, but by the love of God the Father and the Lord Jesus Christ."[9] Thus, in a coined phrase, he says, "wherever Jesus Christ is, there is the whole *ekklesia katholika*."[10]

The mark of the good *episkopos* is his zeal and effectiveness in transmitting the original witness to Jesus Christ to people who must hear it from him. In Ignatius' eyes, this justifies his strong emphasis upon the close communion of bishop and people. The bishop is the principal traditioner of the apostolic tradition. As such, he serves as the chief force for unity in the congregation. "As many as are of God and of Jesus Christ are also with the bishop."[11] "For there is one flesh of our Lord Jesus Christ and one cup in token of union in his blood, one altar, as well as one bishop with the board of elders and the deacons—my fellow servants—to the end that whatever is done is in accordance with the will of God."[12] Yet, not even the bishop is indispensable, as in Ignatius' own case, now removed from his flock in Antioch. But since they have God for their pastor and Jesus Christ for their divine *episkopos,* they will be held together.[13]

Ignatius clearly depends upon the traditionary process both to insure the continuity of the Church and also to guard the Christian message from distortion and heresy. His well-known kerygmatic summaries, in *Trallians* ix, and *Smyrnaeans* i and xii, are striking examples of pastoral theologizing. In *Philadelphians,* he is even more explicit:

> I take refuge in the Gospel which, to me, is Jesus-in-the-flesh. And I also rest back upon the Apostles, as represented by the continuing presbytery of the Church. Let us also cherish the Prophets, because they foreshadowed the Gospel. They hoped in him [Jesus] and waited for him and were saved by their faith in him—and thus they were one with him [Jesus Christ]. Their message is part and parcel of the Gospel of our common hope. . . .[14]

---

8 Cf. Edgar J. Goodspeed, *The Apostolic Fathers* (New York: Harper, 1950), 207–235.

9 *Philadelphians* 1:1.

10 *Smyrneans* 8:2.

11 *Philadelphians* 3:2.

12 *Ibid.,* 4:1.

13 Rom. 9:1.

14 *Philadelphians* 5:1 f.

And, again:

> The priests are good, but the High Priest is better . . . ; he is the door of the Father, through whom Abraham and Isaac and Jacob and the prophets and the Apostles and the Church all enter. All these contribute to union with God. But the Gospel has something unique—the coming of the Savior, our Lord Jesus Christ, his passion and his resurrection. . . . The Gospel is the imperishable fulfillment [of the prophetic expectation]. . . .
>
> I also trust in the grace of Jesus Christ, who will free you from all bondage. Thus I can exhort you not to act in a partisan spirit, but to follow what you have learned in the school of Christ. When I heard someone say: "What I do not find in the official archives, that I do not regard as belonging to the Gospel" and when I answered them, "It is in the Scriptures," they retorted, "But that is just the question." But *my* "official archives" are Jesus Christ himself; the incontestable records are his cross and death, his resurrection and faith through him; on these I rely for justification, thanks also to your prayers.[15]

For Ignatius, *the* Christian tradition *is* Jesus Christ. The traditionary process in the Church functions validly only in so far as she is faithful to *this* Tradition in her various acts of traditioning.

The other "Apostolic Fathers" are in general agreement here with Ignatius; or more precisely, none is in explicit disagreement, so far as we know. The evidence suggests the conclusion that they also understood both the content and authority of Christian teaching to be derived from God's self-revelation in Jesus Christ and renewed in successive generations by the *actus tradendi* in the Church. Their reliance on this communication with the apostolic community enabled them to speak of Jesus' teachings and mission as the historical preface to their faith in him as "both Lord and Christ." Though far inferior to Ignatius in their total grasp of the Christian message, they nevertheless agree with him that the catholicity of the Church is a function of her continuity in and through succeeding time.

By mid-century or thereabouts, the sense of tradition has begun to acquire a fixed focus in a sort of proto-canon of definitive Christian writings. This was not the result of a formal decision in the Church. Justin Martyr, for example, nowhere refers to the Christian literature he cites as "sacred" or even as "Scripture." Only once does he use the traditional lemma—"It is written"—as a preface to a quotation.[16] In the course of his writings, he invokes, as authoritative, texts from all four Gospels (clearly preferring Matthew above the others), from Acts, Romans, I Corinthians, Galatians, II Thessalonians, Hebrews, I and II Peter, and the Apocalypse.

---

[15] *Ibid.*, 9:1 f., 8:1 f.

[16] *Dialogue,* 49:5; cf. Mt. 17:13.

It is a plausible guess that Justin had these texts before him in written form. It is even possible that he had them in some sort of anthology of Christian writings. What matters, however, is the way in which he quotes Old and New Testament texts *together,* and without differentiation as to their authority;[17] nor does he indicate any distinction between written texts and oral sayings. In Justin's view, God's active *Logos* had always been present in human history—*asarkos* in the Old Testament; *ensarkos* in Jesus Christ.[18] Only the Christians have the clue to an understanding of the universal *Logos*—since it is only in the light of the *incarnate Logos* that the eyes of faith see what the Old Testament really means in reference to Christ.[19] Construed in *this* light, both the Old Testament and the Christian tradition communicate their essentially identical message without contradiction. Justin is much impressed by the consilience of these two sources of revelation.[20]

Justin defines the Christian as a man who has undertaken "to follow God and the teachings traditioned by him" (through the apostolic tradition).[21] This fixes the boundary between orthodoxy and heresy, since the heretic feels free to amend or reject the Christian past. On the other hand, the true believer recognizes that his new relation to God in Christ is a replication of the original tradition, in which God came into human history with saving power.[22] Jesus Christ is the Christian's *didagma;*[23] he is the sum and substance of the Christian message.[24]

Justin nowhere uses the noun *paradosis.* But verbal forms of *paradidonai* occur at least ten times in his writings; in each instance they refer to some initiative of Jesus, looking toward the perpetuation of the Christian tradition.[25] Thus Justin understands Jesus' choice of twelve apostles.[26] It is their traditioning of the original tradition that has become the gist of the message which is now to be traditioned in a later age.[27] Justin does not profess to know precisely how the Christian tradition is rightly traditioned from the Christian past to the Christian future. Yet he assumes, without apparent hesitation, the competence of the Christian community in its receiving, main-

---

[17] *Apol.* I 23:1, 48:4, 59:1; *Dial.* 75:3.

[18] *Apol.* I 63:14; *Dial.* 19:6, 63:1 f., 68:5, 141:2.

[19] *Apol.* I 31:5, 36:3; *Dial.* 9:1, 14:2, 29:2, 34:1, 55:3; cf. *Apol.* I 32:2, 50:12; *Dial.* 76:6, 100:2.

[20] *Dial.* 65:2–3, 92:1; cf. 30:1, 119:1, 58:1.

[21] *Dial.* 80:3.

[22] *Apol.* I 14:1, 12:9, 14:5.

[23] *Apol.* I 14:4, 16:8, 17:2; *Apol.* II 2:2, 3:3, 13:2; *Dial.* 35:2, 48:4, 49:3, 69:7, 134:1.

[24] *Apol.* I 40:1, 53:2; *Apol.* II 2:13; *Dial.* 35:8.

[25] *Apol.* I 66:1; *Dial.* 41:1, 49:3, 53:6, 69:7, 70:4 (twice), 117:1.

[26] *Apol.* I 39:3, 50:12.

[27] *Dial.* 53:1, *Apol.* I 42:4, 53:3, 61:9, 66:13, 49:5.

taining, and traditioning of the Christian message. This is derived from its character as a charismatic fellowship, guarded from essential error by the power of its resident governor, the Holy Spirit.

In Justin (and in his fellow "Apologists") there is an atmosphere of implicit reliance upon the *consensus fidelium,* as this is maintained in Christian teaching and worship in the various outposts of the Church in the Graeco-Roman world. This seems natural enough if we realize that these "apologies" of Christianity in this period were very much more concerned with bolstering the morale of the Christians than with converting the Roman officials to whom they were ostensibly addressed.

With Irenaeus and Tertullian, however, we come into a significantly new situation, where the greater danger to the Christian tradition comes from heretics rather than from the persecutors. It is in the refutation of heresy that there emerges for the first time, and in two churchmen of strikingly different temperaments, an explicit doctrine of tradition and Scripture as *twin-touchstones* of Christian teaching and traditioning. In the face of the proliferations and distortions of heretical traditions (the heretics, of course, had *their* traditions, oral and written) the Church had to define the apostolic tradition and its continuity in Scripture and the Church.

Although domesticated in the West, Irenaeus is clearly a spokesman for eastern Christianity—a man who consciously places himself in the Ephesine succession. Of all the theologians of his century, his was the most vivid and intelligible sense of the continuity of the *koinonia* since Pentecost. From this came his confidence that the Church in so remote a time as his still had access to the original revelation of God in Christ—and with it, the power and duty to continue the traditioning of *this* revelation in the time to come. *Paradosis* and *kerygma* are very nearly equivalent terms for Irenaeus.[28] What is more, *paradosis* (and its Latin equivalent *traditio*) is regularly used in the singular. In Irenaeus' mind, this *paradosis* is not an esoteric supplement to the public preaching of the apostles. It is, rather, the apostolic kerygma for later times and other audiences. Irenaeus' highly original notion of *anakephalaiosis* is yet another way of expounding the original message, another exercise in the *agon* of the Christian mind with misunderstanding or ununderstanding.

Thus, for Irenaeus, tradition is the Christian message as it has been received, renewed, and transmitted in and by the Church.[29] This includes both tradition as object (*depositum fidei*) and tradition as process (*actus tradendi*).[30] How-

---

[28] Cf. *Adv. Haer.* III 3:2–3.
[29] Cf. *Adv. Haer.* V, *praef.;* III, 4:1.
[30] Cf. August Deneffe, *Der Traditionsbegriff* (Münster: Aschendorff, 1931), 22.

ever, he never supposes that the teaching *magisterium* in the Church controls the tradition of which she is trustee. The Church's teaching at any given time is bound to concur with the essentials of the Christian tradition in all time because, says Irenaeus, God's revelation is undivided and the Church's present teachers stand in uninterrupted succession to the apostles.[31] This succession belongs to the right ordering of the Church.[32] Its real importance, however, rests in its function as guarantee and medium of the ongoing task of guarding and securing the Christian tradition in the Church in history.[33]

To illustrate this point, Irenaeus gives us a list of the bishops of Rome, without indicating his source of information.[34] In this, the apostles Peter and Paul are reckoned as co-founders and first bishops of Rome. They, in turn, "handed over" the episcopal office to Linus. It is clear, in the context, that Linus was not made an "apostle" but a traditioner of the apostolic tradition.[35] This would seem to say that Linus was commissioned to receive and transmit the apostolic message, not as an apostle but as a traditioner. Thereafter, says Irenaeus, Linus' successors, in known and unbroken line, "have held the legacy of the episcopate." Through this succession—at Rome and elsewhere—"the ecclesiastical tradition and the apostolic preaching have come down to us." In this passage—as elsewhere—the pre-eminence of Rome among the churches is acknowledged—although the notion of the Roman bishop having a *monarchical* primacy seems never to have occurred to Irenaeus.

The bishops are guarded in their guardianship of the apostolic tradition by the power of the Holy Spirit. They are, therefore, the *charismatici* in the Church.[36] There is a *charisma veritas certum* that goes with the office. But the bishops are representatives of the Church as a whole—for it is the Church *as a whole* (*katholika*) that is the medium of the tradition. The Church's true life comes from the life of the Spirit in her midst:

> The preaching of the Church is everywhere consistent, and continues in an even course, and receives testimony from the prophets, apostles and disciples. . . . It is a part of the whole dispensation of God which tends to man's salvation. . . . Having received this preaching from the Church, we preserve it as the Spirit of God renews its youth. For this gift of God

---

[31] Of *episkopoi* or *presbuteroi*, as Irenaeus calls them, without any decisive distinction; cf. *Adv. Haer.* III, 2:2, and 3:1—see also the hendiadys in III, 14:2.

[32] Cf. the notoriously difficult passage in *Adv. Haer.* IV, 33:1–8.

[33] Cf. E. Molland, "Irenaeus of Lugdunum and the Apostolic Succession," *The Journal of Ecclesiastical History*, I (1950), No. 1, 18–20.

[34] *Adv. Haer.* III, 3:3.

[35] *Ibid.*, III, 3:2: *in apostolis Petro et Paulo Roma fundatae et constitutae Ecclesiae, eam quam habebat ab apostolis traditionem.*

[36] *Adv. Haer.* III, 38:1, 18:1; IV, 58:2, 42:1, 40:2.

> (i.e., the apostolic preaching) has been entrusted to the Church, as breath was entrusted to the first man, so that all members receiving it may become alive. . . . The Holy Spirit is the bond of communion which Christ has given to the Church. He is the foretaste of incorruption, the confirmer of our faith, the ladder of ascent to God. . . . For where the Church is, there is the Spirit of God; and where the Spirit of God is, there is the Church, and all grace—for the Spirit is truth. . . .[37]

Possessing the gifts of the Spirit is not equivalent to possessing the power of the Spirit in any magical or thaumaturgical sense. Irenaeus much prefers to stress the witness of the Spirit in the Church as the source of her courage to go on with her task of traditioning, even in the midst of perils, as the ages come and go.

The content of Christian truth, known in the Church, is expressed from time to time in summary form, in what Irenaeus calls the *regula veritatis*.[38] This "rule" is a base line for appraising Christian teaching, including the interpretation of the Scriptures. Irenaeus is well aware that both Scripture texts and oral commentary—and even Homeric verses!—have to be interpreted; and that they are bound to be misinterpreted by people who lack the authentic apostolic traditions.[39] The *regula veritatis* is this right rule of Scripture hermeneutics. This is true because its content is virtually equivalent to that of the apostolic kerygma. What is different is that the *regulae* are *propaedeutic* in form and function. Thus, the rule of truth becomes a sort of canon of the revelation deposited in Scripture.[40]

The apostolic tradition has been transmitted through the episcopate and the Church. It has also been committed to writing. From these writings (Old Testament *and* New Testament, without a clear distinction) we have a *depositum* (a fixed testimony) of the original apostolic tradition. Concurrently, however, there is the *living* witness of the oral tradition in the Church (bishops and doctors) which is, or must be, consilient with the *fixed* witness, if it is to be authentic. Together, the fixed *and* living traditions and traditioners provide the Church with her requisite catechetical instruction and her defense against the heretics. But this tradition can be properly understood only in the Church—because in the Church is the community in which the succession of bishops and teachers verifies the identity of the Christian message from one age to the next. Scripture governs the Church which produced it.[41]

Irenaeus knows and uses a fixed and definite canon of New Testament

[37] *Adv. Haer.* III, 24:1.
[38] *Adv. Haer.* I, 10:1; III, 4:2; V, 17, 18, 20; cf. *Proof of the Apostolic Preaching,* 3.
[39] *Adv. Haer.* I, 9:1 f.
[40] *Adv. Haer.* III, 11:7 (11:1), 12:7 (12:1).
[41] *Adv. Haer.* IV, 42:1 (26:5); V, 20:2 (20:2).

writing.[42] He quotes from every book in the official New Testament except Philemon and III John—and adds no other Christian writings to his canon of authorized books. Yet he nowhere refers to an official action of the Church in selecting its canon. This, too, belongs to the traditionary process: Irenaeus takes the New Testament for granted because it belonged to the tradition he had received.

It is only as we recognize the unity of Scripture—by acknowledging Jesus Christ as its center—that we can begin to understand the meaning of its various parts. If, however, a person denies the unity of the Scriptures—or the centrality of Christ within Scripture—the interpretation of Scripture can only be arbitrary and notional. This is what makes men heretics and what makes heresy so grievous an error.[43]

The *Schallwort* of Scripture is God's redemptive action in Christ. The Church understands this; hence, she is prepared to interpret Scripture in an authentic way.[44] The Church's authority to interpret Scripture does not alter the fact that the Church is bound to the Scripture she interprets. The kerygmatic tradition and the hermeneutical tradition are identical in ultimate reference—and thus confirm and strengthen each other.

The fatal error of the heretics is that they ignore or repudiate the essential message of Scripture. This revelation centers in the Christ-Event, in which all divine revelations are revealed in their true significance. Because the Church understands the Christocentric character of both Scripture and tradition, she is enabled to guide the traditionary process reliably. It is here that Irenaeus' notion of the consilience of Scripture and tradition becomes clearest. Scripture is the locus of the revelation of revelations. Tradition is the process in the Church by which this revelation is renewed in the time of the Church.

Irenaeus was forced to such conclusions by the bland denials, on the part of the Gnostics, of this vital consilience of Scripture and tradition.[45] In Book III of the *Adversus Haereses,* he undertakes to demonstrate the integrity of Scripture and tradition and to show how the written tradition preserves the oral tradition from deviation in later ages.[46]

Because of their conviction that they had come upon a truth superior to Scripture, the Gnostics felt free, as Irenaeus says, to ignore or misinterpret Scripture. In this way they set a new tradition in place of the old. It is against

---

[42] *Adv. Haer.* V, 30:1 (30:1); I, 25:2 (27:3); III, 11:10 (11:7); there was, of course, no problem in connection with the canon of the Old Testament.

[43] *Adv. Haer.* I, 1:15 (8:1); I, 1:20 (9:4).

[44] *Adv. Haer.* II, 41:2 (28:1); 40:2 (27:2); V, 20:2 (20:2).

[45] *Adv. Haer.* III, 2:1.

[46] *Cf. Adv. Haer.* III, *praef.;* III, 5:1.

this that Irenaeus argues that a new tradition (not consilient with Scripture) is false in the very nature of the case:

> . . . the teaching of the church is unconditionally true because it is the revelation embodied in the apostolic tradition; this fact is the integral, formal proof of its absolute faithfulness. If Irenaeus wants to prove the truth of a doctrine materially, he turns to scripture, because therein the teaching of the apostles is objectively accessible. Proof from tradition and from scripture serve one and the same end: to identify the teaching of the church as the original apostolic teaching. The first establishes that the teaching of the church is this apostolic teaching and the second, what this apostolic teaching is.[47]

In Tertullian of Carthage, Latin Christianity emerges as a distinctive new type in the Christian community. This vivid, eccentric man gave the Church in the West a stronger feeling for tradition than she had ever had before.[48] His thought begins and ends—as did Irenaeus'—with the actuality of Jesus Christ as the original and originative *traditum,* to which all Christian truth is related in the Church through the tradition. The apostolic witness is our access to the primordial *traditio.* Tertullian, therefore, introduces the crucial distinction between *traditio* as the constitution of the Church and *traditiones* as those interpretations and customs which the Church has come to cherish but which are not vital to saving faith. *Traditio* is the kerygma and the Church's rule of faith derives from it.[49] *Traditiones* are historical developments.[50]

The verb forms of *tradere,* in Tertullian, normally denote the act of traditioning, whether from God to man in Christ, or from man to man through the Spirit in the Church.[51] In his treatise *On Prayer,* he speaks of Jesus as having traditioned the art of praying to his disciples;[52] in the *Prescription,* Jesus is said to have traditioned to them the original message.[53] Four other verbal usages in this essay refer to the traditionary action of the apostles.[54] Elsewhere he speaks of the production of the Christian Scriptures as an act of tradition suited to the needs of subsequent generations.[55]

---

[47] E. Flesseman-Van Leer, *op. cit.,* 144.

[48] For his most important single text on this question, cf. *De Praescriptione Haereticorum.*

[49] *De praescr.* 21, 22.

[50] *De praescr.* 19; *De bapt.* 1; *De corona* 3 (four times); 4 (six times); *De jejun.* 10:13 (twice); *De pudicitia* 1; *De praescr.* 19; *De pud.* 1; Tertullian understands that where we have traditions, we are then dealing in matters of importance but neither ultimate nor authoritative.

[51] *De test. animae* 5—*a deo traditum est.*

[52] *De oratione* 10.

[53] *De praescr.* 44.

[54] *De praescr.* 22, 28; *cf. Adv. Marc.* IV, 5 (twice).

[55] *Adv. Hermog.* 45.

For Tertullian, the tradition and the Church are dynamic reciprocals in the historical process. The original churches are apostolic foundations and continue as the trustees and bearers of the apostolic tradition. This is not through an uninterrupted succession of bishops but by means of the traditionary witness in the churches. In two instances,[56] Tertullian alludes to episcopal succession as a guarantee of apostolicity, but, generally speaking, his real stress falls on the importance of the succession of the apostolic doctrine.

One of the impulses that drove him into the atypical Montanism that he adopted[57] was his strong feeling that the Roman church had lost its sense of the Holy Spirit's immanent residency in and governorship of the Christian community. In the *De pudicitia* (ca. 217) he pushes the relation of Church and Spirit to the point of virtual identity: "The Church itself, in its proper and primary sense, *is* the Spirit."[58] Tertullian's pneumatology varies in exposition and accent in his various works but he never wavers about the notion that the power which transforms tradition and hearsay into living faith is the Holy Spirit. Moreover, it is the Spirit who illumines the Scriptures to the understanding of the faithful.[59] Even as a Montanist, Tertullian never contended that the "new gifts" of the Paraclete actually superseded the authority of Scripture and tradition. Their principal value had to do with the matter of Christian *discipline* in a new age. Thus the deposit of revelation in Scripture, its re-presentation in tradition, and its inner application by the Spirit are consilient, even if they are not identical in all details. The Spirit's function is to make all of them serve the purpose of presenting Jesus Christ to men in later ages, so as to evoke the response of faith in him.

One of the most important conservative functions of *traditio constitutiva* is to prompt the formulation and re-formulation of *regulae fidei* by the successive teachers of the Church. Tertullian is more interested in this business of the rule and of rule-making than any other Christian writer in the ante-Nicene Church. He uses the phrase more than seventy times and is fond of elaborating its meaning in various ways. The *regulae* are not declaratory creeds nor liturgical confessions; they are not summations of the oral tradition; they are not amendments of, nor supplements to, Scripture.[60] Tertullian distinguishes explicitly between *traditio scripta* and *traditio non scripta,*[61] but

---

[56] Cf. *De praescr.* 32, and also *Adv. Marc.* IV, 5.

[57] Actually quite different from the speculative heresies described and denounced by Hippolytus in the *Refutation,* Book VII, chap. 12, Book X, chap. 21–22.

[58] *De pudicitia,* 21.

[59] Cf. *De Resurrectione* 63 and *De Virg. Vel.,* chap. 1.

[60] Cf. *De praescr.* 44. But see H. E. W. Turner, *The Pattern of Christian Truth* (London, Mowbray: 1954), 352–378, and Reinhold Seeberg, *Dogmengeschichte,* 4th ed. (Graz: Akademische Druck-und Verlaganstalt, 1953), I, 377. By contrast, cf. E. Flesseman-Van Leer, *op. cit.,* 161–173.

[61] *De corona* 3.

the latter, in those contexts not referring to the oral counterpart of the Scripture text, has the typical force of *consuetudines*—established and valued customs in the churches.[62]

The positive uses of the *regulae* have to do with their propaedeutic functions of interpreting the gist of Scripture in the light of the traditions of a given local or regional community. It is, as Tertullian says, "a guidepost to lead men in the way of becoming Christians."[63] In a given *regula,* a catechetical teacher marks out for himself and for his pupils the successive borders of the truth that is certain, of speculation that is allowable, and of heresy. These distinctions are crucial in Christian education if the faith that is taught is to become the faith that is truly believed.

Another aspect of Tertullian's sense of tradition may be seen in his concept of the "prescription" of the heretics. This amounts to a judicial ruling of the heretics out of court—the court of Scripture—since they have no right of appeal to its authority. Tertullian's point, in what seems an arbitrary legal maneuver, is that since the heretics do not subscribe to the central truth of Scripture, they cannot invoke those bits and pieces of Scripture which suit *their* purposes. The other antiheretical writers of the period allow a common appeal to Scripture by any and all—on the assumption that persistent searching of Scripture is bound to lead to truth and to the vindication of the *regulae fidei* (e.g., Origen). Tertullian, in his own peculiar way, had a subtler understanding of the interactions of Scripture and tradition. He realized that the tradition in which a man stands predisposes his hermeneutical approach to Scripture—and this, in turn, affects what he "finds" in the Scripture as he searches for true doctrines. The heretic already stands in a distorted and distorting tradition; hence, his appeals to Scripture will produce distorted conclusions—all the more insidious because of their bland claims to being scriptural. Using a Roman legal tactic which barred a litigant from court if he could not establish his submission to the law governing the case under review, Tertullian proposed to bar the heretics from the court of theological judgment. This is justified because their false traditions cancel their rights of appeal to Scripture.

> We do not make our appeal to the Scriptures nor will we engage in controversy on those points in which a decision is either impossible, or uncertain or not quite certain (*aut nulla aut incerta victoria aut partum certa*).[64]

Thus the *regulae fidei* are the datum planes for the authentic interpretation

[62] Cf. *ibid.,* 4, 5.
[63] *De praescr.* 19.
[64] *Ibid.;* see also 18.

of the Christian tradition. If a man will be guided by the *regula,* he can read Scripture understandingly. He may even contribute to the enrichment of its interpretation (and hence to the *development* of Christian truth) in accord with the tenor and essential meaning of the original *traditio.* The *regula* is, therefore, the rule for biblical *exegesis.*

This recognition that tradition affects hermeneutics and that Scripture alone does not decide the doubtful questions on which the heretics thrive has led certain Protestant scholars to conclude in effect that Tertullian places tradition above Scripture.[65] There is, however, an ampler way of construing the evidence. In Tertullian's view, neither Scripture nor tradition is supreme and neither is efficacious save in dynamic correlation with the other. Both belong to the providential furnishing of the Church for her pilgrimage on earth. It is their consilience which reinforces the Christian's conviction that he has something superior to those with but a single norm—be it Scripture *or* tradition *or* reason! Scripture is infallible and supreme for those who read it with the eyes of faith, who see in it the Christ of the apostolic preaching. But heretics, with their aberrant assumptions, simply abuse the Scripture and stultify its authority.[66] Scripture, by itself alone, suffices for nothing; neither does tradition. Together, they complement each other and re-present the apostolic teaching which is equivalent of nothing less than the divine command itself—which is to say, *revelation in the present moment.* Thus Tertullian affirms a sort of two-natures doctrine of Scripture and tradition—just as, conversely, he drives a deep wedge between the true believer and the heretic.

In Clement of Alexandria and Origen we come upon men of quite different tempers, in a very different theological situation. Neither had a very vivid sense of *historical continuity.* What interested them was the problem of *timeless truth;* and what they were after was the Christian "canon of truth." Both believed Christianity possessed such a normative canon. They saw it lodged in the Scriptures, transmitted in the Christian tradition, interpreted in the Church. But, in Clement of Alexandria, this timeless truth may be rightly understood only by the Christian gnostic, whose insights far surpass the bare faith of the simple believer—without, however, contradicting it. One becomes such a gnostic by means of a progressive discipline of inquiry and illumination which enables one to identify the maieutic clues provided in the Scriptures as to the cosmic meaning of the revelation of God in Christ.[67] Clement seems to have been quite indifferent to the actual history of the Church. He supposes that the tradition of truth has been transmitted from generation to

[65] Cf. E. C. Blackman, *Marcion and His Influence* (London: S.P.C.K., 1948), 94.
[66] *De corona* 4.
[67] Cf. *Stromateis,* VII.

generation, from teachers to pupils—but with no curiosity as to how this actually happened. This transmission of the truth is the true apostolic succession. It has no necessary dependence upon historical succession, since truth is truth whenever and however it appears.

In *Stromateis* I, Clement gives a brief, vague biographical account of his own teachers.[68] Here, and elsewhere, he develops his basic pedagogical theory that Christian truth is *not* traditioned as information. Instead, it involves maieutic teaching and learning, in a significant interpersonal relationship. This means that there is something essentially private in the process of traditioning the Christian *gnosis*. It is, therefore, entirely in character that Clement nowhere produces a summary of the doctrinal content of the Christian *gnosis*.[69]

Clement was quite familiar with the canonical New Testament. He quotes from every book in it save Philemon, II John, and III John. On the other hand, however, he has no notion of a fixed and settled canon. Thus he quotes canonical and apocryphal literature generously and with no clear distinction between the two.[70] And yet, when one asks about the substance and measure of the Christian faith, for Clement the answer is fairly plain: *the faith of the Church,* attested in the Christian Scriptures, traditioned by the generations of Christian teachers, understood (in its fullness) by the Christian gnostic. This does not, however, mean a two-source theory of revelation. Clement, like many another of his fellow Christians, assumed that Scripture and tradition were polar functions of a Christocentric view of truth.

Origen was evidently Clement's student in the catechetical school in Alexandria, though neither mentions this in the writings that we have. In any case, Origen proceeded to develop a strikingly different view of the relation of Scripture and tradition from that of Clement. Harnack's reference to his "unmitigated biblicism" is only slightly exaggerated.[71] Too many of us know him best in his *De Principiis* and *Contra Celsum*. Yet, in his own eyes, he was, first and last, an interpreter of Scripture. This was the task to which he devoted the major fraction of his prodigious talent and energy—and this because of his settled conviction that the Bible, rightly understood, is the sole

---

[68] I, 4; cf. also V, 10; VI, 16; I, 23.

[69] Cf. R. P. C. Hanson, *Origen's Doctrine of Tradition* (London: S.P.C.K., 1954), 63–65, where he tries to infer the main points of secret tradition as Clement understood it. The difficulties which he encounters, and the meager results, testify to Clement's successful reticence.

[70] Cf. *Protreptikos* III, 6, 8; *Strom.* VI, 5; *Hypotoposeis* VIII; *Strom.* I, 17, 19; II, 9; IV, 9: *Excerpta ex Theodoto*. See also Hanson, *op. cit.*, 127, 132.

[71] "Origenes selbst hat in seinem unbedingten Biblicismus stets eine Art von Correctiv gegenüber der Gefahr, völlig auf das philosophischen, Gebiet überzugehen, bessessen." Adolf Harnack, *Lehrbuch der Dogmengeschichte,* 4th ed. (Tübingen: Mohr, 1909), I, 781, n. 4.

and sufficient source of authoritative Christian truth.[72]

His sense—and knowledge of—history was as dim as Clement's; and he shows scant interest in the traditionary process by which the Christian truth had come to him.[73] He had a carefully formulated rule of faith, and it agrees in the main with other *regulae* in the period. He was, and he meant to be, "a man of the church."[74] But his deepest concern is with Scripture and its "rational" interpretation. The Church is bound to Scripture; the rule of faith is a summary of scriptural truth; Scripture is to be interpreted *by* Scripture (with allegory governing "history" wherever the two conflict). In point of intent, therefore, Origen is nearer to the *sola Scriptura* than any other patristic theologian before or after him.

Inevitably, however, this biblical principle ran into its characteristic difficulty: there is no consensus of biblical interpretation. Interpretations vary according to their various hermeneutical traditions. Origen's solution to this dilemma was allegorism—by which he was able to apply the premises of timeless truth (e.g., that God is good, the author of the good and that only) to the anomalies of the biblical text. By this means, the spiritually sensitive Christian can penetrate to the inner truth of the biblical revelation, inspired and guided by the Holy Spirit—and all this without any necessary appeal beyond the Bible to Church tradition or pagan philosophy. Generous as he was toward Gentile wisdom (though not so generous as Clement), Origen decisively subordinated all philosophy and even churchly tradition to the role of confirming testimony to the truth located in Scripture, there to be discerned by the eyes of faith.

Origen does not formally designate a canon of Christian writings, but he does concentrate almost exclusively on what had, in effect, become the canon. His use of apocryphal material is never more than illustrative. He rejects all conceptions of an esoteric or secret tradition, except at one point: the succession of a spiritual elite in the Church, trained to probe deeper than common Christians into the plenary fullness of the revelation deposited in the Bible. On this point, one could scarcely do better than to quote Hanson's admirable summary:

> In Origen there is no evidence for a source of doctrine independent of the Bible. The rule of faith is only independent in as far as it is the

---

[72] Cf. Hanson, *op. cit.*, 182 ff.

[73] Cf. the preface of *De prin.* where he contrasts the authority of the Bible to that of the oral tradition. But see also his commentary *In Joan.*, XXXII, 7 (*PG* 13, 766 ff.) where he quietly approves the Church's right to exclude from its tradition the *pedilavium* as a dominical ordinance (John 13:3–15).

[74] Cf. my article, "Origen and the *Regulae Fidei*" in *Church History,* VIII (1939), No. 3, 212–221.

Church preaching and teaching her faith in continuity with the faith which has from the earliest times been taught and preached by the Church. But he assumes that this preaching and teaching derive their material and evidence from the Bible. He makes no emphatic or frequent appeal to the witness of the apostolic succession of the bishops as a proof of the genuineness of the rule of faith. Where we do find such an appeal in Origen's works, it is usually in those which have survived only in Latin, and it is precisely on such a point as this that we should expect his translators to have altered or supplemented his words. Indeed, we have been able to see examples of their doing something very like this. Or else he appeals to apostolic authority for his use of allegory. But he hardly ever refers to the bishops as trustees of the faith in the way in which Irenaeus did. Origen had had unhappy experiences with bishops. Nor do we find any hint in Origen that the rule of faith could be a substitute for the Bible. We have noted already several times that though he can encourage his advanced students to transcend the rule of faith, he never suggests that they should transcend the Bible. Though he can, when he wants to, use the aid both of the tradition conveyed in Christian institutions and of isolated traditions derived from sources outside the Bible, he gives them no position that could make them serious rivals to the Bible as his sole important source of doctrine. In short, in the matter of tradition outside the Bible, Origen differs markedly from Irenaeus and Tertullian, and definitely, though not so markedly, from Clement of Alexandria.[75]

With Cyprian, we are back again in the atmosphere of Tertullian, but with an important and distinctively new attitude toward the *polity* of the Church. "The Church is established on the bishops":[76] the bishops have both the authority and the responsibility for dealing with novel circumstances in the course of the Church's historical experience—especially those not having specific precedent in Scripture and tradition. Thus Cyprian can claim, in the matter of the Decian *lapsi,* that it is the *consensus episcoporum* which has to decide the matter—rejecting all extremes and crotchets. Again, on the issue of "heretic baptism," Cyprian stands on what he takes to be the historical *consensus episcoporum,* and is thus prepared to correct Pope Cornelius and defy Pope Stephen.[77] Yet the historical fact is that, on this particular point, Stephen had the main weight of tradition on his side. This much was admitted in the 7th Council of Carthage, when Honoratus of Thucca, opposing recognition of heretic baptism, registers his vote with the comment: "We ought rather to follow *truth* than *custom.*"[78] In another case, however (in-

[75] Hanson, *op. cit.,* 191.
[76] *Epistle* XXVI.
[77] *Ep.* LXX.
[78] *The 7th Council of Carthage,* in *The Ante-Nicene Fathers* (Grand Rapids: Eerdmans, 1951), V, 571. Italics added.

fant baptism), Cyprian refers quite complacently to the *consensus episcoporum,* with no explicit appeal to Scripture or history.[79]

For Cyprian, the Scripture is equivalent to revelation itself. He quotes Matthew 10:37–38 (Luke 14:26–27) as "the voice of the Lord through the trumpet of his Gospel";[80] Hosea 8:4 is cited as "the Lord himself speaking in the twelve prophets";[81] "in Deuteronomy the Lord God says . . .";[82] Tobit 4:10 is "an exhortation of the Lord."[83]

This immediate confrontation with God in Scripture is the activity of the Holy Spirit, who inspired the writing of Scripture and who still guards the bishops in their interpretations. There can be no significant doctrinal disagreement among those who share the one Spirit. "Therefore it is clear that [a bishop] who thinks differently from the rest [in a matter involving faith and order] does not hold the truth in the Holy Spirit."[84] There is one Church, one episcopacy, one tradition,[85] which Cyprian calls "God's tradition."[86] Heresies arise when men become estranged from the bishops and "the hieratical college."[87] Heretics are not to be argued with, since their appeals either to Scripture or tradition are attainted. The bare fact of dissent from the *consensus episcoporum* is sufficient evidence of error: men may be condemned on this ground alone.[88]

Within the *collegium episcoporum,* the bishop of Rome is *primus inter pares.* Cyprian acknowledges this freely—but it does not alter the fact that the Pope of Rome stands, with his fellow bishops, under the collegiate authority of the episcopacy as a whole. Only this corporate consensus has the force of *traditio activa.*[89] On this ground, Cyprian was quite ready to oppose the pope, at the imminent risk of actual excommunication.[90] He simply could not conceive of the Church in disunity—even though this bishop and that might be. The Scripture is the written witness to revealed truth; tradition is living witness to the same truth. Where these agree (and Cyprian defines the Church as the place where they do agree) their consilience constitutes an authority against which no private truth has prior rights—not even the sacred

---

[79] *Ep.* LVIII.
[80] *Ep.* XXV, 303.
[81] *Ep.* LIV, V.
[82] *Ep.* LXI.
[83] *Ep.* LI.
[84] *Ep.* LXVI.
[85] *De unitate,* 5.
[86] *Ep.* LI.
[87] *Ep.* LIV.
[88] *Ep.* LIV.
[89] *Ep.* LIV.
[90] Cf. Jules Lebreton & Jacques Zeiller, *The History of the Primitive Church* (New York: Macmillan, 1949), II, 858–860.

honor of a "confessor" or martyr.[91] The natural state of the Church is unity—"sons of God living peaceably, gentle in heart, simple in speech, mutual in affection, linked and bonded to each other in the unanimity of faith."[92] Thus in Cyprian, we see the doctrine which will reappear in later chapters of the history of the Christian tradition: apostolicity consists chiefly in the succession of the apostles' doctrine, traditioned by the *consensus episcoporum* and identified by the consilience of Scripture and tradition.

And yet one also senses in Cyprian a new accent on the notion that the bishops have the right and duty to *make* tradition, to deal with unprecedented situations by setting new precedents—which thus acquire the force of tradition. Thus he insists that the distinction which has developed between clergy and laity is both right and wise. Again, he sees an advantage in the sharper lines of cleavage between ancient truth and some erroneous innovations than earlier generations could have made.[93] Cyprian's "episcopalianism" was something of an anomaly in his own time and was destined quickly to disappear in the West. Nevertheless, its effect was to encourage the evolution of *traditiones ecclesiastici.* That this was recognized at the time—and resisted—may be seen in an anonymous (and "traditionalist") treatise on heretical baptism that stems from the controversy between Cyprian and Stephen.[94] The author is a critic of Cyprian's; his defense of the validity of heretic baptism (understood as clinical) is that it belongs to the Church's tradition and therefore cannot now be set aside. He can, therefore, complain of the Cyprianists that they place themselves above tradition in their presumptuous claim to alter it. This argument, as clumsy as it appears in this particular essay, is yet another echo of the view, now become "traditional," that the Church is bound to the tradition she already has.

And yet, it is *this* view of tradition which soon will fade and the view, portended in Cyprian, will replace it—the Church *makes* tradition and thus may augment the tradition she has received.

It may be significant that there is a comparative silence about the problem of tradition in the literature of the last third of the third century. The sense of tradition in the ante-Nicene Church had been adapted to the conditions of a *religio illicita.* When this began to change—first slowly in the decades between 180 and 313 (despite Diocletian!) and then swiftly in the age of Constantine and thereafter—the roles and functions of tradition and traditions are inevitably changed. Thus, when we come to Athanasius and Hilary, we see the old problem in a drastically new perspective—and changed, in

[91] *De unitate,* 21–23.
[92] *Ibid.,* 24–25.
[93] Cf. *Ep.* LIV.
[94] *On Rebaptism* (ANF) V, 667–678.

some respects at least, unrecognizably from the earlier pattern.

Two examples of this transition in our period may be noted briefly. In an epistle from one Theonas of Alexandria to an imperial chamberlain named Lucian, there is a discussion of the duties of a Christian in a secular office. After the standard exhortations to Christian virtue (in these circumstances, the stress falls on honesty and diligence), Theonas points out that Lucian must be alert to "find occasions to praise the Holy Scriptures." Again, there will be opportunities to speak approvingly of the apostles and the evangelists, "who can be praised as divine oracles." If these gambits arouse interest, then the time will ripen "for introducing a comment about Christ." To be ready for such moments when they come, Lucian must keep himself immersed in the language and spirit of the Scriptures: "Let no day pass by without reading some portion of the Sacred Scriptures, at a convenient time—and when you do, always take time out for meditation."[95] In the context, the Scriptures are viewed as *depositum fidei:* tradition is the legacy of Scripture.

The other example to be noticed is the so-called *Disputatio Archelai,* reported somewhat obscurely by Jerome in *De Virus Illustribus,* LXXXII.[96] Persistent uncertainties with respect to the author and provenance of this odd bit of Christian literature do not obscure the clarity of its witness to the persistence of the notion of the consilience of Scripture and tradition.

In what purports to be a disputation between Manes and Archelaus, Manes begins by professing himself a Christian and proceeds to expound his peculiar views as the *true* interpretation of Scripture. In his refutation, Archelaus' main arguments are drawn, not from Scripture, but from reason and tradition. The basic weight of the orthodox position is that Manes' views are *novel.* Diodorus, who joins Archelaus in the dispute, makes the point that "those who seek to set up any new dogma have the habit of very readily perverting into conformity with their own notions any proofs they desire to take from the Scriptures."[97] The only way to avoid such perversion, Archelaus affirms, is to insist upon the original deposit in the Church of her central and essential teachings. This deposit is, of course, the Bible, but the Bible interpreted by the Church in the manner of the apostolic preachers.

> I understand, then, that [Manes'] chief effort was directed to prove that the law of Moses is not consonant with the law of Christ; and this position he attempted to found on the authority of *our* Scriptures.
>
> Well, on the other hand, not only did we establish [in the first disputa-

[95] *Theonas of Alexandria,* English trans. in *The Ante-Nicene Fathers* (Grand Rapids: Eerdmans, 1951), VI, 158–161.

[96] English trans. in *ibid.,* VI, 179–235; cf. Johannes Quasten, *Patrology* (Utrecht/Antwerp: Spectrum; Westminster, Md.: Newman, 1960), III, 356–358.

[97] *Ibid.,* 213.

> tion] the law of Moses, and all things which are written in it, by the same Scripture; but we also proved that the whole Old Testament agrees with the New Testament and is in perfect harmony with it. They form really one fabric, just as a person may see one and the same robe made of weft and warp together. For the truth is this, that just as we trace the purple in a robe, so, if we may thus express it, we can discern the New Testament in the texture of the Old Testament; for we see the glory of the Lord mirrored in the same. We are not, therefore, to cast aside the mirror, since it shows us the genuine image of the things themselves, faithfully and truly; on the contrary, we ought to honor it all the more.[98]

Not much is said, one way or the other, about the traditionary process, but, at one crucial point, Archelaus argues that Manes stands in a tradition of his own—which is to say that he is a traditioner of a different tradition than the Church's. This Manichean tradition can be traced back, says Archelaus, "to a certain Scythianus who lived in the time of the apostles, and who was founder and leader of this sect (of which Manes is currently the leader)."[99] Here, then, are two traditions set over against each other—the one true, the other false. But which one is which? History, reason, and Scripture form, for Archelaus, a triumviral court, the only one competent to adjudicate such a question.

Both Theonas and Archelaus are avowed biblicists but it is also obvious that their biblical interpretations are products of their own times and traditions. The matrix of their faith is the ongoing life of the Church—in the midst of which they believe that the Lord Jesus stands as center and savior.

But something *has* happened. These men formally exalt Scripture; yet one can scarcely avoid the impression that their typical and distinctive notions of Christian doctrine and the Christian life rest on traditionary developments which have been uncritically assumed to be identical with the gist of Scripture. They profess to uphold the *received* faith as if it were fixed in and attested to by the Scriptures. We are, therefore, on the verge of a two-source concept of revelation, but the two sources are not yet consciously differentiated in the Christian mind. But a step is needed to move into the conscious distinction which will appear in the Nicene Church. When we seek to estimate the ante-Nicene period as a whole, we notice an interesting involution in the pattern of development in the Christian tradition in its oral and written forms. In the beginning, of course, the *paradosis* was oral. Then came the Christian writings, in some of which, as the Church came to believe, the essential content of that *paradosis* had been permanently deposited. Other writings were produced at the same time and the Church proceeded to adjudge them "apocryphal." To all practical intent and purposes, this judg-

[98] *Ibid.*, 215b.
[99] *Ibid.*, 229–231.

ment had been rendered by the middle of the second century—even though final and official action was deferred until the fourth.[100]

It is therefore misleading to interpret Marcion's pro-Pauline canon as the first challenge to the Catholic Church to provide an ampler one of her own. The fact is that the Church had already settled on the basic shape of her written *paradosis* before Marcion, and this in the course of her traditionary activity: preaching, teaching, worship. The *principle* of the canon was established *in* the Church before the *content* of the canon was decided *by* the Church.

Given a written form of the apostolic tradition, plus the elongation of the historical time of the Church, it was inevitable that the function of the oral tradition would change—from repetition to representation, from the conservation of the Gospel to its adaptation in those new situations which kept on arising to confront and confound the Church. This, in turn, gave to the written tradition at least a logical primacy over the ongoing processes of the oral tradition. This was, of course, a relative matter, for the vast majority of ante-Nicene Christians never thought to oppose tradition to Scripture, or vice versa. They took it to be self-evident that both were authentic media of revelation, each with its distinctive value for the Church's mission: to tradition the Gospel in new times to new people. Together, Scripture and tradition gave the Church a joint-agency of continuity and change.

In the ante-Nicene Church, therefore, there was no notion of *sola Scriptura,* but neither was there a doctrine of *traditio solo*. Every new crisis passed gave to the orthodox Christians fresh confidence in the authority of their oral interpretations of the biblical tradition. Thus Scripture and tradition together, centering as they both did around the original *traditum* of God in Christ, sufficed to create a never ending dialogue between *traditio constitutiva* (now forever fixed in Scripture) and *traditiones interpretativae* (the living *magisterium* in the ongoing Church).

There was, however, no avoiding the development of a wide variety of traditions and customs and standpoints in the churches—and this especially in a community in which improvisation and adaptation were prerequisites to survival. But these developments meant that the longer history kept going on, the stronger the probability that the apostolic tradition might be either altered or augmented. It is, therefore, impressive to see how nearly universal was the confidence of the ante-Nicene Christians that all men had equal access to the sources of revelation who had access to the tradition in the Holy Scriptures and to the consilience of oral and written tradition in the Church.

[100] Cf. Alexander Souter, *The Text & Canon of the New Testament* (New York: Scribner's, 1923), 149–204.

This confidence was based on the twin convictions that the apostolic tradition is the prime locus of the revelation of God in Christ and that historical continuity is, so to say, supervised by the Holy Spirit in a dynamic and trustworthy process. History links all later Christians to the originative Event of Christ and to the actual witnesses and interpreters of that Event. History is, therefore, important. But historical knowledge is radically inferior to the knowledge of faith. Hence, the crux of living faith is always the *actus tradendi* wrought by the Holy Spirit, transforming objective knowledge of the apostolic preaching into living faith similar to that of the apostles. It was *this* sense of tradition, this confidence in the continuing activity of God among his people, that nerved these Christians for their ordeals in their times of repression.

It would be fair to say, I think, that in the period we have had under review there is a clear principle of the priority of Christian *community* over any and all principles of rigid doctrinal definition. These Christians are not indifferent to doctrine—they were embroiled in some of the most desperate theological controversies in the entire course of Christian history. But they understood that the main uses of doctrine are heuristic and polemic: the one, to render faith intelligible; the other, to deal with heretical interpretations. Community is the sense of the mutuality engendered in the one body by the one Spirit (cf. Eph. 4:1–17). Its center is in Christ; its life is in the ongoing round of worship and witness; its confidence is in the Christian tradition—the link between the past and the future kept viable by living faith.[101]

Thus the experience of the ante-Nicene Church must be reckoned as an extraordinary achievement: a catholic community that managed to maintain a real residue of its identity and continuity through a period of successive revolutions, within and without—under relentless, nerve-wracking pressures of befuddlement and conflict. There was diversity from the start and it was never overcome. What happened was that the Christians quickly discovered the radical difference between disunity between *rivals* and diversity among *brethren*—the difference between disagreements that deny and those that allow *communicatio in sacris*. One may then speak of this as the first truly ecumenical age of the Church—and still something of a paradigm for our own time.

[101] In this way God's original *traditum* (Rom. 4:25, 8:32) is re-enacted and made contemporaneous to all succeeding ages.

St. Anselm on the Harmony between God's Mercy and God's Justice

GEORGE S. HEYER, JR.
Assistant Professor of the History of Doctrine
Austin Presbyterian Theological Seminary
Austin, Texas

I

Near the end of the first book of the *Cur Deus Homo* Boso, Anselm's interlocutor, voices a complaint that has echoed through the years. He charges Anselm with abolishing not only the hope of man but also the mercy of God.[1] In the course of the dialogue Anselm manages to persuade Boso that he has forgotten neither of these but, while he may also have persuaded later critics that he did not banish the hope of man, Anselm has been less successful concerning the mercy of God. In fact, it has become familiar practice to criticize the chilly, impersonal justice in the *Cur Deus Homo,* a justice never thawed by the warmth of divine mercy. The problem, according to Boso (whose phrases are unfailingly apt), is to explain how man is saved by God's mercy, when God "does not absolve him of sin unless he repays that which he owes on account of it."[2]

The reconciliation of divine justice and divine mercy did not occupy Anselm only in the *Cur Deus Homo*. Nor was the problem merely academic. A glance at the prayers shows that it was very lively indeed. Anselm strews them with anguished appeals to the "strict Judge" to turn from his wrath and show favor to his creature. But how can an absolutely just God hear the cry of such an evil being?[3] The creature stands as a guilty culprit before his judge, trembling at the thought of the sentence he deserves. His own conscience con-

[1] *Cur Deus Homo* I, 23 (*S. Anselmi Opera Omnia,* ed. Franciscus Salesius Schmitt [Edinburgh: Nelson, 1946–1961], II, 91). In following footnotes this edition of Anselm's works will be referred to as A.

[2] *Ibid.*, I, 25 (A II, 96).

[3] *Oratio* 14, ll. 10–11 (A III, 55).

victs him, and he can do no good that will compensate for his evil. No escape presents itself from torments that will neither end nor be eased; he is utterly lost before the just fury of a just God.[4]

What is the sinner to do? One recourse is appeal to the saints and to the Virgin for intercession, and actually Anselm does address a number of prayers to them. Mary is herself the object of three of them, and Anselm seeks her presence as a refuge from the wrath of God.[5] But the very thought of Mary leads him on to contemplate Christ, and in the contemplation of the Virgin and her Son he finds solid comfort.

> For he has brought it about that he himself through maternal generation should be of our nature and that we through the restoration of life should be children of his mother. He does himself invite us to confess ourselves his brothers. Thus our judge is our brother. The Savior of the world is our brother. In short, our God has become, through Mary, our brother. Therefore with what certainty ought we to hope, with what consolation can we fear, we whose salvation or damnation depends upon the will of a good brother and a devout mother![6]

Still, the conflict that Anselm senses between divine mercy and divine justice never lurks far below the surface and as a rule it appears quite openly. In his flight to Mary he, the guilty one, seeks escape from "the just God" and sanctuary with the "mother of the merciful God." Yet even Mary threatens him, for she is "the offended mother," and now he must take flight once more, this time to the "Son of a benevolent mother."[7] There is some suggestion here of the ancient contrast between the angry Father and the compassionate Son. Yet Anselm can also tremble before the Son's wrath as, equally, he can appeal to the Father's mercy. For instance, he contemplates Christ as judge without recollecting him as brother. "Who," he cries, "is called 'the angel of mighty counsel,' who is called Savior?" It is Christ himself. "He is himself the Judge, in whose hands I tremble." Then Anselm exhorts his soul to hope, to hope in the very one whom it fears, to flee to the one from whom it has fled.[8]

When he turns directly to God for mercy, Anselm appeals to him as his creator. In a lustrous passage from the second *Meditation* he writes:

> Remember, just God and benevolent God, remember that thou art merciful, both my creator and my re-creator. Therefore, do not recall, good Lord, thy justice against thy sinner, but be mindful of thy benev-

---

[4] See *Oratio* 13 (A III, 50–54).
[5] E.g., *Oratio* 6, l. 45 (A III, 16).
[6] *Oratio* 7, ll. 137–143 (A III, 23).
[7] *Oratio* 6, ll. 45 f. (A III, 16).
[8] *Meditatio* 1, ll. 78–82 (A III, 79).

> olence toward thy creature. Do not recall wrath against the guilty, but be mindful of pity toward the pitiful.[9]

Passages like this one prevent us from charging Anselm with viewing the Father quite apart from the Son or God quite apart from Christ. He recognizes God here as both creator and re-creator, the author of his being *and* its savior. More telling, however, is the echo of the doctrine which forms one of the cornerstones of the *Cur Deus Homo*. It is that God will not abandon his creation, however deeply it sinks into sin. To do so, he would have to abandon his own purpose and the order which he has himself established. The God St. Anselm envisages would not, could not, do so unfitting a thing. Nevertheless, it is also clear from the previous passage that a benign figure can suddenly alter and assume a dreadful aspect, even as an angry one can turn merciful. This curious ambivalence, while it naturally may be heightened in the prayers, stems from the difficulty Anselm had in forging a union between God's justice and his mercy. Although we find in the *Cur Deus Homo* his most strenuous effort to solve the problem, we must first observe his earlier treatment of it in the *Proslogion*. There, its position, spread across three chapters in the heart of the work, testifies to its importance.[10]

II

Anselm raises the question how God, if he is supremely just, can spare the wicked, who deserve eternal death. The brief answer is that God is good as well as just and that his mercy rises from his goodness. Indeed, Anselm goes one step further and asserts that God is merciful *because* he is just! He writes: "For if thou art merciful because thou art supremely good and art supremely good only because thou art supremely just, truly then thou art merciful because thou art supremely just." So Anselm's faith affirms. But at this place, as at most others in his writings, his faith strives to understand itself. Therefore he adds immediately: "Help me, O just and merciful God, whose light I seek, help me to understand what I say."[11] And with that he turns to explore the harmony between God's justice and God's mercy.

First, Anselm asks if mercy springs from justice because it is just for God to be so good that he cannot be thought of as better. In that case, God must be good not only in punishment but also in forbearance, in making good men out of wicked ones. Still, Anselm continues, it is just for God to punish the

---

[9] *Meditatio* 2, ll. 102–106 (A III, 83).
[10] *Proslogion* 9–11 (A I, 106–110).
[11] *Ibid.*, 9 (A I, 108).

wicked. But how can it be just both to punish and to spare? It depends, Anselm replies, on the perspective. According to their merits, the wicked deserve punishment. But from the standpoint of God's goodness they are justly spared. The case is exactly parallel to that of divine compassion, which Anselm treated in the eighth chapter of the *Proslogion*. God, he wrote, is in himself impassible and does not suffer with others. Yet to the man rescued out of wretchedness God seems compassionate. The effects the man feels appear to be the effects of compassion, though God certainly experiences no emotion.

> For by saving us whom thou mightest justly destroy, in the same way as thou art merciful not because thou feelest an affection but because we feel an effect, so also art thou just not because thou dost reward us according to our deserts but because thou doest what befits thee as the highest good.[12]

Having said that according to God's nature it is just for him to spare the wicked, Anselm next asks if it is not also just, in the same way, for him to *punish* the wicked. The answer is yes, because he who rewards both the good and the evil in accord with their deserts is juster than he who so rewards only the good. Whether sparing or punishing, God always wills justly. Therefore we may say that his mercy springs from his justice, since it is just for him to spare as well as to condemn. But, Anselm confesses, understanding fails at the point of explaining why, among equally evil men, God spares some and condemns others. With that problem, understanding reaches its term.

This attempt in the *Proslogion* to harmonize divine justice and divine mercy suffers from certain weaknesses. We sense Anselm's difficulty when he repeats several times in the course of these chapters the statement that God shows mercy for the very reason that he is just. This was the original deliverance of faith, from which Anselm set out on his quest for understanding. Time and again he circles back to it, not just because it is the ground of his meditation but because he finds it so frustratingly opaque. In its repetition we hear faintly echoed the hope that it may not be so puzzling after all—and the disappointment at forever finding it so. The result Anselm achieves falls short of the goal, for he has juxtaposed justice and mercy, not harmonized them. He has set the two perfections side-by-side, but their relationship is hardly more than tangential. Certainly he has not shown how God's mercy rises and flows from the source of his justice. Instead, Anselm has posited two senses of divine justice—one with a view to man's deserts and one with a view to God's nature. What are we to think of them? Surely he does not mean that two justices reside in a God of utter self-consistency. Yet Anselm's argument

[12] *Ibid.*, 10 (A I, 109).

lends itself to that impression. As we saw, the justice which spares the wicked expresses the goodness of God's nature. But at the same time the punishment of the wicked is demanded by the very *ratio* of justice—and God is himself justice.

It is not mere redundancy to say that Anselm's failure emerges most clearly at the very spot where he admits failure. He first divides men into two categories, the good and the evil; then he cannot answer the question why God chooses certain of the evil ones for condemnation and certain others, who are equally wicked, for redemption. All Anselm can say is that the treatment of the condemned expresses God's justice-according-to-their-deserts, while the treatment of those spared expresses his justice-according-to-his-nature. It is obvious how far short of a true synthesis of justice and mercy this scheme falls. It leaves us with only an external relationship between them, and in the whole enterprise Anselm has run the risk of presenting a God whose right hand does not know what his left hand is doing.

This difficulty over justice and mercy is a symptom of deeper trouble. Anselm has driven a wedge between God's being and his action. It appears in the treatment of compassion, for there, as we noted, God's acts of mercy make him appear compassionate when really he is nothing of the sort. These acts not only fail to reveal God as he is in himself but are even likely to deceive men about his true nature. That is, they may lead men to conclude that God feels emotions. But his compassion is according to our nature, not according to his own, as, contrariwise, God is just according to his nature (and not ours) when he spares the wicked. Exactly the same set of problems would arise if we asked Anselm to show how God's punishment of the wicked demonstrates his mercy. Presumably Anselm would appeal to some second sense of mercy, which would correspond with God's nature, not with the deserts of the wicked ones whom he punishes.

Before leaving these chapters of the *Proslogion,* we must recognize that they have had their defenders. One recent one is Kr. Strijd, who cherishes considerable admiration for them and finds their harmony between divine justice and divine mercy far more convincing than the one that Anselm later wrought in the *Cur Deus Homo.*[13] On the one hand, Strijd prefers the *Proslogion's* more tentative approach to the problem, signalled by Anselm's use of words like *forsitan* and *videri,* instead of *rationabilis*. On the other hand, Strijd prefers the sheer content of these chapters to that of the *Cur Deus Homo* because he believes that in the *Proslogion* Anselm ultimately rests his case upon the goodness, not the retributive justice, of God. Both justice and

[13] Kr. Strijd, *Structuur en Inhoud van Anselmus' "Cur Deus Homo"* (Assen: Van Gorcum, 1957), 108–117.

mercy are said to stem from this goodness and in it they find a higher unity. In the *Cur Deus Homo,* Strijd believes, God's goodness has been shunted aside, while the rewarding and punishing *iustitia dei* has assumed predominance. Finally, this justice in the *Cur Deus Homo* is born not of God's goodness but of the right order of things.

Strijd is entirely right that the *Proslogion* relates both justice and mercy to God's goodness (though not quite so right, as we shall see, about the manner of their relationship). Anselm is explicit: God from his goodness rewards the good and punishes the wicked; but also from his goodness he spares the wicked. The words are there all right. Yet they seem to lack meaning behind them. True as Anselm's insight may be, we do not really see *how* justice and mercy *both* express God's goodness. It is still possible that the solution advanced in the *Cur Deus Homo* lies exposed to the criticisms that Strijd makes. He has taken us back to that original complaint of Boso—that Anselm did away with the mercy of God—and the only way we can fairly evaluate it is by turning to the evidence of the *Cur Deus Homo* itself.

III

The place to begin is the twentieth chapter of Book II. Its heading reads: "How Great and How Just Is the Mercy of God." The chapter is extremely brief, and Anselm pauses in it only long enough to point to the mercy of God enshrined in the Father's assignment to sinful man of the Son's due reward. And this act perfectly harmonizes with God's justice, since nothing could be juster than for God, to whom the price has been paid, to forgive every debt. That is all Anselm says. Now even Strijd raises the possibility that this chapter does in fact produce a sound harmony between justice and mercy. But he rejects the possibility almost as soon as he mentions it. He believes that the use of words like "price" and "debt" in this chapter, as well as such terms as "retribution," "reward," and "merit" in the previous chapter, betray Anselm's sacrifice of mercy at the altar of justice.[14] Nor is Strijd without justice of his own. If we take this chapter *solo*, it does present the aspect of an awkward *deus ex machina,* a kind of afterthought that Anselm tacked onto the *Cur Deus Homo* in order to render lip service to mercy and in order to satisfy Boso, who, actually, gets no chance to reply or object. But surely we cannot take the chapter in this way. Not only must we see it in the context of the entire treatise but we must also consider other references to mercy in the *Cur Deus Homo.* These references do exist and they are important, no matter how frequently Anselm's discussion of justice overshadows them.

---

[14] *Ibid.,* 106 f.

Fairly early in the *Cur Deus Homo*[15] Anselm deals with the suggestion that God might have remitted sins by mercy alone. Such a course, he argues, would be unfitting, for it would involve forgiveness without either punishment or satisfaction. God cannot permit such an irregularity in his Kingdom. Furthermore, forgiveness by mercy alone would lead to the unfitting result of placing both sinner and non-sinner in the same position vis-à-vis God. In addition, it would mean that injustice is freer than justice, for then the former, unlike the latter, would be subject to no law. All agree that the reward God gives for justice is measured by the quantity of justice. It does not befit God, Anselm tells Boso, to do anything without due order. Therefore, it cannot be appropriate to God's freedom or goodness or will to forgive the sinner by mercy alone. This whole stance is clear enough and is much what we should expect Anselm to say. It does not aid us a great deal with our own problem, however, because we need to determine, not whether Anselm believed in redemption by mercy alone, but whether he believed in redemption by justice alone, apart from mercy. It is this latter view that has been ascribed to him. How unrepresentative of him it is we shall see by examining his own words.

Very near the opening of the *Cur Deus Homo* Anselm sets a paean to the merciful and loving God who has so wonderfully restored men from the evils which they deserved to the goods which they in no way merited.[16] That is, he begins by praising God for his mercy and, when he immediately consents to seek rational grounds for the truth, he certainly has not turned his back on the truth of God's mercy. Slightly further on, in the sixth chapter of Book I, Anselm has Boso say: "Surely what you say about how God demonstrated how much he loved you is defended by no reason, if it is not shown that he was able to save man in no other way."[17] The statement simply indicates that the question of God's love is not at issue. What concerns Boso is the *way* in which God expresses his love and he will not be satisfied until Anselm convinces him that God could show it in this one way, and in no other. For Boso, such a demonstration would confirm the love of God. It is not until later, when Anselm has recounted the hopeless situation of man, that Boso begins to worry over the disappearance of mercy. Then, Anselm gives him an answer that deserves careful attention. He says to Boso: "I do not deny that God is merciful, he who saves 'men and beasts,' 'just as' he has multiplied his 'mercy.' We are speaking, however, of that ultimate mercy, by which, after this life, he makes man blessed."[18] God's mercy is demonstrated in his

[15] *Cur Deus Homo* I, 12 (A II, 69–71).
[16] *Ibid.*, I, 3 (A II, 50 f.).
[17] *Ibid.*, I, 6 (A II, 54 f.).
[18] *Ibid.*, I, 24 (A II, 94).

will to make man blessed. Yet, Anselm immediately continues, this blessedness ought to be given only to those whose sins are forgiven; and the sins, in turn, ought to be forgiven only when the debt has been paid. The very next chapter closes Book I with the assertion that men must be saved through Christ, and the stage is now set for Anselm to show in Book II exactly how this redemption through Christ is accomplished. It is a redemption, however, which does not merely satisfy God's justice but also expresses his mercy, since it opens for man a way into everlasting blessedness.

This interpretation is confirmed by additional passages in the *Cur Deus Homo*. Most illuminating of all is the fifth chapter of Book II. Here, Anselm is answering Boso's charge that God is subject to necessity. In his reply Anselm presses the question back to God's original decision to create man for blessedness. It was a free decision, entailing no coercion, and was therefore a matter of pure grace. God did not have to do what he did; he freely undertook this work. As a result, all subsequent action that God performs in bringing to completion his plan must also be attributed to grace. The incarnation is a pre-eminent example. "Nevertheless," Anselm adds, "let us say that it is necessary that the goodness of God, on account of his unchangeableness, finish what he began with man, even though the entire good which he does is grace."[19] What all this means is that Anselm views God's activity as a coherent whole, stretching from creation to consummation and informed by the *ratio* of God's own self-consistency in mercy no less than in justice. In particular, Anselm has bound together the creation and the atonement, a notable theological feat too rarely accomplished. Any critic who accuses Anselm of exalting God's justice at the expense of his mercy can do so only if he narrows his vision to consider the atonement as an isolated doctrine. But that is something which Anselm himself never did.

But even though we conclude that Anselm, far from forgetting divine mercy, allotted a large place to it, we must also admit that the greater stress falls upon God's justice. Such is the case even in the *Proslogion*. Strijd is not quite right when he says that in the ninth chapter of the *Proslogion* Anselm traces both mercy and justice to God's goodness. What Anselm actually presents is the following syllogism: God is merciful because he is good; but he is good because he is just; therefore he is merciful because he is just. In other words, it is not the case that justice and mercy spring from goodness. Instead, the latter two both arise from God's justice, which is their ultimate source. This justice provides the basic premise from which Anselm operates and to which ever and again he returns. The *Cur Deus Homo*, of

[19] *Ibid.*, II, 5 (A II, 100).

course, is the best illustration of this point; in it, the dominance of divine justice is unquestionable.[20] Strijd correctly notes it and he also correctly cites as the ground of it the right order of things. Indeed, the motif of right order (*rectitudo*) lurks in the background of all Anselm's theology. In a work like the *Cur Deus Homo* it appears more prominently, because justice is one prime specification of *rectitudo,* first in God and then derivatively in the lives of creatures. Justice lends itself to this role very well, far better than would mercy. For justice, however it may be defined (and Anselm consistently regards it as "rightness of the will maintained for its own sake"),[21] goes hand in hand with the systematic ordering of thought and action. But mercy is not so. When all is said and done about it, it remains a surd, an uncalculable and perhaps errant virtue that resists rational penetration. Anselm has grounded mercy in divine justice and in placing it there he has submitted it to a certain order. Divine mercy, as Anselm understands it, lacks every trace of caprice or sentiment. God, the eternal and impassible God, feels no emotion.

IV

The true depths of this "setting" for mercy emerge only as we consider the role of the divine Logos, the second person of the Trinity. In him the link between creation and redemption is most tightly forged, and in his person he perfectly unites divine justice and divine mercy. By locating mercy in God's will to create man for blessedness, Anselm associates it most especially with the Logos, because he is both the agent who creates and the model whom the creation resembles.[22] With respect to the atonement, Anselm declares that the second person now comes as God-Man in order to fulfill the very purpose for which, in the beginning, he created man; he acts to realize his own merciful intention. At every step in the doctrine Anselm is careful, of course, to preserve the interests of divine justice. It would be quite wrong, however, to suppose that he espoused in stringently theological fashion the division that we mentioned earlier between just Father and merciful Son. That suggestion is confined to the more ardent temper of the prayers. Furthermore, while in

[20] For discussion of God's justice, according to St. Anselm, see the following articles: Eugene R. Fairweather, "'Iustitia Dei' as the 'Ratio' of the Incarnation," *Spicilegium Beccense,* Vol. I, *Congrès international du IXe Centenaire de l'Arrivée d'Anselme au Bec* (Paris: Librairie Philosophique J. Vrin, 1959), 327–335; Robert D. Crouse, "The Augustinian Background of St. Anselm's Concept *Justitia," Canadian Journal of Theology,* IV (April, 1958), No. 2, 111–119.

[21] See *De Veritate* 12 (A I, 194); *De Conceptu Virginali et de Originali Peccato* 3 and 5 (A II, 143 and 147); *De Concordia Praescientiae et Praedestinationis et Gratiae Dei cum Libero Arbitrio* I, 6; III, 4 and 12 (A II, 256, 268, and 284); *De Libertate Arbitrii* 3 (A I, 212).

[22] *Monologion* 29–34 (A I, 47–54).

some special sense we may appropriate mercy to the Logos, we must not forget Anselm's clear insistence that the Logos is the unique, perfect, and fully divine statement of the Father's thought.[23] The will of the Logos completely expresses the will of the Father, and, to both, both mercy and justice are appropriate. The harmony of these two perfections stands forth only in the light of Anselm's doctrine of the Trinity, and we have had to trace it back to this, its ultimate ground. By doing so, we also catch a glimpse of the integral character of Anselm's thought, for, although he left us no "systematic theology," everything he wrote was informed by a single, conscious viewpoint, best summed up, perhaps, in that passion for right order that has already been mentioned. In a theology so organic as Anselm's it is not possible to touch a single doctrine without being led immediately to others. No wonder that at the end of the *Cur Deus Homo* Boso observes that "through the solution of the single question that we posed, I think that everything that is contained in the Old and New Testaments has been proved."[24] However wide-eyed that remark, it also rings with truth.

---

[23] *Ibid.*, 29 (A I, 47 f.) See also *De Processione Spiritus Sancti* 1 (A II, 181).
[24] *Cur Deus Homo* II, 22 (A II, 133).

The *A Priori* in St. Thomas' Theory of Knowledge

GEORGE A. LINDBECK

Associate Professor of Historical Theology
The Divinity School
Yale University
New Haven, Connecticut

I

The structure of human knowledge as described by Aquinas is in some respects remarkably Kantian. For this reason, it also leaves room for some characteristic emphases of modern existentialism. To be sure, neither Kant, nor Heidegger, nor Jaspers is in any sense St. Thomas *redivivus*, but the opposition between him and these recent thinkers is by no means as complete as is often supposed, and efforts to develop a Thomism which incorporates Kantian and existential concerns are not necessarily a betrayal of what Aquinas himself taught.

This thesis may sound novel; actually it is not at all original. Joseph Maréchal of Louvain,[1] with his attempt to synthesize Thomism and Kantianism, started a development which has become influential in Europe, and which now also borrows extensively, even though critically, from modern phenomenology and existentialism, and even to a certain extent from nineteenth-century idealism.[2] As has been emphasized in a recent article which is

---

[1] Maréchal, *Le point de départ de la métaphysique*, Cahier 5: *Le thomisme devant la philosophie critique* (Bruges: Beyaert, 1922–1949).

[2] For the metaphysics of the movement, see esp. Emerich Coreth, *Metaphysik. Eine methodisch - systematische Grundlegung* (Innsbruck - Wien - München: Tyrolia - Verlag, 1961); for its relation to existentialism, Bernard Welte, *Der philosophische Glaube bei Karl Jaspers und die Möglichkeit seiner Deutung durch die thomistische Philosophie: Symposion 2* (Freiburg im Breisgau: Alber, 1949), in French translation, *La foi philosophique chez Jaspers et saint Thomas d'Aquin* (Paris: Desclée-De Brouwer, 1958); for the connections with idealism, Emerich Coreth, "Metaphysik als Aufgabe," in *Aufgaben der Philosophie* (Innsbruck: Rauch, 1958), 1–100; and for the interpretation of St. Thomas, Karl Rahner, *Geist in Welt: zur Metaphysik der endlichen Erkenntnis bei*

the best introduction in English to the philosophical character of this development,[3] what we have here is a movement, not a school with a fixed philosophical position. It might be described as the equivalent among Thomist philosophers of the *aggiornamento,* the bringing-up-to-date, of Roman Catholicism recommended by the late Pope John XXIII. Its representatives are unmistakably Thomistic in their metaphysics, but methodologically, especially epistemologically, they differ sharply from their fellows.

In risking a brief, general description of this variegated movement, it is useful to contrast its representatives with what is probably the other major group of contemporary Thomists. These might be called, for the sake of brevity, the "Gilsonians," because they have been so influenced by the undoubted pre-eminence of Etienne Gilson[4] as the leading contemporary historian of St. Thomas' thought that their own philosophical position, by and large, resembles rather closely what he says was that of St. Thomas. (As long as we are using misleading school labels, we might add that they could also be called "Maritainians," because Gilson, by his own avowal, has been greatly influenced by Jacques Maritain.[5] Further, it should be mentioned that on the epistemological point which concerns us here, the followers of Gilson and Maritain are in basic agreement with the dominant Thomism of a past generation such as was represented, for instance, by Reginald Garrigou-Lagrange.[6])

The "Maréchalians" generally accept the historical work of Gilson and his

---

Thomas von Aquin, 2nd ed. (München: Kösel, 1957). Among many other German works which could be cited, I shall mention only two by Gustav Siewerth, *Der Thomismus als Identitätssystem* (Frankfurt a.M.: Schulte-Bulmke, 1961), and *Die Apriorität der menschlichen Erkenntnis nach Thomas von Aquin* (Freiburg im Breisgau: Alber, 1948), 89–167. French-language authors who have been influenced by Maréchal include Nicolas Balthasar, *La méthode en métaphysique* (Louvain: Institut supérieur de philosophie, 1943), *Mon moi dans l'être* (Louvain: Institut supérieur de philosophie, 1946), Louis de Raeymaeker, *La philosophie de l'être* (Louvain: Institut supérieur de philosophie, 1946), Aimé Forest, *Du consentement à l'être* (Paris: Montaigne, 1936), André Hayen, *L'intentionnel dans la philosophie de Saint Thomas* (Paris: Desclée-De Brouwer, 1942), Ferdinand van Steenberghen, *Ontologie* (Louvain: Institut supérieur de philosophie, 1946). The positions of most of these last-named authors are described by Georges van Riet, *L'épistemologie thomiste,* 2nd ed. (Louvain: Bibl. philosophique de Louvain, 1951).

[3] Bernard Lonergan, "Metaphysics as Horizon," *Gregorianum,* XLIV (1963), 307–318.

[4] See esp. his *L'être et l'essence* (Paris: Vrin, 1948), and *Being and Some Philosophers* (Toronto: Pontifical Institute, 1952).

[5] Particularly indicative of Maritain's resemblances to Gilson are his *Court traité de l'existence et l'existant* (Paris: Hartmann, 1947), and his *A Preface to Metaphysics: Seven Lectures on Being* (London: Sheed and Ward, 1948).

[6] *God: His Existence and Nature* (St. Louis: Herder, 1945–1946). For further explanations of the epistemological similarities and differences in regard to the knowledge of *esse* of Gilson, Maritain, and Garrigou-Lagrange and their associates, see my essay, "Participation and Existence," *Franciscan Studies,* XVII (1957), 1–22, 107–125, esp. 16 f. and 20 f.

associates, and their own version of the Thomistic doctrine of being incorporates all the major features of what the best contemporary scholarship presents as St. Thomas' own teaching. However, they unconditionally reject as both philosophically unacceptable and historically inaccurate the kind of anticritical, dogmatic realism which other Thomists attribute to Aquinas. There is no reason, they maintain, for rejecting Kant's question, for refusing an epistemologically critical approach. Once the problem is raised, the only philosophically responsible thing to do is to seek to establish epistemological realism, rather than simply blindly assert it.

Having accepted the Kantian question, one must accept the Kantian method, that is, one must seek by means of transcendental deductions to discover the necessary conditions of human knowledge. When properly handled, this method produces results far more positive than any of which Kant dreamed. It can be shown that his critical idealism is untenable and that it must be replaced by critical realism. Realistic convictions regarding the objective reality of the *Ding-an-sich,* of *noumena,* indeed of the whole vast range of metaphysical entities described in St. Thomas' doctrine of being, can be shown to be just as much necessary, *a priori* conditions of human knowledge as are space and time and the categories of the understanding. Kant, it is said, failed to go this far, failed to reach a realistic metaphysics, because his starting point was too limited, not because of a bad method. He undertook to ascertain the necessary conditions for representation only, rather than for the entire activity of intellection, including its indispensable dynamic and "existential" dimensions.

It is, to be sure, difficult to take account of all relevant aspects of the process of cognition, especially when the philosophical tradition, as at the time of Enlightenment, is narrow and distorted. In order to become aware of the full range of phenomena which needs to be explained, it may be necessary to have one's attention widened by the riches of the *philosophia perennis* from Parmenides to the present, as well as by the depths of existential concern opened up by religious passion. Thus, even though philosophy is a purely rational activity, it may be existentially dependent on faith which can, so to speak, open the philosopher's eyes to aspects of experience which, while recognizable to natural reason, are easily ignored. At any rate, once the philosopher has developed an adequate phenomenological account of what is involved in intellection, it is possible for him to show, contrary to Kant, that the God of natural theology is not simply a regulative idea of pure reason, but rather that there is an *a priori,* nonobjective *Vorgriff* (anticipation) and "openness" to the *ens realissimum et infinitum* as the "horizon" of all possible beings. This is a necessary condition for our knowledge of finite entities. It is not itself an object of direct knowledge, but it finds expression in myths, symbols, and analogies which are explicated and clarified by the traditional philosophical descriptions and "demonstrations" of the existence of God. However, this natural knowledge of God is never more than purely formal, a knowledge of him as the ultimate precondition for cognition and existence. Like all the formal conditions for knowledge, it can receive concrete and determinate content only through sense experience, that is, only through the revelation of God under the conditions of space and time in history.[7]

It is not our business in this essay to give a philosophical evaluation of these efforts to rise from an existential phenomenology of human knowledge, by means of a Kantian transcendental deduction, to a Thomistic doctrine of being. Nor shall we deal with the considerable and, from a Protestant point of view, beneficial effects which this approach has had on theological treatments of faith and reason, nature and grace.[8] Our concern is with the plausibility of the historical claim that St. Thomas Aquinas does not reject, but at least to a certain extent supports, the view that metaphysical knowledge is *a priori.*

Because of limitations of space, it will be necessary to summarize, rather than present at length, the textual evidence. There are many scholars whose textual knowledge equips them far better than I am to do this work, but they apparently do not read, and certainly have not discussed in print, the arguments which seek to show that Aquinas' thought is open to a post-Kantian reconstruction. For them the issue is apparently foreclosed, presumably because they have been completely convinced by works such as Gilson's *Réalisme thomiste et critique de la connaissance*[9] that there is an irreducible opposition between Kant and Thomas. The result is what seems to me the scandalous neglect of some really brilliant exegesis of St. Thomas. I think especially of Karl Rahner's *Geist in Welt,*[10] to which I am particularly indebted, because while this, like all the writings of this movement, is philo-

---

[7] The above description is based mostly on Welte, Coreth, and Rahner. See n. 2.

[8] In addition to numerous essays scattered throughout Karl Rahner's *Schriften zur Theologie,* 5 vols. (Einsiedeln-Zürich-Köln: Benziger, 1954–1962), see Carlos Cirne-Lima, *Der personale Glaube* (Innsbruck: Rauch, 1959), and, in English, Gerald A. McCool, "The Primacy of Intuition," *Thought,* XXXVII (1962), 57–73. The most thorough study of this theme of which I know is an unpublished doctoral dissertation, presented at Yale University in 1962, by Eugene Arthur TeSelle, Jr., *Thomas and the Thomists on Nature and Grace: An Interpretation of the Theological Anthropology of Thomas Aquinas in the Light of Recent Scholarship.*

[9] Paris: Vrin, 1939.

[10] The first edition of this book appeared in 1939. See n. 2 for the reference to the second, slightly revised edition which I have used.

sophically oriented, it is also packed with careful textual analyses. To ignore it seems to me very nearly equivalent to dismissing Bultmann without a hearing because of an *a priori* conviction that his use of Heidegger must inevitably vitiate everything he writes about the New Testament.

However, as the example just mentioned reminds us, exegetical breakthroughs are at first almost always exaggerated. Thus the proponents of the new interpretation of St. Thomas tend to picture him as a man who, handicapped by inadequate intellectual tools, was groping toward their own views. Often, it seems to me, the most that can be shown is that he left room for them, that he did not exclude them. Contrary to what Rahner suggests,[11] respect for his genius should not lead us to assume that he had philosophical reasons for his statements when purely historical explanations suffice. It may be, to put it strongly, that some of the resemblances between him and his present-day reinterpreters are in reality purely verbal because they have different reasons than he had for saying what they do. In short, from the strictly historical point of view which I have tried to adopt in this essay, they rely far too much on philosophical arguments about what Thomas "should" and therefore "must" have meant.

Unfortunately, therefore, I shall not be able to appeal to their direct support as much as I would like. The stimulus comes from them, the hypothesis which we shall examine was suggested by them, but the pattern and details of my argument are generally different. Further, my hypothesis is much more limited than theirs. Maréchal, Rahner, and Siewerth have advanced interesting claims regarding the *a priori* status of time and space for St. Thomas, and they, as well as others, explore the repercussions throughout the system of their epistemological proposals. Such investigations are beyond the scope of this essay.

Limiting ourselves, then, to what Aquinas considers properly intellectual knowledge, the discussion will proceed in two stages. I shall argue in the first and shorter part, that Aquinas' Aristotelian insistence on the *a posteriori* character of all knowledge was directed against the objective *a priorism* of Augustinian Platonism and does not exclude a Kantian nonobjective variety. Expressed differently, this would suggest that all Aquinas says about the sense origin of knowledge can be understood as summed up in the principle that there is no human cognition apart from the *conversio ad phantasma*. This is pretty much the equivalent of the Kantian affirmation that concepts without percepts are blind, and from it both our philosophers drew the conclusion

---

[11] *Geist in Welt,* 13.

that there are no innate ideas, nor ways of directly apprehending pure intelligibles. Thus they both reject Platonistic *a priorism* and, from the point of view of this conflict with Platonism, they both accept the *a posteriori* character of all knowledge, i.e., all knowledge has a sensory component. Further—and this is the decisive point—even though Aquinas talks as if he rejects all kinds of *a priori* knowledge, he does not in fact exclude the kind that Kant later proposed. The result is that it is possible to read with perfect logical consistency a good many Kantian and post-Kantian views into St. Thomas. It must be admitted, however, that this goes against what might be called the rhetorical grain of much of his writing.

However, the second stage of our argument advances further. Not only is it logically possible to introduce a certain amount of Kantian *a priorism* into Aquinas' epistemology, but much of what he says, especially about the knowledge of being and of its first principles, suggests that he himself has already done this. From the point of view of his opposition to medieval Augustinianism, these things are known *a posteriori,* but he seems to recognize in them the peculiar characteristics which would make them *a priori* from a Kantian perspective. Or, to put it in another way, Aquinas rejected only that part of his Platonic heritage which he explicitly says he did: he rejected only *a priori* objects of knowledge, and he continued to accept, in the form of a nonobjectifiable *a priori,* a good deal more Platonism than is immediately apparent.

Once again, it would be surprising if this were not so, for a thinker generally shares the assumptions of his age except in so far as he overtly rejects them. Yet this means that the second part of our argument cannot be completely conclusive. We shall perhaps be able to show, not only that there is nothing against a certain kind of *a priori* in St. Thomas, but also that there is some evidence for it, but we shall not be able to cite texts in which St. Thomas positively asserts it. This, of course, is what has made it possible for generations of readers to be convinced by the "rhetoric" of his presentation that he held nothing of the sort.

Before we begin summarizing the textual support for this argument, it will be well to emphasize a point which has already been mentioned. On the question of epistemological realism *versus* idealism, Aquinas is obviously not in the least Kantian. In the medieval context, this issue was never considered, and it is utterly independent of the problem of the *a posteriori* versus the *a priori.* The Augustinians and the Aristotelians were both equally "realistic" in the epistemological sense of the word. Their disagreement was entirely on how we come to know the objectively real natures of things as these exist in themselves independently of our minds, not on the fact that we do know them. It is important to insist on this, for probably the biggest single obstacle to the theory we are investigating is the uncritical assumption that because Aquinas was vigorously realistic, believed so strongly that our minds really know, really penetrate, beyond the phenomena to the trans-sensible metaphysical essences of things, he could not possibly have any significant epistemological resemblances to Kant.

Now perhaps *a priorism* and epistemological realism are philosophically irreconcilable (though Maréchal, Rahner, *et al.* vigorously deny this), but it is historically anachronistic to attribute such an opinion to St. Thomas. He never attacked the *a priorism* of his Augustinian opponents on the grounds that it would logically lead to idealism (which, after all, had not yet been invented); and therefore, conversely, it is historically absurd—whatever it may be philosophically—to argue, as is done by Gilson, from Aquinas' realism to an anti-Kantian interpretation of his *a posteriorism.*

This *a posteriorism,* as I shall now try to show in more detail, can be understood as wholly directed against Platonism. It excludes only nonsensible cognitive objects, only the view that the content, or part of the content, of intellectual knowledge has a nonsensory origin. It does not exclude the possibility, which Kant was later to develop, that the "form," the intelligibility, of objects of intellectual knowledge is contributed by the mind. It at least leaves open the question of whether the necessity and universality of certain concepts and judgments, such as those which express knowledge of being and its first principles, come from the side of the intellect rather than of sensible things. Stated briefly, then, my first thesis is that Aquinas does not reject the view that intelligibility is "projected" into the sensible content of our knowledge rather than "extracted" from it.

This, as I have already mentioned, seems difficult to reconcile with the language which Aquinas generally uses. He normally speaks of the process of cognition as one in which the agent intellect "dematerializes" and "universalizes" the essences of material things, thus making the potentially intelligible into the actually intelligible. Once this is done, the essence or its likeness, the *species intelligibilis,* is "assimilated" into or "informs" the mind.[12] Further, the standard name for this process is "abstraction." Such terms suggest with apparent irresistibility that, not only the material content, but also the intelligibility of things is "extracted" from sense experience rather than "projected" into it.

---

[12] A glance at, e.g., Ludwig Schuetz, *Thomas-Lexicon* (Paderborn: Schoeningh, 1895), under such terms as "cognitio," "abstractio," "species," "informatio," etc., will provide many illustrations of the kind of usage referred to here.

II

The first thing to do if the thesis we are exploring is to be taken seriously, is to escape from the limits imposed by the different ways of pictorializing the problem.[13] Admittedly, St. Thomas constantly uses extractionist and assimilationist imagery, but he was not bound by it. He also uses the language of projection, and clearly says that neither of these two ways of speaking is to be taken literally. Our conclusion will be that, from the point of view of our problem, both are hopelessly ambiguous. We cannot settle the problem of the *a priori* by arguing from Aquinas' metaphors.

In saying that St. Thomas sometimes uses the language of projection, we are referring to the illuminationist imagery which he borrows from the Augustinians. He habitually speaks of the "light of the agent intellect," and that phrase already is a combination of Augustianian and Aristotelian, extractionist and projectionist, motifs. It may seem exaggerated to say that the mere use of the image of light suggests that intelligibility is actually projected by the mind into the objects of knowledge. Couldn't one just as well say the light reveals an intelligibility which is in some sense pre-existent in them? The difficulty with this is that according to Aquinas' physics, light makes a contribution to the objects which it irradiates. It contributes their color. It cannot be seen in and of itself, but only as the color of the bodies on which it shines,[14] and color, in turn, "is nothing else than incorporated light (*lux incorporata*)."[15]

This physical conception of light clearly influences the way in which he speaks of the light of the agent intellect. "Since everything which is understood is known by the power of the intellectual light, in so far it is thus known, it includes in itself the intellectual light as that in which it participates (*includit in se intellectuale lumen ut participatum*)."[16] "The light is contained in the perceived object of knowledge (*lumen contentum in cognito percepto*)."[17] The light of the agent intellect is "the act of these intelligibles (*actus ipsorum intelligibilium*)."[18] It is the "form" of what is given to the intellect through the senses.[19] Finally, a passage which makes completely

[13] While he would scarcely agree with the later course of my argument, A. D. Sertillanges has an eloquent page on this point in his *Saint Thomas d'Aquin,* Vol. 2 (Paris: Alcan, 1922), 168.

[14] E.g., *De Verit.* 14, 8, ad 4.

[15] I *Sent.* 17, 1, 1, c.

[16] *De Verit.* 9, 1, ad 2. Cf. S.T. I, 79, 3 ad 2.

[17] *Ibid.*

[18] *S.T.* I, 87, 1, c.

[19] III *Sent.* 14, 1, 1, 12, ad 2.

explicit the parallelism between physical and intellectual light: "A thing is understood only as it is illuminated by the light of the agent intellect and received into the possible intellect. Thus just as corporeal light is seen in everything colored, so the light of the agent intellect is seen in every intelligible, though not as an object of knowledge, but as a medium of knowledge."[20] We draw no conclusions from these passages, but simply point out that they could easily be interpreted as referring to something like the Kantian forms and categories of the understanding which are not in themselves representable objects of knowledge, but rather bestow intelligibility on sense data by forming them into objects of which they themselves then appear as constituents.

It must be stressed that these illuminationist descriptions refer to exactly the same process of understanding that Aquinas in other places speaks of in terms of abstraction. There is only one passage of which I know which suggests that *abstrahare* and *illuminare* are not completely interchangeable,[21] and in this case the imagery of light is apparently used in an unusually extended sense to refer to the way in which the intellect informs and shapes sensibility even on the preintellectual level.[22] The rest of the time, however, he simply says that the intelligible light "makes actually intelligible" (*facere intelligibilia actu*)[23] and this, in turn, is the technical expression for abstraction.[24] Sometimes he completely fuses the two ways of speaking as when he writes of the power of this light "to separate the intelligible species from the phantasms."[25]

Because this kind of illuminationist language has been cited as evidence that Aquinas did affirm something like a Kantian *a priori,*[26] let me emphasize once again that we are at present arguing only that he did not deny it. His use of illuminationism shows that one cannot argue against an *a priorist* interpretation of his thought by appealing to his often crudely extractionist formulations. In his own thinking, extractionist and projectionist imagery do not conflict, because he knew very well that they are both metaphorical. "The word 'light' was first used to signify that which makes something manifest to the sense of sight, and then afterwards its meaning was extended to whatever makes manifest in any order of knowledge. If, therefore, one takes 'light' in its first imposition, it is used metaphorically in regard to spiritual

[20] I *Sent*. 3, 4, 5, c.
[21] *S.T.* I, 85, 1, ad 4.
[22] Rahner, *op. cit.,* 228.
[23] *Ibid.,* 229.
[24] See *S.C.G.* II, 76 and 96, *S.T.* I, 54, 4, c. and 79, 3, c., etc.
[25] *De Sp. Creat.* 10, ad 6.
[26] Rahner, *op. cit.,* 219–232, esp. 227.

realities."[27] So also abstraction "does not mean that one and the same form which was first in the phantasms is afterwards in the possible intellect in the way in which a body is taken from one place and transferred to another."[28] Indeed, the way to correct the misleading connotations of abstractionist imagery is to use that of light: "The agent intellect does not make things actually intelligible as if by infusing them into the possible intellect . . . [but] in the way in which light actualizes colors, not as if it may possess them, but in so far as it in some way gives them visibility (*non quasi habeat apud se, sed inquantum dat eis quodammodo visibilitatem*)."[29]

So far we have not discussed the application of the fundamental Aristotelian concepts of act and potency, form and matter, to the process of cognition. However, they do not help us decide between the two alternatives which we have outlined. On the one hand, they make it possible to say, for instance, that the same form which is actually intelligible in the intellect exists in a potentially intelligible form in corporeal things.[30] This certainly seems to reduce the active molding role of the mind to a minimum. It positively incites one to imagine that the agent intellect simply strips away a veil of matter and then imprints an otherwise unchanged form upon the wax tablet of the soul. However, the correctness of such analogies depends on what kind of potentiality for being known characterizes sensible things. Is it purely material and passive, or is it more actively determining? In one passage, St. Thomas says that sensible knowledge is not "the cause of intellectual cognition, but rather the matter on which it acts."[31] If taken literally, this pushes us to the opposite extreme of picturing the mind as constructing the world out of the unformed material supplied by the senses (and, indeed, even of giving it existence because, according to Thomas, form rather than matter is the source of *esse*).[32]

The truth seems to be that Aquinas changes and mixes his metaphors with the utmost *insouciance*. The meaning they have depends on the context, and this is never supplied by the *Critique of Pure Reason*. Presumably, therefore, the quantitative dominance of abstractionist and assimilationist imagery in his writings does not tell us where he stands in reference to our contemporary philosophical battles. Rather, it simply indicates that he was a medieval Aristotelian opposing medieval Platonism, and that this kind of language helped him to make clear that it is the proper business of the human mind to deal

[27] *S.T.* I, 67, 1, c.
[28] *Comp. Theol.*, 88.
[29] *Ibid.* Cf. Maréchal, *Point de départ* 5, 148 ff.
[30] E.g., *S.T.* I, 79, 3, c.
[31] *S.T.* I, 84, 6, c.
[32] E.g., in the passage just cited and in *S.T.* I, 75, 5, ad 3.

with the stuff of the physical world. This alone supplies the basic raw material for all our knowledge, and it is impossible to escape, no matter how hard we try, into some distant empyrean of pure intelligibles. If this is so, then Aquinas' *a posteriorism,* his contention that all our knowledge is abstracted from the material world, is simply a rather metaphorical way of asserting what he says more precisely in his doctorine of the *conversio ad phantasma.*

Let us recall what St. Thomas himself asserts before commenting on it. The *conversio* is necessary to every act of human intellection. The only way of thinking anything, of making it an object of thought, of representing it to ourselves, is by means of phantasms, the sensory images of the imagination. Thus we know nothing except as we see it in sense data, except in the process of coming to know material things. The proper object of the human mind is the quiddity, the nature, of corporeal existents. There are no pure intellectual objects of thought, whether these be innate ideas or nonsensible realities outside the mind. We can, of course, know immaterial realities of which there are, properly speaking, no phantasms, but in order to do so, they must be objectified in the phantasmal, the sensory. That is why metaphysical knowledge depends on analogies or comparisons with sensible bodies of which there are phantasms and why there is, to use a modern phrase, a sensible symbolic component even in our thinking of the divine. There is no need for a lengthy documentation of the assertion that all these consequences follow from the *conversio ad phantasma.* Everything that we have said is repeated over and over again by St. Thomas.[33]

Now as far as I can see, there is nothing in Aquinas to require us to interpret even the most sweepingly *a posteriori* assertions as implying more than this *conversio.* Take, for example, the famous adage *"Nihil est in intellectu, quod non prius erat in sensu."*[34] This can be interpreted as simply meaning that everything we know, whether its origin is sensible or intellectual, *a posteriori* or *a priori,* becomes an object of knowledge only by being seen in and through the phantasms. In the imagery of illumination which Aquinas employs, the *a priori* is known only as reflected in phantasms (or to be precise, in intelligible essences which have a phantasmal component or base). We have already seen Aquinas asserting that this is the only way in which we can become aware of something which definitely was for him *a priori,* viz., the light of the agent intellect. This also must first be *in sensu,* in the sensible faculty of the phantasmal imagination, before it can be known. Thus the *conversio ad phantasma* makes it necessary to say that whatever is known

---

[33] Most fully, perhaps, in *S.T.* I, 84, 7.
[34] Cf. *S.T.* I, 84 f.

a priori for Aquinas, whether this is more or less than for Kant, is also first in the senses. In short, the Thomistic principle of the sense origin of all knowledge can easily and consistently be understood as basically equivalent to the Kantian view that concepts without percepts are empty, but this does not exclude the possibility of asserting that concepts themselves are in part *a priori*.

Is it possible to go further than this? The conclusion of this first part of our argument is simply that the Maréchalian and post-Maréchalian modernizations of St. Thomas do not contradict what he himself held. Gilson and others who argue differently clearly go beyond the texts and advance philosophical speculations about what the Angelic Doctor should have said or must have meant. If one sticks to the strictly historical evidence, then these modernizations must be considered legitimate developments of Thomism in the sense that there is nothing in Aquinas' own position calculated to exclude them. But are they more than that? Does he give them any positive support?

While it seems to me that he does, it must once again be emphasized that the evidence is inconclusive. Interpreters such as Maréchal and Rahner exceed the limits of the historically demonstrable at least as much as do Thomists of the opposite orientation. Indeed, they are quite frank about this, as when Rahner says that "the direction of the questions directed at Thomas is predetermined by a systematic concern . . . [which] is conditioned by the problematic of present-day philosophy. . . . Whoever is convinced of the influence of the *philosophia perennis* on at least the greater philosophers, cannot, at least not from the outset, reject such a modern *Fragestellung* as improper in an historical work."[35]

This seems to me quite wrong. Even those who, like myself, are philosophically sympathetic to the notion of the *philosophia perennis* should try not to let this influence their historical work. Yet it must be admitted that these improperly speculative historical attempts to reconcile Aquinas with modernity have clarified important and difficult points by showing that certain contrasts between medieval and modern arguments which certainly look like contradictions are not that because they have different starting points and objectives. What must be objected to is simply the excessive ease with which this no-man's land of noncontradiction is filled with premonitions and anticipations of Kant and Heidegger.

This does not deny that there are some anticipations, although inconclusive ones. A good many texts suggest that if the modern notion of the *a priori* had existed in St. Thomas' day he would have applied it to the knowledge of being *qua* being, to other first conceptions and to first principles. This,

---

[35] Rahner, *op. cit.*, 14.

as we have already shown, could be true even though he says that "we know even indemonstrable principles by abstraction from the sensible."[36] There is, we must repeat, a Thomistic sense in which our knowledge of anything, even of the unquestionably *a priori* light of the agent intellect, is abstracted. When Aquinas applies this word to being, he makes it quite clear that it then signifies something quite different than it usually does. It can be argued, plausibly even if inconclusively, that it refers to a kind of abstraction appropriate only to knowledge of what is *a priori*. This is important because, as we shall see, the status of being is decisive for first conceptions and first principles in general. If that is *a priori,* so are these. Further, the role of being and of first principles in abstracting essences, in making all other things intelligible, is described in terms so closely parallel to what is said of the agent intellect and its intelligible light that it is by no means far-fetched to suggest that they are in fact identical. My problem is that Aquinas nowhere does explicitly identify them, and consequently I do not think his writings provide a decisive answer to the modern question regarding the epistemological status of first conceptions and first principles, even though they do tend to favor the newer rather than the older interpretation.

In giving the barest sketch of the textual evidence supporting this conclusion, let me recall that first principles are self-evidently necessary truths[37] such as the principle of contradiction[38] and, to cite a favorite example, the principle that the whole is greater than any of its parts.[39] Aquinas never discusses them systematically nor gives a complete list, but it is safe to say that they include all the truths which Kant considered *a priori* as well, obviously, as a good many others, such as those which affirm epistemological realism. The first conceptions are the terms of the first principles[40] and they, first conceptions and first principles together, are described as depending on our knowledge of being; they are additions to *ens*.[41]

III

Postponing the discussion of *ens,* let us now see what Aquinas has to say about the relation between first principles and the agent intellect. There are many texts which illustrate the close connection between them. For example: "There is in every man a principle of knowledge, viz., the light of the agent

---

[36] *S.C.G.* II, 83.
[37] *S.T.* I–II, 58, 2.
[38] *S.T.* I–II, 94, 2, c.
[39] *Ibid.*
[40] *Quodl.* 8, 4, c.
[41] *De Verit.* 1, 1, c. and *S.C.G.* II, 83.

intellect, by which certain universal principles of all sciences are naturally known from the beginning. When someone applies these principles to the particular realities which are experienced and remembered through the senses, then by his own discovery he acquires knowledge of that which he did not know, proceeding from the unknown to the known."[42] The first principles "are in us as *quasi* instruments of the agent intellect."[43] "They are related to the agent intellect as its instruments by which it makes things intelligible."[44] The impression left, especially by the last quotations, is that the process of abstraction, of "making things intelligible," consists, at least in part, in the application of first principles to the data of the senses.

This, however, still leaves open the question of the manner in which these first principles originate from or are produced by the agent intellect. According to what we have labeled the "extractionist" view, they are abstracted from material things in much the same way as any other essential or quidditative feature. The only difference is that they are abstracted first. Stated in this naïve, though by no means uncommon way, the position is obviously untenable. We have seen Aquinas say that abstraction, "making things intelligible," consists at least in part in the application of first principles to the particular things known through the senses. But first principles themselves obviously cannot have been abstracted in this way. They cannot themselves be instances of the application of first principles to sense data, because then they would not be "first," and we would be involved in an infinite regress to ever higher principles. This would seem to be both formally inadmissible and also intuitively absurd. What, for instance, could be higher than the principle of contradiction, the terms of which are "one" (*unum*) and "other" (*aliquid*) which, in turn, are *passiones entis* or transcendental properties of being?

Yet it must be admitted that Aquinas does not himself clearly exclude extractionist interpretations of the origin of first principles. We may find it even more difficult to imagine what such interpretations would mean in their case than in reference to lower level essences. We may point out that if Aquinas thought of the first principles as forms first immanent in matter and abstracted simply by stripping away individualizing materiality, he was in fact violating his own warnings against taking abstractionist imagery literally. However, this is inconclusive, for Aquinas may very well have been guilty of just such an error. Lulled by his own metaphors, he may have failed to notice that, by his own account, our knowledge of first principles and of other essences must originate in very different ways.

---

[42] *S.T.* I, 117, 1, c.
[43] *De Verit.* 10, 13, c.
[44] *De Anima* 5, c.

On the other hand, it is also possible that the traditional illuminationism was still so deeply ingrained in him and his readers that statements tended to embody the meaning they would have in an illuminationist context, save in so far as this was specifically prevented. If so, Aquinas' insistence on the sense origin of first principles would not have an extractionist meaning. Consider, for instance, the statement that "the knowledge of principles is received from the senses, even though the light by which the principles are known is innate."[45] If Aquinas understood this in an illuminationist manner as, indeed, he could without contradicting his doctrine of the *conversio ad phantasma,* it would mean that the first principles are the reflection in sense data of the light of the agent intellect. That light in its visible, its knowable, form would be identical with first principles as these are exemplified in sense experience.[46] The first principles, as the "imprint" of the light on experience, are the "instruments" for the abstraction of determinate essences; that is, they constitute the general formal structures exemplified in objects of knowledge; they are the general rules in terms of which sense experience is organized.

These observations, it is hoped, may indicate that this is a viable line of interpretation. It even comes close to receiving direct textual support, especially when Aquinas speaks, as we have noted, of the intelligible light as contained in objects of knowledge. However, we have also pointed out that the metaphorical character of these passages makes it impossible to base any decisive argument upon them.

What we have so far done is preliminary. The real test of our hypothesis comes in what Aquinas says about the origin of the knowledge of being. This, as we have seen, is basic to the knowledge of the first principles so that its ultimate source must also be theirs. If they are reflections of the light of the agent intellect, so also must be *ens*. More than that: the intelligible light itself must be either being, or else some kind of prereflective, preconscious awareness of being—in the phrase of Karl Rahner, a *Vorgriff auf esse,*[47] an "anticipatory knowledge" of existence.

As we shall see more clearly later, the second alternative is the only one which would be plausible in a Thomistic context. It is impossible to identify the agent intellect, which is in a sense from the very beginning "all things," with the limited being, the limited act of existence, of the human knower. Further, it cannot very well be conceived as unlimited because this would, in effect, make it identical with the immediate presence of God himself to the human mind, and Aquinas insists against the Augustinians that the agent

---

[45] *In Boet. de Trin.* 3, 1, ad 4.

[46] See n. 15 to 19.

[47] Rahner, *op. cit.,* 167 ff., *passim.*

intellect is not itself the divine light, but only a "participation" in it.[48] This leaves us, then, with the hypothesis that the knowledge of being of which we can become consciously aware is a projection, a reflection, in our sense experience of the *a priori,* anticipatory knowledge of being which is either identical with or a part of the agent intellect.

The extractionist alternative, of course, is to think of the being which is known by the mind as originating in material objects and mediated through, rather than reflected in, sense experience. This is a somewhat unsatisfactory way of phrasing the contrast between the two options because it may give the impression that according to the projectionist position, the intellect does not know the being, the existence, of material entities themselves, but simply attributes *ens* and *esse* to them. Actually, however, what this view proposes is that the *a priori* anticipation of being "in general" is what enables human beings to recognize the objects of sense experience as instances of it.

Fortunately for our purposes, there is a consensus among contemporary Thomists about most aspects of the doctrine of being and of our knowledge of it. Rahner and Gilson, for example, describe the metaphysical structure of being, both human and divine, in similar terms. And, if one abstracts from the single question of ultimate origins, of the *a priori* versus the *a posteriori,* they also basically agree on the character of our knowledge of being. In the paragraphs which follow it is possible simply to summarize the assured results of recent historical work, and to cite even fewer texts than usual.

IV

The meaning which "being" has in this discussion is the so-called "existential" one which is now just about universal in leading Thomist circles. It is scarcely necessary to say that "existential" in this context has nothing to do with modern philosophical existentialism. Anyone who is in the least familiar with Gilson and Maritain—who have done most to familiarize at least English-speaking readers with this aspect of the Thomistic doctrine of being—is aware that we are here concerned with Aquinas' emphasis on the *esse,* the *actus essendi.*[49] This is the central actuality in every substance. It is because of a thing's "to be" (*esse*) that it is called a being (*ens*). In creatures, this act of existence is distinct from the essence which limits it and is in potentiality to it. In God, *esse* and *essentia* are identical, or, to put it another way, God is

[48] God does not illuminate men by his own light, but "by imprinting on them the natural light of the agent intellect." *De sp. creat.* 10, ad 1. For the texts in which this natural light is called a participation in the divine light, see Maréchal, *Point de départ* 5, 322–325.

[49] See n. 4 and n. 5.

the unlimited, infinite act of existence. He is being itself, the *ipsum esse,* the all-encompassing fullness of reality. All other things exist only as limited participations in his pure actuality. Consequently, the deeper one penetrates into the existential depths of beings, into the noumena behind the phenomena, the closer one comes to a knowledge of God.[50]

We must now expand our suggestion that what Aquinas has to say about the knowledge of *ens* is, in general, what we would expect on the basis of the hypothesis that this knowledge is the primary and fundamental reflection in our cognitive experience of the light of the agent intellect. We have already mentioned that this knowledge, like the agent intellect itself, is said to be the source of first principles and consequently of all intellectual knowledge. It is the *conceptio prima.*[51] In trying to understand what this means, we must constantly remember that the concept of being of which Aquinas speaks is not the *summum genus* of the logician; it is not the widest and emptiest of all notions. It is not that minimal facticity, that simple thereness, which constitutes the logical class of widest extension and least intension. Before the time of Scotus, it would seem that "being" never referred to this. For Aquinas, the primary notion of *ens* is one which contains all entitative differences, all possible reality, in a confused state. He sometimes describes the acquisition of knowledge in terms of the progressive clarification of what one knows vaguely and implicitly from the very beginning. That is why it is axiomatic that, for the philosophical tradition of which he was a part, the first known is the most universal, viz., being.[52] In short, to say that *ens* is the *conceptio prima* seems to be equivalent to asserting that the basis of all knowledge is a vague but powerful awareness of the unlimited intensional riches, extensional breadth, and existential depth of reality. Some Thomists like to say that, for Aquinas, being is comparable to the all-encompassing "horizon" of which modern existential phenomenology speaks.[53] Such a horizon is *a priori* in the sense that it is not an object of experience or knowledge, but is rather the locus for these.

This is equivalent to saying that knowledge of *ens* is indirect, nonobjective, nonconceptual, a constituent in our knowledge of the objects of sense experience rather than something known independently in and of itself. This is a second way in which it resembles what we have seen Aquinas saying about the knowledge of the intelligible light and, therefore, a further confirmation

[50] Etienne Gilson's most recent summary of his research on Thomas' doctrine of divine and creaturely being is found in *Elements of Christian Philosophy* (New York: Doubleday, 1960), 100–135.

[51] E.g., *S.T.* I, 5, 2, c. and 11, 2, ad 4.

[52] *S.T.* I, 85, 3.

[53] This is true of all the German-language authors listed in n. 2.

of the suggestion that it is a reflection of that light. Despite his use of the word *conceptio,* Aquinas does not believe that there is such a thing as a "concept" of being in the usual sense of the word.[54] One cannot have a clear and distinct idea of it. It is indefinable by such logical devices as genus and difference. Its meaning is constantly shifting, depending on its context; in other words, *ens* is analogous rather than univocal. Yet it is not simply a syncategorematic term, in the sense of medieval logic, nor systematically ambiguous in the sense of Russell's and Whitehead's *Principia Mathematica.* It is used, not primarily because of the syntactical requirements of the language, but in order to refer to the fundamental objective reality of things.

To say that the knowledge of being is nonconceptual is equivalent, for Aquinas, to asserting that it is judgmental.[55] It is through the process of judging, of "composing and dividing," of formulating propositions either implicitly or explicitly, that our knowledge of being is expressed. Our knowledge of existence is therefore radically different from our knowledge of essence. The essence, the quiddity, the "whatness," of a thing is known only in and through concepts, in and through an *apprehensio* which Aquinas calls *simplex* because it is not judgmental, even though, from the point of view of its internal character, it may be extremely complex. In contrast, existence, *esse,* being, is intellectually grasped only through the activity of judging that such and such is in fact so and so.

It is desirable to digress for a moment in order to dispose of a possible source of misunderstanding. In view of the primacy of the knowledge of *ens,* one would expect judgment to be referred to as the first act of the intellect, but actually Aquinas follows the traditional usage of calling it the second act. He explains, however, that what is named the first act, the *simplex apprehensio* or *intellectus incomplexus* through which essences are grasped, actually occurs in a context of judgments, i.e., of comparison of things, which, to be sure, may be wholly implicit.[56] The formation of the universal concept of red, for instance, takes place through a complex process of "dividing" a color from its subject and "composing" it with other instances of the same color. It is only when one adopts the logician's point of view and considers knowledge in its fully articulated form as a body of explicit judgments, that

---

[54] It is once again Etienne Gilson who has discussed this point most fully. See his *Le thomisme,* 5th ed. (Paris: Vrin, 1948), 61–68, *Réalisme thomiste et critique de la connaissance* (Paris: Vrin, 1939), 213–239, and the works already cited in n. 4: *L'être,* 249–310, and *Being,* 190–215.

[55] *Ibid.,* but esp. the last two references in the above footnote. This provides another point of contact with the intelligible light of the agent intellect, because this is first of all, according to Aquinas, the source of judgments rather than of the apprehension of essences. *De Malo* 16, 1, 2, c.

[56] E.g., *S.C.G.* I, 59.

acquaintance with the meaning of terms seems to be prior to the combining of these into propositions. In much of what he says, Aquinas abandons this abstract standpoint and describes the so-called first act of the intellect as standing in a relation of reciprocal causation to the so-called second act. It is, therefore, entirely consistent for him to describe the knowledge of *ens,* of the independent existence of things, as basic to the knowledge of essences. Consequently, the Cartesian and Kantian questions regarding the external existence or noumenal reality of apprehended essences cannot arise. The very structure of our knowledge forbids this because, as we shall see more clearly later when we deal briefly with the theory of abstraction, the precondition for the abstraction of essences is our primordial awareness of existence.

Existence, it must now once again be emphasized, never does become a direct, thematic object of knowledge, not even when it is isolated for attention by the metaphysician. Some of Aquinas' descriptions of metaphysical knowledge are easy to misunderstand. He speaks of different levels of abstraction, and seems to place these on a continuous, ascending scale. There is, first of all, the abstraction of the essences of natural species such as man; second, that of mathematical quantity; and third, that of metaphysical realities which lack even mathematical quantitativeness. These last are "being, oneness, potency, and act and other things of this sort which can exist without any matter as is evident in immaterial substances."[57] This may give the impression that the mode of cognizing metaphysical objects is the same as for other objects. Only the objects themselves seem to be different, the metaphysical ones being more abstract, more general, farther removed from sensory concreteness than the others. However, Aquinas clearly indicates that this is not the case when he says that, in contrast to other sciences, metaphysics arrives at its objects by making judgments of a certain type rather than by forming a special kind of abstract concept. Metaphysics indicates its objects by negative judgments, by *separatio,* rather than by selective attention to the form as contrasted with sensible matter, or to the universal as contrasted with the particular.[58]

The metaphysician, in other words, can indicate what he is talking about only by denying that the concepts he uses are adequate to his referents. He tries to explicate by means of concepts a knowledge of existence, of being, which is nonconceptual. He must do this, because it is only by means of concepts drawn from material things that anything can be represented to the human mind.[59] But this mode of signification, appropriate to material things,

[57] *S.T.* I, 85, 1 ad 2.
[58] *In Boet. de Trin.* 5, 3.
[59] E.g., *S.T.* I, 13, 1 and 3.

must be separated from the *significatum,* from that which is signified, viz., existence as this comes to be known in and through the very act of judging. Since this *separatio* cannot be performed representationally or conceptually, it must be done by means of propositions which indicate that the reference of the names and concepts which apply, for instance, to Being Itself or God, is a reality which they are not normally used to denote.[60] This is the explanation and the meaning of the Thomistic thesis that all metaphysical knowledge is analogous, and it is equivalent to the assertion that there is only nonobjective knowledge of nonsensible realities including, of course, the light of the agent intellect.

So much, then, for the description of the nature of the knowledge of *ens* according to Aquinas. We have pointed out, at a number of points, that it supports the *a priorist* interpretation of this knowledge, but before we sum up this evidence, we must note certain additional indications that the agent intellect can be best understood as an "openness" to being which is the direct source of our knowledge of being.

Aquinas, for instance, speaks of the actuality of a thing as its light, presumably meaning that it is its intelligibility.[61] This suggests the possibility of interpreting the intellectual light, i.e., the agent intellect, as the intelligibility of the highest form of actuality, viz., *esse*. This would mean that the agent intellect is simply the intelligibility of *ens* present *a priori* to the mind. In agreement with this is the fact that St. Thomas speaks of the agent intellect as that which is supremely actual in the cognitive order,[62] namely, as always in act.[63] To be sure, these statements do not contradict the traditional Thomistic epistemology, but they do seem to make more sense in the context of the hypothesis we are examining. They make more sense because they go beyond the traditional explanation. This stops with the repetition of the Thomistic truism that the potentially knowable can become actually knowable only through the agency of something already in act. The newer view provides an intelligible account of the nature of this "something" by describing it as a kind of openness to the full actuality of being.

The reading is further supported by Aquinas' description of the agent intellect as a participation in the divine light, that is, the divine intelligence.[64] As God's *intelligere* is first of all knowledge of himself, of the fullness of being,[65] participation in this is most naturally understood as a sharing in

[60] *S.C.G.* I, 30. Cf. for this paragraph, Rahner, *Geist,* 197–209.
[61] *In Lib. de Causis* 6 (Parma ed. XXI, 729 b). Cited from Rahner, *op. cit.,* 221, n. 37.
[62] E.g., *S.T.* I–II, 50, 5, ad 2.
[63] E.g., *S.T.* I, 79, 4, ad 2.
[64] E.g., *S.T.* I, 79, 4, c., and 84, 5, c.
[65] E.g., *S.T.* I, 14, 4.

God's own knowledge of being and of himself. If this interpretation is adopted, the puzzling statement that God is known implicitly in everything that is known[66] can be easily explained. It simply means that the *a priori* anticipation of the divine plenitude which is the agent intellect is a precondition for every act of knowledge.

Once again, it is admittedly possible to give these texts an *a posteriori* interpretation, but on the surface they suggest some kind of *a priori* knowledge of God. Such knowledge would not, of course, be in the form of an innate idea or concept of the kind which could serve for an Anselmic ontological argument. St. Thomas unequivocally rejects this.[67] However, as we have repeatedly pointed out, this rejection of objective *a priori* knowledge does not logically entail opposition to a nonobjectifiable or nonconceptualizable variety.

There are still other textual arguments which could be advanced in favor of the thesis that Aquinas indirectly asserts an *a priori* knowledge of the infinitude of being. For example, the natural desire for the beatific vision is said to presuppose some kind of knowledge of the beatifying object, God. It is true that St. Thomas explains that this is a confused knowledge which is quite incapable of serving as the basis for a demonstration of God,[68] but it would seem that the sort of *a priori* knowledge of which we are speaking is quite sufficiently vague to satisfy that condition. This is a question which we cannot pursue because it would lead us into a set of problems which have been the subject of extensive and inconclusive debate among Thomistic commentators for hundreds of years.[69] I shall, therefore, simply record my belief that this doctrine of natural desire does lend credence to the theory that there is an *a priori* knowledge of being.

V

We shall now attempt a final estimate of the arguments in favor of this theory. We have seen that knowledge of being is indirect, nonobjective, and judgmental just as in the case of the agent intellect. Further, it is the source of the intelligibility of all other things as is true also of the agent intellect. It is by definition the cognition of unlimited being, implicitly including God himself. Correspondingly, the agent intellect, on its part, is described as a kind of intellectual participation in the unlimited actuality of the

[66] *De Verit.* 22, 2, ad 1.
[67] E.g., *S.T.* I, 2, 1, c.
[68] *Ibid.*, ad 1.
[69] For recent literature, see "Desiderium naturalis" in *Lexikon fuer Theologie und Kirche* (Freiburg: Herder, 1959). To the references given there, add the unpublished dissertation by TeSelle mentioned in n. 8.

divine being. When one keeps these considerations in mind, it must be admitted, I think, that the *a priorist* interpretation of Aquinas' position makes more philosophical and logical sense than do the alternatives. The easiest way to combine his various strands of analysis into an intelligible whole is to say that our consciously accessible knowledge of being is a reflection in experience of the light of the agent intellect, and that this latter must, therefore, be understood as a preconscious anticipation or openness to the fullness of being, to God.

The case for the logical and philosophical superiority of this way of reading of St. Thomas would be considerably strengthened if space allowed attention to certain other aspects of the arguments of its proponents. I think especially of Karl Rahner's analysis of the nature of abstraction.[70] He rejects the traditional view, represented, e.g., by Cajetan, according to which the universal form is first abstracted from the singular, and only afterward, in a separate act, does the *conversio ad phantasma* take place. On the contrary, Rahner holds that abstraction is the single, indivisible act of the illumination of the phantasm by the agent intellect. Through this illumination, the phantasm appears against the background, within the horizon, of the infinite fullness of being. The concrete singular given in the phantasm is thereby seen as limited, as capable of indefinite repetition, and as having a form which is more universal than it. In the words of one of Rahner's interpreters, "To grasp the limitedness of the singular . . . is, *eo ipso,* to become aware of the universal."[71] Even this brief a comment may indicate the usefulness of the *a priorist* interpretation of St. Thomas' thought in clarifying certain points which, in the form in which they are usually explained, appear opaque to the modern reader.

It must be granted, of course, that the philosophical merits of a given reading of a man's thought, including this particular interpretation of Aquinas, are no guarantee of its historical accuracy. Yet the historian is well-advised to assume that the great thinkers of the past were not fools, even by modern standards, and therefore, when all other things are equal, he may properly favor the philosophically meritorious interpretation.

These conditions seem to be fulfilled in reference to the theory which we are exploring. As far as I can see, there are absolutely no positive arguments against it. Aquinas nowhere states that the primary, basic knowledge of being in general is derived by universalizing abstraction from our sensory knowledge. Indeed, it is difficult to conceive what a sensory knowledge of an *actus*

[70] Rahner, *op. cit.,* 146–153 and 243–270.

[71] Gerald A. McCool, "The Primacy of Intuition," *Thought,* XXXVII (1962), 67. Cf. by the same author, "The Philosophy of the Human Person in Karl Rahner's Philosophy," *Theological Studies,* XXII (1961), 537–562, esp. 540.

essendi would be. Gilson admits this, in effect, when he argues that the sensory origin of the knowledge of existence—as something which transcends phenomena—must simply be asserted in order to avoid a skepticism repugnant to the healthy intellect. This must be allowed even though the reality and character of this knowledge can neither be logically demonstrated nor conceptually described.[72] It may be urged in this connection that St. Thomas simply does not raise the question regarding the derivation of that awareness of the existential depths of being which he explicates in his metaphysics.[73] Thomists advance many different theories on this crucial point, but none of them is based directly on the texts. They all consist of speculative arguments about what Aquinas would or could have said if he had ever dealt with the problem.

This, to be sure, is true also of the theory we are examining. The most it can claim to show is that it is possible St. Thomas assumed, either unreflectively or as too obvious to need mention, that knowledge of being and of first principles is projected into, rather than abstracted from, sense experience. As we have previously noted, the predominance of extractionist imagery in the Aquinate's writings has led many generations of commentators to suppose the contrary, but they have overlooked three points to which we have repeatedly referred. First, this imagery is directed against Augustinian objectivizing *a priorism* and can be interpreted as asserting no more than does the *conversio ad phantasma,* viz., that sense experience provides all objects of knowledge. Second, Aquinas uses the language of illumination enough to make the projectionist interpretation possible. Third, the predominance of illuminationism in his time would have made this interpretation the normal one wherever it was not explicitly excluded. Our conclusion, therefore, is that the purely historical evidence supports this projectionist, *a priorist* interpretation at least as much as it does any other and, under these circumstances, its philosophical superiority properly swings the balance in its favor —though not conclusively.

It is impossible to be emphatic on a question like this because those whose philosophical palates are displeased by anticipations of Kant will disagree, and rightly so. The purely historical arguments do not suffice to decide the case against them. But those who find it impossible to do philosophy as if the last two centuries had never existed will agree that it makes as much sense historically, and more sense philosophically, to read Aquinas as one who, like Kant, deobjectivized, without abandoning, the Platonic *a priori* in order to do justice to the role of sense experience in knowledge.

---

[72] Etienne Gilson, *Réalisme thomiste,* 163–228. Cf. Lonergan's comments in the article cited in n. 3, 311–313.

[73] In the article cited in n. 6.

The Role of *Consensus* in Richard Hooker's Method of Theological Inquiry

EGIL GRISLIS

Associate Professor of Historical Theology
The Divinity School
Duke University
Durham, North Carolina

The literary activity of Richard Hooker occupies the last two decades of the sixteenth century. During this period he produced his major work, *Of the Laws of Ecclesiastical Polity,* along with treatises and sermons of which only a few survive. In defense of the Church of England against the attacks of the Puritans, Hooker gave rigorous thought to methodological procedure in theological inquiry. In this task, his attention was focused on reason as it is assisted by grace and employed within the Church for the formulation of correct doctrine. To this end Hooker adopted the classical idea of *consensus.* This study is concerned to give a systematic account of Hooker's endeavors.

I

Two major themes in Hooker's thought constitute the basic foundation of his understanding of *consensus.* One is his hierarchical view of reality, and the other his concept of sin. In developing both of these themes Hooker remains largely within traditional boundaries. His description of the structure of the universe abounds with commonplace ideas current in the English Renaissance.[1] Similarly, his analysis of sin depends on traditional insights that for centuries had been a part of the Augustinian heritage of the Church. Yet when this is said, it must also be observed that Hooker's dependence on

[1] Herschel Baker, *The Image of Man* (New York: Harper Torchbooks, 1961); Hiram Haydn, *The Counter-Renaissance* (New York: Grove, 1960); Theodore Spence, *Shakespeare and the Nature of Man* (New York: Macmillan, 1961); E. M. W. Tillyard, *The Elizabethan World Picture* (New York: Modern Library Paperbacks, published by Random House, n.d.).

the past is a creative one.[2] Consequently, the hierarchical view of the universe and the doctrine of sin stand in so subtle a juxtaposition as at times to be mistaken for a simple internal contradiction.[3] Although this study attempts to show that such a contradiction does not in fact prevail, the problem thus highlighted may serve as a significant vantage point from which to explore the deeper meaning of the two basic themes in Hooker's thought.

Turning our attention first to Hooker's understanding of the structure of the universe, we must note that the principle of hierarchy has been very consciously placed at the center of his account. In the famous and often quoted sentence of one hundred and ninety-six words, Hooker puts it this way. What would happen, "if nature should intermit her course, and leave altogether though it were but for a while the observation of her own laws"? Having traversed the entire universe, the question ends with the same inquiry now referred to man: "what would become of man himself, whom these things now do all serve?" Hooker's reply is immediate: "See we not plainly that the obedience of creatures unto the law of nature is the stay of the whole world?"[4] Moreover, the law of nature itself is continuously dependent upon the eternal law of God. This means that wherever we discover purposeful order at work, it is always dependent and subordinate, and ultimately reaches back to God himself. By the same token, Hooker is also prepared to say that genuine order is established only by patterning the temporal order according to its ultimate origin. It is on account of such a perspective that the term "law" is so highly significant for Hooker. He defines it often, but most clearly in two statements: law is "a directive rule unto goodness of operation"[5] "which superior authority imposeth."[6] Or, according to Hooker's longer definition, we can say that law is "that which doth assign unto each thing the kind, that which doth moderate the force and power, that which doth appoint the form and measure, of working."[7]

In a more detailed analysis than could be elaborated fully but here must be only sketched, Hooker sets forth the following levels of law.

The *eternal law* is "that order which God before all ages hath set down

---

[2] H. F. Woodhouse, "Permanent Features of Hooker's Polity," *Anglican Theological Review,* XLII (1960), No. 2, 164–168.

[3] Gunnar Hillerdal, *Reason and Revelation in Richard Hooker* (Lund: Gleerup, 1962); cf. n. 47.

[4] *The Works of that Learned and Judicious Divine, Mr. Richard Hooker: With an Account of His Life and Death by Isaac Walton.* Arranged by the Rev. John Keble. Sixth edition. (Oxford: Clarendon, 1874), I:3:2–I, 207 f., which means Book I, chapter 3, section 2, in volume I on page 207 f.

[5] I:8:4–I, 228.

[6] I:3:1–I, 205.

[7] I:2:1–I, 200; cf. John S. Marshall, "Hooker's Doctrine of God," *Anglican Theological Review,* XXIX (1947), 82 f.; Dionisio De Lara, "Richard Hooker's Concept of Law," *Anglican Theological Review,* XLIV (1962), No. 4, 380–389.

with himself, for himself to do all things by."[8] Here, speaking about the source of all law whatsoever, Hooker is emphatic that God's eternal law is "with himself" as well as "for himself." Thus he denotes the essential difference between the relation of law to God and its relation to other creatures. All created levels of reality are under the law which exercises its functions upon each level from without. But since the divine existence is not contingent, God cannot be ruled by an external force. Therefore, in speaking about the eternal law, we must always remember that "the being of God is a kind of law to his own working: for that perfection which God is, giveth perfection to that he doth."[9] Or, alternatively, it can be said that the eternal law is made by God "to himself" in such a way that God forever remains the sole "cause and author" of everything that may be done by this law.[10] In this way, claims Hooker, the divine freedom is not "any wit abated, let, or hindered . . . because the imposition of this law upon himself is his own free and voluntary act."[11]

Having thus defined the eternal law, Hooker then proceeds to designate it as the *first eternal law,* in order to distinguish it from a *second eternal law.* While making this distinction, Hooker acknowledges that he is indeed familiar with the Thomistic view of eternal law as God's law for all of his creatures.[12] Although basically in agreement with such a tradition, Hooker nevertheless desires to amplify it. Accordingly, he now proposes the designation "second eternal law" for the eternal law in its relation to all creation. The second eternal law is, then, the first eternal law as revealed in the structure and life of the universe. As Hooker poetically records in Book V: "All things which God in their times and seasons hath brought forth were eternally and before all times in God, as a work unbegun is in the artificer which afterward bringeth it into effect."[13] When the second eternal law is finally analyzed in more detail, he prefers to speak about three major areas where one may observe its working, viz., as *natural laws, celestial laws,* and *laws for men.*

In his definition of the *law of nature* Hooker again uses traditional categories even though with a slight modification. Instead of applying the law of nature to the entire creation, Hooker limits the range of this law to the nonvoluntary agents which keep the law "unwittingly, as the heavens and the elements of the world, which can do no otherwise than they do."[14] The institution of the law of nature Hooker refers to the moment of creation, viewing

[8] I:2:6–I, 204.
[9] I:2:2–I, 200.
[10] I:2:5–I, 203.
[11] I:2:6–I, 204.
[12] I:3:1–I, 204 f.
[13] V:56:5–II, 248.
[14] I:3:2–I, 206.

the divine declarations recorded in the Book of Genesis as indications of "the infinite greatness of God's power." He views them also as a witness to the fact that the institution of the laws of nature took place completely by the free choice of God.[15] Once the law of nature has been thus promulgated, it remains in effect, so that ordinarily nature does not depart from it.[16] The only exceptions to this are the occasional "swervings" which are caused by a divine malediction in punishment for man's Fall.[17] Of course, since nature possesses neither will nor reason, it is not conscious of the law which it follows. Yet nature observes its law with such "dexterity" and "skill" that "no intellectual creature in the world were able by capacity to do that which nature doth without capacity and knowledge."[18] This is obviously possible only because nature is continuously guided by God:

> Who is the guide of nature, but only the God of nature? "In him we live, move, and are." Those things which nature is said to do, are by divine art performed, using nature as an instrument; nor is there any such art of knowledge divine in nature herself working, but in the Guide of Nature's work.[19]

Moreover, as each level of nature works toward the achievement of its own perfection, it is directed by the law of nature "to prefer the good of the whole before whatever their own particulars."[20] Thus the hierarchical structure of the universe is highly dynamic and most visible precisely where all created things are "by wonderful art and wisdom sodered [*sic*] as it were together with the glue of mutual assistance, appointing the lowest to receive from the nearest to themselves what the influence of the highest yieldeth."[21] Although men and angels as voluntary creatures do not come under the immediate direction of the law of nature, the significance of this law for men can hardly be overstated. Hooker believes that human reason can greatly profit by the careful observation of the works of nature. And when the whole of mankind does this, understanding has a genuinely objective foundation: It is such understanding as is, in fact, brought to men by God himself through the instrumentality of nature. As Hooker puts it, propounding thereby a principal support for belief in the *consensus gentium*:

> The general and perpetual voice of men is as the sentence of God himself. For that which all men have at all times learned, Nature herself must

[15] I:3:2–I, 206.
[16] I:3:4–I, 209.
[17] I:3:3–I, 209.
[18] I:3:4–I, 209.
[19] I:3:4–I, 209 f.
[20] I:3:5–I, 211.
[21] V:76:9–II, 454.

> needs have taught; and God being the author of Nature, her voice is but his instrument. By her from Him we receive whatsoever in such sort we learn.[22]

The second area of the second eternal law, here merely to be mentioned, is the *celestial law* which is beheld and obeyed by the angels. The third area of the second eternal law, however, applies specifically to men and contains the *law of reason* as well as the *divine law*. The law of reason is "that which bindeth creatures reasonable in this world, and with which by reason they may most plainly perceive themselves bound."[23] Or, following another definition given by Hooker, we can say that "the Law of Reason or human Nature is that which men by discourse of natural Reason have rightly found out themselves to be all for ever bound unto in their actions."[24] Of the three basic characteristics of the laws of reason we should note, first, that they closely resemble the purposeful and harmonious working of nature itself; secondly, that the laws of nature are "investigable" by human reason "without the help of Revelation"; and, thirdly, that the laws of nature have been universally known by all men. Obviously, here again we touch the foundation of Hooker's belief in the *consensus*. Quoting Sophocles, Hooker himself defines the law of reason: " 'It is no child of to-day's or yesterday's birth, but hath been no man knoweth how long sithence.' It is not agreed upon by one, or two, or few, but by all." In stating this, Hooker does not intend to suggest that every human being knows or could verbalize the full range of the law of reason. He is, however, affirming that each man possessed such a capacity potentially; viz., "this law is such that being proposed no man can reject it as unreasonable and unjust."[25]

In this third area of the second eternal law Hooker also includes *divine law*. This law is intended exclusively for men and cannot be known in any other way except "by special revelation from God."[26] As supernatural law that transcends creaturely finitude, the divine law guides men toward infinite "felicity and bliss." Its guidance prevails in time, and will continue eternally, in order to satisfy the soul of man "with everlasting delight" in union with God.[27] When Hooker attends to the content of the divine law, he observes that during man's earthly lifetime his natural capacities do not suffice for a full understanding of his ultimate quest. Because this quest "exceedeth the reach of sense," and is even "somewhat above capacity of reason," it is with a

---

[22] I:7:3–I, 227.
[23] I:3:1–I, 205.
[24] I:8:8–I, 233.
[25] I:8:9–I, 233.
[26] I:3:1–I, 205.
[27] I:11:2–I, 255.

"hidden exultation" that man "rather surmiseth than conceiveth" it. Even so, "very intentive desire thereof doth so incite it, that all other known delights and pleasures are laid aside, they give place to the search of this but only suspected desire."[28] But regardless of the intensity of the desire, the search would never be successful if divine revelation were not afforded as a gift.[29] This, then, is how Hooker defines divine law, or, as he sometimes calls it, supernatural law:

> Laws therefore concerning these things are supernatural, both in respect of the manner of delivering them, which is divine; and also in regard of the things delivered, which are such as have not in nature any cause from which they flow, but were by the voluntary appointment of God ordained besides the course of nature, to rectify nature's obliquity withal.[30]

Finally, Hooker's account of law includes *positive human law* which is formulated by men as they gather those insights from the law of reason and the divine law that are called forth by the specific needs of a given society.[31] In this category he includes the laws of a commonweal, the laws of the Church, and the laws of nations. Although these laws cannot be discussed here in any detail, their significance for the present study is considerable, since Hooker's discussion of their formulation serves as a case-in-point indication of some of his thoughts about the practical operation of a *consensus.*

At the same time, however, it is important to note that the hierarchical structure of the law although important is not the only basis upon which Hooker attempts to build his idea of consensus. Hooker also possesses a clearly stated doctrine of sin that is indispensable for a full assessment of the careful qualifications that he has introduced into the traditional view of the hierarchical structure of the universe. In other words, we must recognize that Hooker's preponderant concern with law and order as basic in all reality has not blinded his eyes to the disorder and misery of human existence. Of course, it must be admitted that the scope of Hooker's concern at this point is somewhat narrow. He pays little attention to the problems of physical suffering, doubt, and despair. Yet this is understandable, since his main involvement is with the Puritan revolt against the Church of England, and consequently with the investigation of those sinful attitudes that have to do with the individual's refusal to participate in the established order of society. Nevertheless, even such a limited range of attention suffices to reveal Hooker's understanding of the actual condition of fallen man.

---

[28] I:11:4–I, 257 f.
[29] I:11:6–I, 261.
[30] I:11:6–I, 262.
[31] I:3:1–I, 205.

In the Fall Hooker finds the ultimate source of human sin. Analyzing the Fall in reference to both angels and men, he depends upon traditional insights for the description of the fall of the former, and his own emphases when describing the latter. The angels fell when, pridefully disregarding their role in the hierarchical order of reality, they began to adore themselves instead of God.[32] Continuing their rebellion against God, one of the fallen angels approached Adam, and subtly "took advantage" of the fact that, since the purpose of a supernatural law may not always be known to man, Adam did not know why he was forbidden to eat from the tree of knowledge.[33] Although Adam was deceived, the responsibility of sin was his own.[34] This Hooker explains in analogy with the causes of human error in general. Thereby, he inadvertently reveals how darkly he views sin and how weak is man despite the fact that he abides in a world pervaded by law. Strictly speaking, it is always true that "evil as evil cannot be desired." Yet what is in reality evil may be mistaken for good.[35] When reason errs in this manner, "we fall into evil."[36]

At the same time, for a full understanding of the dynamics of the act of sin, more than epistemological categories are needed. Aware of this, Hooker suggests that man is guilty when he commits sin on the grounds that he has neglected to prepare himself so as to be able to avoid errors due to ignorance. Now, by ignorance, Hooker does not mean a morally neutral nescience, but a sinful neglect to gather available and needed knowledge.[37] And this neglect he views not as accidental, but as due to human sloth, rooted in original sin. For sloth arises from a "divine malediction" which leads man to prefer "rest in ignorance before wearisome labour to know."[38] The scope of this affliction Hooker indicates by observing that in the Fall human reason has been "darkened" to such a degree that no man can ever reach saving knowledge except by divine intervention.[39] Hooker does not deny that man can still employ his reason in the natural realm with at least some measure of success. But instead of concerning himself at length with the capacities of fallen reason in describing how that reason operates, his primary concern is, rather, to show how grace has restored nature. In so far as he emphasizes the accomplishments of sin-afflicted reason, they are primarily negative and serve to underscore Hooker's profound understanding of sin.

[32] I:4:3–I, 214.
[33] III:10:1–I, 384.
[34] V Appendix I:5–II, 541.
[35] I:7:6–I, 223.
[36] I:8:1–I, 225.
[37] V Appendix I:5–II, 542; cf. I:9:1–I, 238.
[38] I:7:7–I, 224; cf. V Appendix I:8–II, 544.
[39] Sermon I–III, 471; I:12:2–I, 263; Sermon II:2–III, 484 f.; Sermon III–III, 600.

Thus Hooker can observe that men are afflicted with inordinate self-love: "Nature worketh in us all a love to our own counsels. The contradiction of others is a fan to inflame that love. Our love set on fire to maintain that which once we have done, sharpeneth the wit to dispute, to argue, and by all means to reason for it."[40] Likewise, the preference of "their own private good before all things, even that good which is sensual before whatsoever is most divine"[41] is characteristic of the majority of men. We are also "prone . . . to fawn upon ourselves and to be ignorant as much as may be of our own deformities."[42] Similarly, when men experience some blessings from God, they are inclined to think that they have deserved them.[43]

Inadvertently men themselves admit that such is indeed their true condition. In pointing to this, Hooker reminds his readers of the universally known fact that "no man can be presumed a competent judge what equity doth require in his own case.[44] And when an equitable judgment is pronounced, men should not be expected to accept it gladly. This must be especially taken in account at the formulation of laws for the guidance of society:

> Laws politic, ordained for external order and regiment amongst men, are never framed as they should be, unless presuming the will of man to be inwardly obstinate, rebellious, and averse from all obedience unto the sacred laws of his nature; in a word, unless presuming man to be in regard of his depraved mind little better than a wild beast, they do accordingly provide notwithstanding so to frame his outward actions, that they be no hindrance unto the common good for which societies are instituted: unless they do this, they are not perfect.[45]

Consequently, Hooker's definition of authority includes the practical provision which he regards as absolutely necessary:

> Authority is a constraining power, which power were needless if we were all such as we should be, willing to do the things we ought to do without constraint. But because generally we are otherwise, therefore we all reap singular benefit by that authority which permitteth no man, though they would, to slack their duty. It doth not suffice, that the Lord of an household appoint labourers what they should do, unless he set over them some chief workmen to see they do it.[46]

In view of Hooker's devotion to order and reason it must be especially emphasized that his awareness of the ubiquitous human inclination to per-

---

[40] Preface 2:5–I, 138.
[41] I:10:6–I, 244.
[42] I:12:2–I, 263.
[43] Sermon III–III, 625.
[44] V:9:4–II, 40.
[45] I:10:1–I, 239 f.
[46] VII:18:5–III, 267.

verse use of reason is in no way merely marginal. Throughout his writings he consistently and repeatedly acknowledges the radical effects of sin on human life. As a result, if one merely observes what Hooker has to say about the hierarchically ordered universe on the one hand, and human sin on the other, it may indeed appear that the tensions within his thought are beyond reconciliation. Hooker himself, however, is not at all aware that his description of sin entails a denial that man may recognize and utilize the hierarchical structure of law as Hooker has portrayed it. And this need not be judged as an oversight on his part. Rather, it is due to the fact that Hooker consciously and steadfastly acknowledges the overarching role of grace. Consequently, his analysis of the role of reason in the life of the Christian Church is made in regard to three, rather than merely two, points of reference. That is to say, Hooker describes reason, first, as grounded in nature; secondly, as affected by sin; and thirdly—and most important of all—as redeemed by grace.[47] Therefore, it is only to grace-redeemed reason that Hooker ascribes the ability to draw knowledge from the hierarchical structure of reality. Such a qualification, it should be noted, does not destroy the apologetic value of Hooker's work within the setting of his age. He is after all addressing himself to Puritans whom he regards as fellow Christians albeit misguided ones.

---

[47] John Tulloch, *Rational Theology and Christian Philosophy in England in the Seventeenth Century* (Edinburgh and London: Blackwood, 1874), I, 53, describes Hooker's work as "an enduring monument of all the highest principles of Christian rationalism." Paul Schuetz, *Richard Hooker, Der grundlegene Theologe des Anglikanismus* (Goettingen: Mittelstelle für Mikrokopie angeschlossen an den Verlag Vandenhoeck & Ruprecht, 1952), 46–59, thinks that Hooker has separated reason from revelation, asserted the primacy of reason, and the dependence of faith on reason. Cf. also Hans Leube, *Reformation und Humanismus in England* (Leipzig: Deichert, 1930), 12, and Ernst Jenssen, "Das Licht der Vernunft (reason) in der Theologie Richard Hookers," in *Solange es "heute" heisst; Festgabe für Rudolf Hermann zum 70. Geburtstag* (Berlin: Evangelische Verlagsanstalt, 1957) 147–152. Peter Munz, *The Place of Hooker in the History of Thought* (London: Routledge and Kegan Paul, 1952), 62, although admitting that Hooker "must not be mistaken for a modern rationalist," nevertheless thinks that he has "wiped out" the Thomistic distinction between faith and reason as operative in supernatural and natural spheres respectively, and "established the complete autonomy of human reason over the whole of life." Just as one-sided a claim from the opposite direction is made by Gunnar Hillerdal who suggests that Hooker while teaching the primacy of grace succumbs to the fallacy of a circular argument. Bringing in the final evaluation of Hooker such an outspoken expression as "pious delusion," Hillerdal claims that Hooker began his work as a philosopher relying on reason without any reference to grace, but eventually came to admit the need for grace to redeem reason, before reason can be properly utilized. Questions Hillerdal: "Is not a circle inevitable? Reason is supposed to clarify revelation. However, the particular aid of God must first quicken reason!" *Op. cit.*, 95, cf. 148 f. For my criticism of Hillerdal and outline of Hooker's position, see "Richard Hooker's Image of Man" in *Renaissance Papers 1963* (Printed by Charles E. Tuttle, Japan, 1964, for The Southeastern Renaissance Conference), 73–84.

II

Within such a framework Hooker then proceeds to elaborate the nature and functions of reason. The episemology to which Hooker subscribes is, of course, in large measure dependent upon St. Thomas. Like St. Thomas, Hooker denies that man is naturally possessed of an innate knowledge of God.[48] Rather, starting from "utter vacuity" the human mind acquires knowledge "by degrees." Therefore Hooker can compare the human soul to "a book wherein nothing is and yet all things may be imprinted."[49] Or Hooker can say that "into the world we come as empty of the one as of the other, as naked in mind as we are in body."[50]

At the same time, the human mind is potentially capable of obtaining knowledge. And that the mind actually seeks knowledge is due to the fact that "a natural thirst after knowledge is ingrafted in" all men.[51] It is interesting to note that Hooker lays considerable stress upon the intensity of the desire for knowledge. He insists that the human mind is "by nature speculative" and therefore "delighted with contemplation in itself."[52] But Hooker does not say that reason without grace can satisfy its deepest desires.

Also, after St. Thomas, Hooker assumes that to the human mind "the main principles of Reason are in themselves apparent."[53] This assumption, which Hooker nowhere defends but always takes for granted, must be explored further. On the one hand, it is obvious that Hooker desires to qualify the notion of the self-evidence of these main principles in the light of what has been said about the effects of the Fall. Therefore he suggests that not every man is actually aware of these principles. In accord with his view that sloth blinds men to the truth, Hooker explains that the cause "that so many thousands of men" are ignorant of such self-evident principles is due to "lewd and wicked custom."[54] On the other hand, however, Hooker obviously shuns the impossible position of affirming that sin has totally annihilated essential humanity. Consequently, although the Fall has destroyed "original perfection," the "powers and faculties" of the human mind "retain still their natural manner of operation."[55] In regard to self-evident principles, this means that fallen man lacks the necessary initiative to seek them out. When he is con-

[48] V:21:3–II, 86.
[49] I:6:1–I, 217.
[50] I:10:2–I, 241.
[51] I:7:7–I, 224.
[52] I:8:5–I, 229.
[53] I:8:5–I, 228.
[54] I:8:11–I, 235.
[55] V Appendix I:2–II, 539.

fronted with these principles, then his "mind doth presently embrace them as free from all possibility of error, clear and manifest without proof."[56] Yet such an embrace does not save. In other words, Hooker's unwillingness to assert the need for grace in the acknowledgment of self-evident principles does not result in any exaltation of the capacities of unredeemed reason.

But what then has he done? The answer to this question may be given at two levels. For the most part, it appears that Hooker adheres to a relatively unsophisticated insight of common sense that, after all the debilitating effects of sin are acknowledged, man is not completely "void of brain."[57] Even the Puritans themselves who have begun to treat " 'the star of reason and learning' " as if it were "an unlucky comet" are in fact still employing reason: "they never use reason so willingly as to disgrace reason."[58] There are other passages where Hooker penetrates somewhat more deeply. He appears to be conscious of the fact that the affirmation of the continuing humanity of fallen man presumes more than the human capacity for the basic laws of logic. It presumes that even fallen man retains some ethical consciousness. Hooker, for instance, is convinced that everyone to whose attention it is brought will be compelled to assent to the proposition "that the greater good is to be chosen before the less."[59] Likewise, Hooker believes that numerous less general axioms will be accepted without any demand for further proof, as that, " 'God to be worshipped'; 'parents to be honoured'; 'others to be used by us as we ourselves would be by them.' "[60]

Yet even such an acceptance of the ability of sinful reason to recognize self-evident ethical principles is ultimately no acknowledgment of their soteriological efficacy. In fact, any such claim is directly opposed by Hooker at all times. Thus, in the last analysis, Hooker has not admitted unredeemed reason into the construction of his theological system. This can most clearly be seen in Hooker's analogous attempts to evaluate the capacities and functions of human will when yet untouched by the operation of grace. The will, indeed, has also retained its "natural manner of operation" after the Fall but with the qualification that, although it is "framable to good things," it is not "able to frame" itself.[61]

The bearing of this distinction becomes apparent as soon as we turn to Hooker's understanding of the actual dynamics of the operation of human will. There we note that Hooker distinguishes between appetite and will. He

[56] I:8:5–I, 228.
[57] Sermon III–III, 603.
[58] III:8:4–I, 365.
[59] I:8:5–I, 228.
[60] I:8:5–I, 229.
[61] See n. 53.

defines appetite as a "natural desire" whose object is any "sensible good." The fact that an object of desire is such a "sensible good" is discoverable only by reason.[62] But once reason has prescribed the proper direction for action the will is at liberty to exercise its essential function of choice. In describing this choice, Hooker makes it manifest, on the one hand, that he desires to defend the freedom of the will. He quotes St. Augustine with approval: *"Voluntas, nisi libera sit, non est voluntas."*[63] On the other hand, however, Hooker drastically limits the range of this freedom by introducing a distinction between aptness and ableness. This distinction is presented in Book I and again in greater detail in the Appendix to Book V.[64] It is, accordingly, characteristic of Hooker's early as well as late theological position. As he puts it: "You peradventure think aptness and ableness are one: whereas the truth is, that had we kept our first ableness, grace should not need; and had aptness been also lost, it is not grace that could work in us more than it doth in brute creatures."[65] Or, as he finally sums up his position in response to Puritan criticism:

> I conclude therefore, the natural aptness of man's will to take or refuse things presented before it, and the evidence which good things have for themselves, if reason were diligent to search it out, may be soundly and safely taught without contradiction to any syllable in that confession of the Church, or in those sentences of holy Scripture by you alleged, concerning the actual disability of reason and will, through sin, whereas God's especial grace faileth.[66]

Since the operation of the human mind involves the exercise of both will and reason, Hooker's outspoken denial of any saving ability to the sinful will is tantamount to denying any such ability to reason as well. And, on several occasions, Hooker actually articulates this implication. He suggests that men who are totally forsaken by grace are also totally incapable of right thinking. Speaking about the Puritan extremist Hacket and his two followers, "those poor seduced creatures" who had been executed for rebellion, Hooker states that God "gave them over to their own inventions, and left them made in the end an example for headstrong and inconsiderate zeal no less fearful, than Achitophel for proud and irreligious wisdom."[67] Similarly—in apparent reference to Machiavelli and other "wise malignants"[68]—Hooker informs us that "they lose themselves in the very maze of their own dis-

[62] I:7:3–6–I, 221 f.
[63] V Appendix I:1–II, 537.
[64] I:7:6–I, 222; cf. V Appendix I:1–II, 537.
[65] V Appendix I:1–II, 538.
[66] V Appendix I:9–II, 545.
[67] V Dedication 6–II, 5.
[68] V:2:4–II, 22.

courses, as if reason did even purposely forsake them, who on purpose forsake God the author thereof."[69] And in the Appendix to Book V Hooker can observe that "they, who, being destitute of that spirit which should certify and give reason, follow the conduct of sensual direction, termed the *wisdom* of the flesh, must needs thereby fall into actions of plain hostility against God."[70] That such people follow the judgment of the senses in preference to reason, is not due to any innate inability. It must rather be stated that their condition is a direct consequence of their sin, since

> the wittiest, the greatest in account for secular and worldly wisdom, *Scribes, Philosophers, profound disputers,* are the chief in opposition against God: such in the *primitive Church* was *Julian, Lucian, Porphyry, Symmachus,* and others of the like note, by whom both the natural law of God was disobeyed, and the mysteries of supernatural truth derided.[71]

Clearly then, if men are to benefit from the hierarchical structure of the universe, the grace of God must first restore their sinful minds and continuously aid them in all their efforts. When this does occur, then nature again is perceived as an instrument of God and therefore a source for the knowledge of God. Then instead of an irreconcilable tension between nature and sin, it is possible to see a divinely sustained harmony between nature and grace.[72]

Despite Gunnar Hillerdal's claims to the contrary, the primacy of grace is basic to Hooker's perspective and not a later qualification of his early and unqualified exaltation of reason.[73] Of course, Hillerdal is correct in observing that the most thorough discussion of grace is found in the Appendix to Book V and was written late in Hooker's life.[74] Nevertheless, the position in essence is affirmed throughout his writings.

What Hooker means by grace may be best seen in reference to the conflicting Pelagian and Augustinian understanding of grace. Over against Pelagius, Hooker refuses to define grace exclusively as "external incitements unto faith and godliness, which the Law, the Prophets, the Ministers, the works of God do offer."[75] Turning to the familiar proof-text, "I stand at the door and knock," Hooker defines as the work of grace not merely the outward proffer of the message of salvation, but also the inward response of its acceptance, the opening of the door.[76]

---

[69] V:2:4–II, 23.
[70] V Appendix I:9–II, 544.
[71] V Appendix I:9–II, 545.
[72] I:14:4–I, 271.
[73] Hillerdal, *op. cit.*, 117.
[74] *Ibid.*, 121, 135, 137–147.
[75] V Appendix I:10–II, 546.
[76] V Appendix I:3–II, 540.

Furthermore, over against traditional Catholicism, Hooker objects to the definition of grace as "a divine spiritual quality" which is "received into the soul."[77] Apparently, he desires to avoid the use of categories of substance and, instead, follows the traditional Protestant approach, which views grace in personal and redemptive terms. Hooker points to God himself as the source of all grace and suggests that grace must be defined as God's "undeserved love and favour,"[78] or "his favour and undeserved mercy toward us."[79] At the same time, Hooker seeks to retain the Catholic emphasis on grace as resident and, hence, objectively present power in the soul of the believer. Nevertheless, in order to avoid all suggestion of teaching an impersonal and thinglike view of grace, Hooker introduces a very profound reference to the Holy Spirit and points out that the gift of grace given inwardly is nothing else but the "bestowing of his Holy Spirit which inwardly worketh."[80] Since the Holy Spirit is the third Person of the Trinity, the experience of him is necessarily personal and inward, yet at the same time also an objective gift. The objective efficacy of this gift Hooker describes in terms of the saving "effects" of the Holy Spirit's working.[81] Viewing sanctification in such personal terms and recognizing it as the gradual redemptive work of the Holy Spirit whereby "Christ imparteth plainly himself by degrees,"[82] Hooker has once more focused his attention upon the Church as the unique place where the Holy Spirit is at work and therefore broken reason can actually be restored. The traditional Catholic emphasis on the objective nature of sanctification thus serves to assure the continuation of grace-redeemed reason within the Church. At the same time, once Hooker understands grace as an undeserved gift and its recipient a sinner so long as he lives on this earth, the possibility of the abuse of reason within the Church remains.

Such an understanding of the nature and work of grace Hooker now attempts to relate to the condition of fallen man. Hooker's first explicit acknowledgment of the need for grace to redeem human nature before the latter can perform its functions is set forth somewhat vaguely. He speaks of the need for the "perpetual aid and concurrence of that Supreme Cause of all things," both for "man and any other creature" if they are properly to "perform the functions allotted" to them. That Hooker is here concerned with grace and that he does not merely echo the traditional view of the relation between primary and secondary causation, is indicated by the context. For Hooker

[77] Sermon II:5–III, 487.
[78] V Appendix I:16–II, 545.
[79] V Appendix I:16–II, 552.
[80] V Appendix I:16–II, 552.
[81] V Appendix I:16–II, 552.
[82] V:56:10–II, 253; cf. V:66:9–II, 347.

suggests that when "the benefit" of the "perpetual aid and concurrence" is withdrawn as a just punishment for sins, then

> there can no other thing follow than that which the Apostle noteth, even men endued with the light of reason to walk notwithstanding "in the vanity of their mind, having their cogitations darkened, and being strangers from the life of God through the ignorance which is in them, because of the hardness of their hearts." And this cause is mentioned by the prophet Esay, speaking of the ignorance of the idolaters, who see not how the manifest Law of Reason condemneth their gross iniquity and sin. "They have not in them," saith he, "so much wit as to think, 'Shall I bow to the stock of a tree?' 'All knowledge and understanding is taken from them; for God hath shut their eyes that they cannot see.' "[83]

The same insight is accented by Hooker more emphatically in Book III. He proclaims that it is the Spirit of God which does "aid and direct men" in their use of reason.[84] And while the reference here is admittedly limited to the formulation of laws for the use of the Church, there are frequent instances in Hooker's writings where it is affirmed that the laws of nature cannot be rightly discovered "without the grace of God assisting us in the search."[85] As Hooker finally states with precision: "let precedent grace be a spur to quicken reason, and grace subsequent, the hand to give it; then shall good things appear as they are, and the will, as it ought, incline towards them."[86]

III

Having followed Hooker's attempts to delineate the proper context for the use of reason, we must now assert that such a discussion does not intend to establish the exclusive sufficiency of grace-redeemed reason for attaining correct doctrinal formulations. Instead, its purpose has been merely to insure the legitimacy of the use of reason alongside revelation in order to state as a matter of principle:

> There are but two ways whereby the Spirit leadeth men into all truth; the one extraordinary, the other common; the one belonging but unto some few, the other extending itself unto all that are of God; the one, that which we call by a special divine excellency Revelation, the other Reason.[87]

The data supplied in this manner Hooker regards as "complete" in the sense

[83] I:8:11–I, 236.
[84] III:8:18–I, 380.
[85] V Appendix I:7–II, 543.
[86] V Appendix I:8–II, 544.
[87] Preface 3:10–I, 150.

that revelation and reason "jointly and not severally" contain all that men must know for their "everlasting felicity."[88]

However, Hooker also very clearly distinguishes between reason and revelation. He points to the ultimate superiority of revelation, and thereby to his own basic preference for exegetical rather than speculative theology. He affirms repeatedly that "to find out *supernatural laws,* there is no natural way, because they have not their foundation or ground in the course of nature."[89] These supernatural laws, of course, are supplied in Scripture. At this point Hooker proceeds very carefully. On the one hand, he holds that the Scriptures "are with such absolute perfection framed" that they do not lack "any thing" without which salvation could not be obtained.[90] On the other hand, however, Hooker obviously refuses to identify every scriptural passage with the supernatural law. To do this would be to disregard the fact that the Scriptures also contain natural as well as ceremonial law,[91] and to overlook the need to employ reason in order to reach a *consensus* as to which scriptural portions are the divine law in the first place!

Aside from such qualifications, Hooker's main point remains. It is the affirmation that "the mysteries of our religion are above the reach of understanding, above discourse of man's reason, above all that any creature can comprehend."[92] Hooker means that, on the basis of either first principles or the laws of reason and nature, man is not capable of proving the truth of divine revelation.[93] Therefore divine truth must be accepted by belief which "consisteth not so much in knowledge as in acknowledgment of all things that heavenly wisdom revealeth."[94] Nevertheless, even on this level where Hooker's primary concern is to acknowledge the ultimate superiority of revelation, reason is in no sense superfluous. As a rule, suggests Hooker, reason is not incapable of understanding what it is that the Scriptures call upon men to acknowledge. When such incapacity prevails, as it may, the proper course of action is "to believe that which he hath not given us capacity to comprehend, how incredible soever it may seem, yet our wits should submit themselves, and reason give place unto faith therein."[95] At other times human reason may lack perfect understanding, yet still be capable of some insight.[96] In any case,

---

[88] I:14:5–I, 271; cf. VIII:6:5–III, 400.
[89] V Appendix I:2–II, 543; I:12:3–I, 264; V Appendix I:14–II, 551; Sermon II:26–III, 516.
[90] I:13:3–I, 267.
[91] I:14:1–I, 268.
[92] V:63:1–II, 305.
[93] V Appendix I:14–II, 551.
[94] V:63:1–II, 305; cf. V Appendix I:9–II, 544.
[95] VI:6:11–III, 92.
[96] V:52:1–II, 222.

to reject the measure of understanding that is available to men, Hooker views as sinful ingratitude and an unnecessary stricture as well, since the legitimacy of grace-redeemed reason has been already established.[97] And, turning to his Puritan opponents, Hooker reminds them that in actual practice even they cannot avoid the utilization of his theological position which they have officially scorned. They do in fact accept as scriptural, and therefore as correct, numerous doctrines despite the fact that they are "nowhere to be found by express literal mention, only deduced they are out of Scripture by collection."[98] Likewise, the Puritans invariably transgress against their own precepts when they "gather out of Scripture general rules to be followed in making laws"[99] and employ reason in doing so. Moreover, Hooker points out that the actual meaning of scriptural words is not taught by divine revelation but is discovered through human learning and reasoning.[100] Hooker sees this most acutely on those occasions where passages of Scriptures are employed as sources for deducing scriptural proof. He therefore asks the despisers of reason, "what warrant have they, that any of [the scriptural proofs] doth mean the thing for which it is alleged?"[101] Indeed, in all exegetical disputes "between true and false construction, the difference reason must shew."[102] Yet to point this out, insists Hooker, in no way implies that the task of human reason would be to improve the content of Scripture; rather, the role of reason must be always limited to that of "a necessary instrument, without which we could not reap by the Scripture's perfection that fruit and benefit which it yieldeth."[103] By appealing for the need to utilize reason in the interpretation of revelation, Hooker has not intended to introduce an infallible authority. He is deeply aware how readily reason can go astray and instead of a *consensus* produce widely ranging disagreement. However, despite such liabilities, he sees reason as an indispensable instrument which, when restored by grace, can and must be employed within the Church for the interpretation of supernatural truth.

With like efficacy, and yet with equal possibility of error, reason can also be utilized in the natural realm. When this is done, however, it must be kept in mind that Scripture does not need the addition of any doctrines of man's salvation "as in supply of the Scripture's unsufficiency."[104] Rather, reason is to be introduced for the regulation of those activities of human life that have

[97] VII:11:10–III, 213.
[98] I:14:2–I, 269.
[99] II:7:4–I, 363.
[100] II:7:3–I, 321.
[101] II:7:9–I, 329.
[102] III:8:16–I, 378.
[103] III:8:10–I, 371.
[104] II:8:5–I, 334.

not been specified by revelation. That these are numerous is the main force of much of Hooker's contention against the Puritans. In an eloquent *reductio ad absurdum* Hooker proclaims:

> Make all things sin which we do by direction of nature's light, and by the rule of common discretion, without thinking at all upon Scripture; admit this position, and parents shall cause their children to sin, as oft as they cause them to do any thing, before they come to years of capacity and be ripe for knowledge in the Scripture: admit this, and it shall not be with matters as it was with him in the Gospel, but servants being commanded to go shall stand still, till they have their errand warranted unto them by Scripture.[105]

Hooker sees no basic contradiction between insights gained from creation and revelation. Therefore, he can look to revelation and reason as mutually complementary sources of knowledge. It is also consistent with such a perspective to claim that revelation has no need to contain any such directives as can be obtained by the use of reason—even though for special human benefit it often does.[106] In other words, to the insight of St. Paul "that nature hath need of grace," Hooker is prepared to add "that grace hath use of nature."[107] Or, as Hooker puts it elsewhere, "when supernatural duties are necessarily exacted, natural are not rejected as needless,"[108] and "to be ripe in faith" does not require "to be raw in wit and judgment."[109]

It is to be observed that the basis of such an understanding of the functions of reason as we have noted is the hierarchical structure of reality. As the Christian, living in the Church and under the healing process of grace, comes to recognize this, Hooker believes he must thereby acknowledge the revelatory function of all reality. And, since all created reality is potentially capable of pointing to its ultimate source, viz., the Logos or the Wisdom of God, to meditate on the nature of creation can also mean meditation upon that Wisdom who is the Author of reason as well as of revelation. It was Wisdom, observes Hooker, that instructed Adam in Paradise and later informed David and Solomon. In this task, "some things she openeth by sacred books of Scripture; some things by the glorious works of Nature: with some things she inspireth them from above by spiritual influence; in some things she leadeth and traineth them only by worldly experience and practice." Yet, regardless of the particular way in which Wisdom may teach men on any one given occasion, "we may not so in any one special kind admire her, that we dis-

---

[105] II:8:6–I, 335.
[106] III:4:1–I, 358; cf. III:7:2–I, 362; III:11:5–I, 394.
[107] III:8:6–I, 367.
[108] I:12:1–I, 262.
[109] III:8:4–I, 366.

grace her in any other; but let all her ways be according unto their place and degree adored."[110]

At the same time, while exalting the omnipresent Wisdom, Hooker admits that there are men who despite their great learning have failed to learn true wisdom. Whereas the objective ground for such a condition is sin and the absence of grace, its subjective manifestation is an inordinate self-love. Such "wise men," who are actually anything else but what they claim to be, "wholly addicted unto their own wills, use their wit, their learning, and all the wisdom they have, to maintain that which their obstinate hearts are delighted with, esteeming in the frantic error of their minds the greatest madness in the world to be wisdom, and the highest wisdom foolishness."[111]

Hooker's recognition of the presence of such men prompts him to form a cautious estimate of the final value of doctrinal *consensus*. If one compares Hooker with Whitgift at this point, it is instructive to observe that Whitgift never seems to realize that learned men could be utterly mistaken in their agreement. Writing against Cartwright, Whitgift untiringly appeals to wise and learned men, primarily relying on Calvin, Augustine, and Zwingli—in that order—but also including numerous references to his contemporaries, Bullinger, Beza, Bucer, and Musculus. He appeals also to Cyprian, Chrysostom, and Ambrose of the Early Church. Not once, however, does Whitgift attempt to determine the basis by which he has recognized these men as wise and learned and their agreement as normative for others. By contrast, Hooker is on principle opposed to indiscriminate deference to authorities. It is in fact this error of which he accuses his Puritan opponents. He compares them with the continental Anabaptists in order to show that their position is as absurd as it is dangerous. The Anabaptists, Hooker asserts, had always insisted that they were relying on Scripture alone. But in reality they merely used Scripture to justify their own preconceived opinions.[112] Indeed, so deceived were the Anabaptists by their special pleading that they finally convinced themselves that "they might lawfully have their six or seven wives apiece."[113] Thus the Anabaptists are alarming examples of what can happen to those who, pretending to seek truth, follow no higher guide than subjective preference. In summary Hooker affirms the principle:

> where . . . singularity is, they whose hearts it possesseth ought to suspect it the more, inasmuch as if it did come of God, and should for that cause prevail with others, the same God which revealeth it to them, would also give them power of confirming it unto others, either with miraculous

[110] II:1:4–I, 289 f.; cf. III:8:9–I, 370.
[111] III:8:9–I, 370 f.
[112] Preface 8:7–I, 185.
[113] Preface 8:12–I, 190.

> operation, or with strong and invincible remonstrance and sound Reason, such as whereby it might appear that God would indeed have all men's judgments give place unto it. . . .[114]

This sharp contrast between the theological insufficiency of private opinion and the superior validity of insights shared by all genuinely wise and judicious men is found throughout Hooker's writings. On the surface, Hooker sometimes leaves the impression that his contrast of singularity with the *consensus* is tantamount to a claim that the majority cannot be wrong. On such occasions Hooker looks down upon his opponents in scorn, and eloquently rebukes them for preferring their "methinketh"[115] to the *consensus* of the Church. For example:

> a man whose capacity will scarce serve him to utter five words in sensible manner blusheth not in any doubt concerning matter of Scripture to think his own bare *Yea* as good as the *Nay* of all the wise, grave, and learned judgments that are in the whole world: which insolency must be suppressed, or it will be the very bane of Christian religion.[116]

When Hooker attempts to articulate his fundamental objections to Puritan subjectivism, he proceeds beyond mere contrast to define the valid *consensus* in greater depth. As Hooker reflects upon the doctrinal *consensus* that exists among the Puritans, he recognizes that it has not been reached without some probable opinion.[117] And sometimes a *consensus* is nothing more than a precipitous adoption of an unexamined viewpoint that actually happens to be wrong. As a case in point Hooker refers to the agreement that exists among the churches that follow Calvin on matters of church government; they are but "daughter churches" that "speak their mother's dialect" rather than possessing of a genuine *consensus*.[118] And re-examination of one's convictions, while helpful, does not necessarily assure the exclusion of all error. Says Hooker: "Men's consultations are always perilous. And it falleth out many times that after long deliberation those things are by their wit even resolved on, which by trial are found most opposite to public safety."[119] An analogous insight can be obtained from the formulation of positive laws. Despite good intentions and careful deliberation, "that which is supposed behoveful unto men, proveth oftentimes most pernicious."[120] Likewise, Hooker admits that the general councils of the Church can err,[121] even though they otherwise provide an excellent opportunity for reaching a *consensus*.

---

[114] V:10:1–II, 41.
[115] IV:4:2–I, 430.
[116] II:7:6–I, 327.
[117] Preface 6:6–I, 171; cf. Preface 6:3–I, 168; Preface 6:6–I, 170.
[118] Preface 4:8–I, 162; cf. Preface 4:6–I, 160.
[119] III:11:9–I, 398.
[120] IV:14:1–I, 480.
[121] Preface 6:3–I, 167.

The recognition that the reasoning of many is still liable to error and therefore possessed of truth with only a greater measure of probability, does not dispose Hooker to forsake the idea of the *consensus*. Judiciously, Hooker points out that in cases where "proof infallible" is not available, "probable persuasions" are to be preferred to such "that have in them no likelihood at all." Here it is important to observe that Hooker is desirous of defining "probable persuasions" with a good deal of latitude. For example, if in a dispute one side has "no kind of proof appearing," but the other can show that it agrees with "a number of the learnedest divines of the world," the latter is to be preferred, because "to their very bare judgment somewhat a reasonable man would attribute, notwithstanding the common imbecilities which are incident into our nature."[122] At the same time, Hooker emphatically insists that wise and learned men are preferred only when no specific argument militates against them and when, preferably, some probable reason is in their favor. To follow even apparently "wise" men completely without reason or against the conclusions of reason is simply "brutish."[123] Moreover, on several occasions Hooker explains why he pays heed to wise and learned men. "Men of common capacity and but ordinary judgment" are not capable of paying objective attention to all the various details that must be considered.[124] As a rule, the "multitude" follows its own preconceived preferences and ignores all contrary evidence.[125]

But, however much the insights of wise men may be preferable to those of a multitude, in the last analysis it must be asserted that even the wise need occasional correction. Hooker looks for this correction in three directions. In the first place, Hooker advises search for the truly learned in each generation among those who have reached a mature age. Hooker explains his dictum that "wisdom and youth are seldom joined in one" as follows: "sith the aged for the most part are best experienced, least subject to rash and unadvised passions, it hath been ever judged reasonable that their sentence in matter of counsel should be better trusted, and more relied upon than any other men's."[126]

Secondly, Hooker believes that the *consensus* will be strengthened if the wise and old men are selected from within the structure of the Church. Presumably such an approach has the advantage that it does not require an

---

[122] II:7:5–I, 324.
[123] II:7:6–I, 325; cf. Richard H. Wilmer, Jr., "Hooker on Authority," *Anglican Theological Review*, XXXIII (1951), No. 2, 102–108.
[124] I:10:7–I, 245; cf. VIII:6:2–III, 410.
[125] V Dedication 8–II, 7; cf. VII:19:2–III, 275.
[126] V:7:1–II, 30.

arbitrary selection but readily utilizes already present resources. In a lengthy and crucial passage, Hooker puts the whole matter as follows:

> To them which ask why we thus hang our judgment on the Church's sleeve, I answer with Solomon, because "two are better than one." "Yea simply (saith Basil) and universally, whether it be in the works of Nature, or of voluntary choice and counsel, I see not any thing done as it should be, if it be wrought by an agent singling itself from consorts." The Jews had a sentence of good advice, "Take not upon thee to be a judge alone; there is no sole judge but one only; say not to others, Receive my sentence, when their authority is above thine." The bare consent of the whole Church should itself in these things stop their mouths, who living under it, dare presume to bark against it. "There is (saith Cassianus) no place of audience left for them, by whom obedience is not yielded to that which all have agreed upon."[127]

Thirdly, Hooker suggests that a *consensus* formed over the centuries may serve as a final and most helpful corrective. Hooker writes in the concluding sentences of the first volume of his *magnum opus*: "what can we less thereupon conclude, than that God would at leastwise by tract of time teach the world; that the thing which he blesseth, defendeth, keepeth so strangely, cannot choose but be of him?"[128]

Under these conditions the certainty obtained is of high probability, thinks Hooker, yet it is always something less than absolute. In principle, thinks Hooker, the *consensus* is infallible: viz., "the general and perpetual voice of men is as the sentence of God himself."[129] But in actual experience, as Hooker well knows, there is no infallible guarantee that a perfect *consensus* has actually been attained. Thus, in the end, the value of *consensus* is that it supplies the highest available probability.

Yet Hooker does not end the discussion of the range of reason at this very point. Concerned as he is with the preservation of unity within the Church of England in the face of growing Puritan dissent, and familiar with the endless contentions concerning even the least significant aspects of the doctrines and liturgy of the Church, Hooker knows that he must say a mere definitive word. He believes that in fact such a word can be said. Defining the Church as a "society," Hooker sees in its organic structure the necessary resources to cope with the problem at hand.

Hooker thinks that, on the one hand, there is in all men an innate desire to live in society with other men "a life fit for the dignity of man."[130] On the

[127] V:8:3–II, 34 f.
[128] IV:14:7–I, 488; cf. IV:14:1–I, 480 f.
[129] I:8:3–I, 227.
[130] I:10:1–I, 239; cf. F. J. Shirley, *Richard Hooker and Contemporary Political Ideas*

other hand, Hooker also believes that fathers have "a supreme power" within each family as a gift from nature before the formation of society.[131] When a society is actually formed, this supreme authority held by fathers is by a compact transferred to the government of the society.[132] This is done in the knowledge "that no man might in reason take upon him to determine his own right" since in doing this he would necessarily be "partial" to himself, "and therefore . . . strifes and troubles would be endless, except they gave their common consent all to be ordered by some whom they should agree upon. . . ."[133]

Now, in so far as the Church is also a society, the role of authority within it is analogous to that of the state. That is, the Church must exercise its authority to end contentions. "Nature, Scripture, and experience itself" teach precisely how this can be accomplished: viz., "by submitting itself unto some judicial and definitive sentence, whereunto neither part that contendeth may under any pretence or colour refuse to stand."[134] Of course, Hooker knows well enough that such a position is not demonstrable or always reliable:

> God was not ignorant that priests and judges, whose sentence in matters of controversy he ordained should stand, both might and oftentimes would be deceived in their judgment. Howbeit, better it was in the eye of His understanding, that sometime an erroneous sentence definitive should prevail, till the same authority perceiving such oversight, might afterwards correct and reverse it, than that strifes should have respite to grow, and not come speedily unto some end.[135]

The practical realism of Hooker has this result: it becomes quite clear that he is completely convinced of the necessity for enforcing the *consensus* of the Church.[136] In light of Hooker's insistence on the highly useful character of reason when it is aided by grace, the authoritarian note that now appears may be disappointing to those who see genuine parallels between Hooker's advocacy of *consensus* and our contemporary openness to theological discussion in ecumenical context.[137] While this may be admitted, it nevertheless should

(London: S.P.C.K., 1949); Ernest William Talbert, *The Problem of Order. Elizabethan Political Commonplaces and an Example of Shakespeare's Art* (Chapel Hill: University of North Carolina Press, 1962); Arthur C. McGrade, "The Coherence of Hooker's Polity: The Books on Power," *Journal of the History of Ideas,* XXIV (1963), No. 2, 163–182.

131 I:10:4–I, 242.

132 I:10:1–I, 239; cf. VIII:6:11–III, 412.

133 I:10:4–I, 242.

134 Preface 6:1–I, 166.

135 Preface 6:3–I, 168.

136 Preface 6:3–I, 168; cf. V:8:2–II, 34; Answer to Travers–III, 587.

137 See my article, "Richard Hooker's Method of Theological Inquiry," *Anglican Theological Review,* XLV (1963), No. 2, 190–203; cf. John T. McNeill, *Books of Faith and Power* (New York: Harper, 1947), 88.

be noted that Hooker's readiness to advocate enforcement of the *consensus* upheld by the Church of England is not without its constructive aspects for his situation.

Hooker is a political realist who seeks to defend a reasonably equitable status quo against the dangers of conflict in the name of a new reformation. If any genuine reformation of the Church should be needed—a possibility that Hooker does not rule out—then it should proceed from within the hierarchy of the Church. Consequently, the average Christian should be concerned with "the weightier matters of the law, 'judgment, and mercy, and fidelity.' "[138] If such Christians are commanded by the Church to observe laws "which in their hearts they are steadfastly persuaded to be against the law of God," then their duty is to "suspend" this "persuasion" for the time being—otherwise they offend against God.[139]

Hooker commends such a course, not because he is opposed to all change on principle or out of subservience to the powers that be, but because he truly believes that the Church of England has established as good a *consensus* as is practically possible under existing circumstances. Moreover, Hooker is not commending a course of action on grounds that it is most expedient.[140] Instead, he is concerned to bring to light his central conviction that doctrinal unity cannot be achieved without the concord assured in a hierarchically structured Church. Hence Hooker's ultimate intent is not to rule out the legitimate rise of a Luther or a Calvin. He never denies that an individual can reach valid insights which may benefit the entire Church. What he denies is that doctrinal truth could permanently remain the exclusive property of a few individuals. Precisely because truth is not the private discovery of man, but above all, the divine gift which is grounded in the love and power of God, it is capable of so inflaming men's hearts as not to be permanently ignored. Thus what Hooker seeks is not to stifle individual thinking, but so to nurture men's minds that they may seek to relate themselves—through the hierarchically structured Church that spans the centuries—to that final goal of the human life, the saving truth of God. It is at this point, as we have noted, that Hooker's practical realism becomes most visible. While the quest for truth continues, and the *consensus* is in the process of being perfected, there

---

[138] Preface 6:5–I, 170.

[139] Preface 6:6–I, 170; cf. IV:14:6–I, 486 f.; Answer to Travers–III, 587.

[140] Henry Thomas Buckle, *History of Civilization in England* (New York: Appleton, 1867), I, 248, asserts the very opposite: "His defence rests neither upon tradition, nor upon commentators, nor even upon revelation; but he is content that the pretensions of the hostile parties shall be decided by their applicability to the great exigencies of society, and by the ease with which they adapt themselves to the general purposes of ordinary life."

is need for authoritative decisions that must be proclaimed as well as enforced if the Church is not to dissolve into a multitude of mutually opposed sects. The need for an occasional sacrifice of one's own convictions does not frighten Hooker. He does not view truth as a rare find that would occur only at great intervals of time and could be easily and permanently lost.

Thus, Hooker looks at the hierarchically structured universe, the divine revelation in Scripture, and the presence of wise and judicious men throughout the centuries. And, against the chaos of his own immediate world, he remains hopeful that the doctrinal and organizational unity of the Church will prevail. At times his vision may be limited and too readily inclined to identify the views of the Church of England and his own convictions with the true *consensus*. At times also Hooker may look too much to the past without envisioning the creative possibilities of many new solutions. But in the end Hooker redeems himself by the remarkable ability to translate his personal humility into theological categories: instead of appealing to his own insights, he points to the wisdom of others and forever subordinates himself to the judgment of the true *consensus*. Yet Hooker is not only humble; he is also courageous. He is aware that the *consensus* can become known only to the relentless searcher who questions and interprets, and who must finally decide what the wisdom of the ages is. Hooker never claims that in this task his decisions have always been the best and his system infallible; nor does he deny it. In the last analysis, Hooker is great enough not to reflect upon his own greatness, but instead to keep his gaze steadfastly upon the wisdom of God, wherever it may be found.

Spinoza on Theology and Truth

WILLIAM A. CHRISTIAN

Professor of Religious Studies, Fellow of Timothy Dwight College
Yale University
New Haven, Connecticut

I

On the title page of his *Tractatus Theologico-Politicus* (1670) Spinoza describes the treatise as "containing some discussions by which it is shown not only that freedom of philosophizing can be granted without detriment to piety and the peace of the commonwealth, but that it cannot be taken away without taking away the peace of the commonwealth and piety itself."[1] From the structure of the treatise (chapters I–XIII) it appears that his interest in piety is at least formally subordinate to his interest in a political problem. He moves from a discussion of Scripture (chapters XVI–XX) to a discussion of faith and philosophy (chapters XIV–XV) and finally to a discussion of freedom in a political community. The heading of the last chapter is: "It is shown that in a free state it is permitted to anyone to think what he chooses and to say what he thinks." Spinoza was mainly concerned to show that freedom of

[1] Carl Gebhardt, ed., *Spinoza: Opera* (Heidelberg, 1924–1926), III, 3. This edition is designated in subsequent references as "G." References are to Vol. III if no volume number is given. Page numbers refer to pages of the volume (outer margins), not pages of the treatise (inner margins). "E" refers to Vol. I of *The Chief Works of Benedict de Spinoza,* trans. by R. H. M. Elwes (New York: Dover, 1951). It is unfortunate that this is the only complete English translation of *Tractatus Theologico-Politicus* which is generally available, because it was made long before the Gebhardt edition. Elwes used Bruder's text (1843). See also Benedict de Spinoza, *The Political Works,* ed. and trans. by A. G. Wernham (Oxford: Clarendon, 1958), who gives a Latin text facing his translation. But Wernham includes only certain parts of the theological treatise, mainly the last chapters. "S" stands for Spinoza, *Selections,* ed. by John Wild (New York: Scribner's, 1930), which gives the W. H. White translation of the *Ethics.*

thought and expression is necessary to the welfare of a political community.

Much of his argument for this conclusion consists in an interpretation of the Bible.[2] But I shall concentrate on another part of his argument, namely his theory of the relation between theology and philosophy. This theory, which he speaks of as "the main object of the whole work,"[3] is that "between faith, or theology, and philosophy, there is no intercourse (*commercium*) or, if you like, affinity. . . . For philosophy has no aim (*scopus*) except truth; faith, on the other hand, has no aim except obedience and piety."[4] Faith, or theology, does not aim at truth but only at obedience and piety; philosophy does not aim at obedience or piety but only at truth. For this reason, Spinoza's argument runs, it is impossible that theology should conflict with philosophy. Therefore churchmen can have no good reason to hold that the state should restrict the liberty of philosophers.

Let us agree for the sake of our own argument that there is indeed an important difference between faith (and theology) and philosophy. And let us agree more specifically that theology aims at piety, though some speculative theologians would claim it is a purely theoretical discipline. And, of course, one can still ask: *How* does theology aim at piety? Further, let us agree that philosophy aims at truth, although some philosophers might argue that philosophy is concerned only with meaning and not with truth.

For I want to concentrate on one of the negations involved in Spinoza's distinction, namely that theology does not aim at truth. I shall take this to imply that theological assertions do not make truth-claims, and that truth is no concern of the theologian *qua* theologian (as someone might say, analogously, that truth is no concern of the poet, *qua* poet). Then I shall argue that Spinoza's ultimate thesis, that freedom of thought is necessary to public welfare and to piety, does not logically require this negation. I wish to argue not that Spinoza's ultimate thesis is wrong (for I agree with it most heartily), and not *mainly* that his fideism (if we may call it that) is wrong, though I think it is wrong,[5] but that his thesis does not require his fideism. In other words, I want to show that a defense of freedom of thought does not require skepticism about the possibility of truth-claims in religion.

In Spinoza's argument for this negation many threads of thought are woven—and sometimes badly tangled—together. Some of its main points are

---

[2] See Walter E. Stuermann, "Benedict Spinoza: A Pioneer in Biblical Criticism," *Proceedings of the American Academy for Jewish Research* XXIX (1960–1961), 133–179.

[3] G 174; cf. E 183.

[4] G 179; cf. E 189 and see also 194.

[5] See William A. Christian, *Meaning and Truth in Religion* (Princeton: University Press, 1964).

as follows: When we study the Scripture without prejudice we find that its fundamental aim is to excite and strengthen piety (or religion, or devotion to God). That is why it consists mainly of narratives, laws, and exhortations. And that is why the prophets were men of vivid imagination rather than great intellectual power. The revelations described in the Scripture were aimed at making men more obedient to God, not at changing their opinions about God.

The fundamental teaching of the Bible is that obedience to God consists in justice and charity to one's neighbor. This is the essential rule of piety. We may think of other scriptural doctrines as accommodations to the prevailing beliefs of the people, calculated to move them to do justice and charity and thus obey God. So the Scripture leaves us absolutely free to philosophize on speculative questions. This agrees well with our experience, for we find many simple people who lead pious lives but are not skilled in reasoning about such questions.

The argument becomes firmer when we come to Chapter XIV, in which "what faith is, who are faithful, and the fundamentals of faith, are determined, and faith is finally distinguished from philosophy."[6] Faith is defined as nothing else than ". . . thinking such things about God that if they are disregarded there is no obedience to God, and such that if there is obedience to God these things are necessarily given."[7] This definition is crucial to Spinoza's argument, as we shall see. From it he draws two consequences: first, that faith does not bring salvation through itself but only by reason of obedience (quoting James 2:17); and second, that he who is truly obedient necessarily has true and saving faith. And from these, he says, it follows further that we cannot judge that anyone is faithful or unfaithful except by his works.

This last consequence is calculated to support Spinoza's ultimate thesis about freedom of thought in the commonwealth. For if no one can be judged to be faithful (or unfaithful) by reference to any of his opinions but only by reference to his actions, it follows that the state cannot restrict freedom of thought *on the ground that* some opinions are incompatible with religious faith. This follows because, if we take this last consequence strictly, no opinion someone "M" may have can be taken as counting against (or for) a proposition of the form "M has faith."

A further consequence of this definition of faith is that faith "requires

---

[6] G 173.

[7] ". . . de Deo talia sentire, quibus ignoratis tollitur erga Deum obedientia, & hac obedientia posita, necessario ponuntur." G 175; cf. E 184. Spinoza claims to derive this definition from Scripture. See E 183 f. This claim, it would seem, is a thesis in Biblical theology. The question is: Does "God commands justice and charity" state the *summa,* the main point, of the Bible as a whole? Much hangs on this question. Certainly countertheses have been proposed and defended, for example theses claiming that the *summa* of the Bible is not a precept but a gospel.

dogmas which are not so much true as pious, that is, such dogmas as move the heart to obedience."[8] The point is expressed more severely a few lines later where, instead of the comparative *"non tam . . . quam,"* Spinoza uses an adversative expression (*non . . . sed*). The definition of faith "does not expressly demand true dogmas, but such as are necessary to obedience, that is to say dogmas which confirm the heart in love towards one's neighbor." Thus it seems that someone can have saving faith even if his dogmas are not true. So the kind of thinking about God in which faith consists does not necessarily involve having true beliefs about God. It consists in having beliefs which issue in obedience. Since people vary widely in their dispositions and opinions, a doctrine which moves some to devotion may move others to contempt.

But there are some dogmas which obedience to God posits absolutely and without which obedience is absolutely impossible. These dogmas belong to the "catholic faith." They are as follows:[9]

I. That God, that is to say a supreme being supremely just and merciful, or in other words an exemplar of true life, exists.

II. That he is one. (Spinoza adds that this dogma is necessary because devotion, admiration, and love arise only from the excellence of one thing over others.)

III. That he is omnipresent, or (*vel*) that all things are manifest to him.

IV. That he has supreme right (*jus*) and dominion over all things, and does not do anything from external compulsion but from his absolute good pleasure and grace alone.

V. That worship of God and obedience to him consists only in justice and charity, which is to say love towards one's neighbor.

VI. That all and only those who obey God by this manner of living are saved; the rest who live under the rule of their pleasures are lost. (Spinoza adds that if men did not believe this firmly, there would be no reason [*causa*] why they would prefer to submit to God than to their pleasures.)

VII. Finally that God pardons sins to those who are penitent.

All these dogmas are necessary conditions of obedience to God. Notice that Spinoza is deducing these doctrines from the concept of obedience to God taken in conjunction with the general character of human nature. He could do this without *asserting* them. Men being what they are, it is necessary for them to think about God in this way, *if* they are to be obedient to God.

---

[8] ". . . non tam . . . vera, quam pia . . ." G 176, l. 18; cf. E 185. Cf. ". . . non tam veritatem, quam pietatem." G 179.

[9] G 177 f.; E 186 f.

But *only* these dogmas are necessary. Questions which go beyond these dogmas have nothing to do with faith, for example:

A. what God, i.e., the exemplar of true life, is (*quid Deus, sive illud verae vitae exemplar sit*), whether for example he is fire or a spirit or light or thought, etc.;[10]
B. in what way (*qua ratione*) he is the exemplar of true life, whether for example because he has a just and merciful disposition (*animum*), or because all things exist and act through him and consequently it is through him that we understand and see that which is true, just, and good;
C. (whether) God is everywhere by virtue of (*secundum*) his essence or by virtue of his power; (whether) he directs things out of freedom or by the necessity of nature; (whether) he prescribes laws like a prince or teaches them as eternal truths;
D. (whether) man obeys God from freedom of choice or from the necessity of the divine decree; and
E. (whether) the reward of good men and the punishment of evil men is natural or supernatural.[11]

It does not matter, as far as faith is concerned, how anyone understands these matters, so long as he does not draw some conclusion in order to give himself an excuse for being less obedient to God. Indeed each man must adapt (*accommodare*) the dogmas of faith to his own understanding and interpret (*interpretari*) them in that way which he thinks will enable him to embrace them without hesitation but with the complete consent of his heart, so that consequently he may obey God with the full consent of his heart.

From this discussion of faith Spinoza moves to a discussion of theology in Chapter XV in which he shows "that theology is not subservient to reason, nor reason to theology, *and* the way (*ratio*) in which we persuade ourselves of the authority of the sacred Scripture."[12] The function of theology is to show the object (*scopum*) aimed at by Scripture, namely the pattern and the manner of obeying (*rationem et modum obediendi*), which is to say (*sive*) the dogmas of true piety and faith. Theology thus understood, if one considers its precepts or rules of life, agrees with reason and, if one considers its intent

---

[10] Cf.: "The Scripture does not teach, professedly and as an eternal doctrine, what God is, and in what manner he sees and provides for all things, and similar matters." G 102 f.; cf. E 104.

[11] G 178; cf. E 187 f. Spinoza's own answers to these questions are made quite explicit in the treatise. See E 14, 25, 43–46, 57–65, ch. VI (Of Miracles), 200, 202, 211, 248, 270, 276 f.

[12] G 180.

and end, is in no respect repugnant to reason and therefore is common to all men.[13]

But the function of theology is not just to discover what the Bible teaches, by critical study. Theology *asserts* the dogmas of faith, and Spinoza singles out one of these for special attention, namely that men are saved even by obedience alone, and calls it the cornerstone (*fundamentum*) of theology.[14] Now we cannot demonstrate by reason whether this proposition is true or false. Therefore revelation was necessary. But once it has been revealed we can use our judgment to embrace it with, at all events, *moral* certainty (*morali saltem certitudine*).[15] Spinoza's reasoning for this conclusion is, to say the least, not altogether clear,[16] but some of his points are as follows: This doctrine gives great consolation to those who are not able to find consolation by reason. It has benefited the state (by strengthening public morality, presumably). It would be absurd to admit nothing as true, for the sake of ordering life wisely, which could be called into question in *some* way or other, or to suppose that most of our actions are not highly uncertain and full of hazard.[17] Finally, since all men can obey, and since very few acquire the habit of virtue by the leading of reason alone, we should doubt of the salvation of nearly all men if we did not have this testimony of Scripture.[18]

II

Now we are in a position to raise some questions about the force of Spinoza's negation concerning theology and truth. The major problem is as follows: Theology not only defines but asserts the dogmas of faith. This would seem to mean that it claims they are true. But if theology makes truth-claims,[19] how can it be said that it has no aim (*scopus*) except obedience and piety?

The most promising line of exploration is to look for some way of construing the dogmas of faith as assertions which do not make truth-claims.

[13] G 185; E 195.

[14] G 185.

[15] G 185. See on moral certainty E 28 f., 270 (n. 8), and George H. R. Parkinson, *Spinoza's Theory of Knowledge* (Oxford: Clarendon, 1954), 156 f.

[16] See on this passage Frederick Pollock, *Spinoza, His Life and Philosophy* (2nd ed., London: Duckworth, 1899), 338 f., and Elmer E. Powell, *Spinoza and Religion* (2nd ed., Boston: Chapman and Grimes, 1941), 299–301.

[17] G 187.

[18] G 188.

[19] The question here is not whether Spinoza himself is willing to assert the dogmas of faith (with suitable interpretations of them) or not, but whether, if some theologian (or anyone at all) should assert them, this assertion would amount to making a truth-claim.

Our problem is not how to interpret the content of the dogmas. Spinoza suggests various possible ways of adapting and interpreting them,[20] as we have seen, and says that the faithful man is free to interpret them in any of these or in other ways. That is why our problem is not how to interpret them but rather how to construe them. In what *way* are they significant, and how can their significance be independent of any of these interpretations? In other words, what *kind* of thinking about God (*de Deo sentire*) is necessary for obedience?

It would not do to say that the dogmas of faith fail to be truth-claims because we can have only moral certainty about them, if being morally certain means being certain enough for practical purposes that something is *true*. For then the dogmas of faith would be genuine truth-claims, even though judgments that they are in fact true or false must rest on experience and not on mathematical demonstration, and hence would be only probable, not absolutely certain.

We might say that though the dogmas of faith are not as they stand, without interpretations, genuine truth-claims, they constitute a matrix for truth-claims. Truth-claims are made when interpretations of the dogmas are offered and asserted. Without interpretations, we do not know just what is being claimed. As they stand the dogmas are too vague to be genuine truth-claims. At one point Spinoza says that Scripture *does* have some doctrines which are of speculation alone (*solius . . . speculationis*), but they are very few and very simple.[21]

This suggestion has some merit, but what keeps the dogmas from being truth-claims is not exactly their vagueness; it is the way they are introduced. Not only do they appeal to experience (instead of to pure reason); it seems they are proposed with a practical purpose in view and are instrumental to this purpose. So we might claim at most that they are practically necessary, human nature being what it is, to lead most men to be moral. But this is very different from claiming they are true. A number of passages, along with some we have already noticed, suggest that religious doctrines not only have a bearing on morality but themselves have a moral *significance*.[22]

In his preface Spinoza tells us that as he pondered the nature of prophecy he concluded that "the authority of the prophets has weight only in those

[20] E.g., as interpretations of I, "God is fire" and "God is thought."

[21] G 168; cf. E 176. See also G 77; E 77, but cf. G 77 f.; E 78.

[22] It would be interesting to explore similarities and contrasts between the treatise and Kant's *Religion within the Limits of Reason Alone,* and such present-day theories as Richard B. Braithwaite, *An Empiricist's View of the Nature of Religious Belief* (Cambridge: University Press, 1955).

questions which bear on the practice of life (*usum vitae*) and true virtue; for the rest, their opinions have little to do with us."[23] The prophets were ignorant of, and had contrary opinions about, "things which bear on speculation alone and not on the practice of life and charity."[24] Speaking of certain speculative doctrines he says,

> Although experience can give no clear knowledge (*cognitionem*) of these things, and cannot teach what God is and in what way (*qua ratione*) he sustains and directs all things and has concern for men, it can still teach and enlighten men as much as suffices for impressing obedience and devotion on their hearts.[25]

"The divinity of Scripture must be established from this fact alone, that it teaches true virtue."[26] All the arguments of Moses "are not drawn from the armory of reason but are only ways of speaking by which he expressed the decrees of God more effectively and pictured them more vividly."[27] The chief point (*summa*) of religion as preached by the Apostles "consists above all in moral lessons (*documentibus moralibus*), as does the whole doctrine of Christ."[28] "God sought no other knowledge of himself through the prophets than knowledge of his divine justice and charity, that is, such attributes of God as men can imitate by a certain way of living."[29] What everyone is required to know is "that God is supremely just and supremely merciful, which is to say that he is the one and only exemplar of true life (*unicum vera vitae exemplar*)."[30] So

> we conclude that intellectual knowledge of God, which considers his nature so far as it is in itself and as a nature which men cannot imitate by a certain way of living, nor take as an example, for the sake of instituting the true way of living, is in no way relevant to faith and revealed religion. . . .[31]

The knowledge of God aimed at in the Scripture is necessary "not for science but for obedience."[32]

---

[23] G 9; cf. E 8.
[24] G 42; cf. E 40.
[25] G 77 f.; cf. E 78.
[26] G 99; cf. E 100.
[27] G 153; cf. E 159.
[28] G 156; cf. E 162.
[29] G 170; cf. E 179.
[30] G 171; cf. E 179.
[31] ". . . concludimus, intellectualem Dei cognitionem, quae ejus naturam, prout in se est, considerat, & quam naturam homines certa vivendi ratione imitari non possunt, neque tanquam exemplum sumere, ad veram vivendi rationem instituendam, ad fidem, & religionem revelatam nullo modo pertinere. . . ." G 171; E 180.
[32] G 172; cf. E 181.

> Theology determines the dogmas of faith only so far as is sufficient for obedience; but in exactly what way they should be understood in respect of truth (*ratione veritatis*) it leaves to be determined by reason, which is really the light of the mind, without which it (the mind) sees nothing but dreams and fictions (*figmenta*).[33]

Against this background for understanding the significance of the *dogmata fidei* let us take a further step by considering their structure. Their central concept is the concept of God. Now let us ask: How is this concept *introduced,* in the statement of the dogmas? What initial footing in experience or thought is it being given? Dogma I reads as follows: *"Deum, hoc est ens supremum, summe justum, et misericordem, sive verae vitae exemplar existere."*[34] Keeping in mind the other references to God as "exemplar of true life" we already have noticed in the treatise, it looks as though *"verae vitae exemplar"* is being used in Dogma I not to express an additional attribute of God but as a way of introducing the concept of God. What is the concept of God a concept *of?* What sort of concept is this? It is a concept of an exemplar of the true life. This is how the concept of a supreme being gets its initial significance. It arises in moral experience as a projection of the moral ideal.[35]

If this is the way the concept of God is being introduced, then we can construe the dogmas of faith in the following way. The kind of thinking about God (*de Deo sentire*) which is necessary for obedience is thinking about an exemplar of true life. This is imaginative thinking,[36] controlled by the idea of

---

[33] G 184; cf. E 194 f.

[34] G 177.

[35] In the preface to Part IV of the *Ethics* Spinoza says that "good" and "evil" are only notions we form from comparing one thing with another. Nevertheless they are useful terms for the following reason: "We desire to form an idea of man as an exemplar of human nature, which we may contemplate." (. . . ideam hominis tanquam naturae humanae exemplar, quod intueamur, formare cupimus. . . .) So in the following pages he will mean by "good" that which we know is essential to our approaching more and more to the exemplar of human nature we propose for ourselves, and by "evil" that which we know to impede us from representing (*referamus*) that exemplar. Then we shall speak of men as more or less perfect in so far as they approach this same exemplar more or less. G II, 208; cf. S 285 f.

[36] See Ep. XIX (1665): "Scripture . . . continually speaks in a human manner. . . . the prophets composed whole parables. First of course they represented God in the form of a king and lawgiver, because he revealed the means of salvation and perdition, of which he was the cause. The means, which are nothing but causes, they called laws, and drew them up in writing in the manner of laws . . . and they ordered all their words according to this parable more than according to truth, and expressed God in the form of a man throughout. . . ." G IV, 92 f.; cf. *The Correspondence of Spinoza,* trans. and ed. by A. Wolf (London: Allen and Unwin, 1928), 149 f. See Ep. XXI (1665), G IV, 132; A. Wolf, *op. cit.,* 180.

But see also *Ethics* IV, lxviii: "If men were born free they would form no concept of good and evil, as long as they were free." (And hence would have no need of the notion of an exemplar.) But "the hypothesis of this proposition is false." G II, 261; cf. S 347.

a supremely just and merciful being whom we ought to obey. In defining the dogmas of faith theology is filling out, so to speak, this imaginative idea.

This would explain how theology differs from speculative thought. For intellectual knowledge of God "considers his nature so far as it is in itself and as a nature which men *cannot* imitate by a certain way of living, nor take as an example, for the sake of instituting the true way of living."[37] And *that* is why intellectual knowledge of God "is in no way relevant to faith and revealed religion." The root of the difference between theological thinking about God and speculative thinking about God is not that they come to different conclusions of the same logical kind, and certainly not to conflicting conclusions. (Spinoza is explicit on the impossibility of conflict between the dogmas of faith, considered apart from interpretations of them—some of which are superstitious—and reason.) The root of the difference is that they are different kinds of thinking. Hence they use different modes of expression. "When we speak philosophically we should not use the expressions (*phrasibus*) of theology, for . . . theology represents God throughout, and not by accident (*passim, nec temerè*), as a perfect man."[38] Theology is imaginative thinking arising in moral experience and controlled by the idea of God as the exemplar of true life. Piety is action guided by this idea. Philosophy is speculative thinking about God as he is in himself.

It would follow that the dogmas of faith are not truth-claims. They are explications of a certain image which naturally arises in the course of living a good life. But they do not really purport to tell us what is in fact the case.

So what keeps the dogmas of faith from being truth-claims is not exactly their vagueness. They are not vague speculative claims because they are not speculative claims at all. Therefore, and in this way, Spinoza's negation about truth in religion would remain in force. Truth-claims about God would be made only when the dogmas of faith are interpreted, but these interpretations are not themselves dogmas of faith.

Here we should pause to notice one sort of truth-claim which, on Spinoza's own showing, theology must make, even though this admission would not affect his main point. Consider the following statement:

A. The *summa* of Scripture is that God commands justice and charity.

Spinoza himself argues for a proposition of this kind. And some such premise, either this or some positive alternative about the *summa* (or *funda-*

On Spinoza's doctrine of imagination see George H. R. Parkinson, *op. cit.,* ch. VII. But it would be interesting to explore further Spinoza's view of the positive role of imagination in moral life, beginning with the passage cited from the preface to Part IV of the *Ethics.*

[37] G 171, italics mine.

[38] Ep. XXIII (1665), G IV, 147 f.; cf. A. Wolf, *op. cit.,* 190.

mentum) of Scripture, is essential for deducing any dogmas of faith. So it seems that theology must make *some* truth-claim or other about the central intent of the whole of Scripture.

But contrast with A the following:

B. God commands justice and charity.

C. God is the one substance of which all other things are modes.

D. Human blessedness consists in the intellectual love of God.

These express propositions not about Scripture but about God, or human blessedness. So these claims are different from A. A could be asserted without assent to B, or to C or D, or indeed without assent to any proposition about God or human blessedness. For A could be argued by Biblical scholars who are religious humanists, or Theravada Buddhists, or even not religious at all. Analogously, political scientists who are not Communists could argue for or against interpretations of the Soviet constitution, and scholars who are not Roman Catholics, nor Christians, nor even religious, could argue for or against interpretations of *The Divine Comedy*.

It follows that A could be asserted without assenting to the dogmas of faith. It could be true that this or that is what the Bible says, but at the same time what the Bible says could be untrue. To go further, it might be the case that A makes a truth-claim and yet B does not even make a truth-*claim*. So even if theology makes some truth-claim in a statement like A, it does not follow from this that the dogmas of faith are truth-claims. So Spinoza's main point would remain.

III

Now let us consider an objection to the way we have construed the significance of the dogmas of faith in the treatise. We have construed them as explications of an imaginative idea which arises naturally in the course of moral life, an idea which is essential to leading the good life, at least for most men. The objection is that Spinoza's own thought, in the treatise and elsewhere, is in fact fundamentally hostile to this idea. So he cannot mean to give the dogmas of faith as much positive significance as we have done.

I am concerned with Spinoza's *argument* in the treatise, that is to say with what Leo Strauss calls the "obvious reasoning."[39] Certainly the reasoning in the treatise is highly involved and often tortuous. There is much that is ironical and much that seems devious. As a result many contradictions can be produced, as Strauss has done. His rule for resolving these contradictions,

[39] Strauss, "How to Study Spinoza's *Tractatus Theologico-Politicus*," *Persecution and the Art of Writing* (Glencoe, Ill.: Free Press, 1952), 201.

namely that "every statement of such an author which agrees with views vulgarly considered sacred or authoritative must be dismissed as irrelevant, or at least it must be suspected even though it is never contradicted by him,"[40] is much too simple, and his use of the distinction to which it leads him, between the "obvious reasoning" of the treatise and its "hidden reasoning," does something less than justice both to Spinoza's truthfulness and to his perspicacity. If Spinoza had meant to mislead some of his readers into thinking that he agreed with the orthodox theology of his time, would he have explained his own concepts of God and human blessedness as clearly as he does in the treatise?[41] And if he expected to mislead his readers in this way he was badly mistaken, as the history of the reception of the treatise shows.

In any case, as Strauss would agree,[42] the first step to understanding what Spinoza thought is to understand the argument he presents, and this is my intention. So the question I wish to consider is whether Spinoza's argument in the treatise rejects the idea of God as exemplar of the true life, or whether the argument permits it as an image which is natural to the mind, though falling short of the standard for intellectual understanding. In the former case, we should have to say that his argument was fundamentally hostile to faith as he defined it. In the latter case, the argument is at least permissive of the imaginative thinking involved in faith, though the mind cannot rest content with this kind of thinking. Hence interpretation of the dogmas of faith is still required.

Now if we take the argument as hostile to the exemplar concept, one consequence would be as follows. The dogmas of faith, of which this is the central concept, would come nearer making a truth-claim than if the argument were permissive of this concept. For presumably this rejection would be based on some principles of judgment, and hence something more than an expression of personal disinclination. It would be a negative *judgment*. And where there are judgments, whether affirmative or negative, there are truth-claims.

The principal evidence for the objection we are considering is that in the treatise, as well as elsewhere, Spinoza rejects anthropomorphic conceptions of God as a being who can be imitated, or obeyed. In Chapter IV he raises the question whether "by the natural light we can conceive God as prescribing laws for men like a legislator or prince."[43] His answer is that we cannot, since the will of God and the intellect of God are in reality one and the same.

---

[40] *Ibid.*, 177; cf. 170.

[41] See the reference in n. 11 above, and his impassioned outbursts against superstition, as in E 4, 7, 27.

[42] Strauss, *op. cit.*, 201.

[43] G 62; cf. E 62.

If Adam had understood this, he would have seen that the forbidden fruit involved an eternal necessity and truth. Instead he took the revelation as a law, "that is, as a statute which entails gain or harm, not from necessity and the nature of the action performed, but solely from the pleasure and absolute authority of some prince."[44] Similarly, Moses perceived the conditions for uniting the Israelites

> not as eternal truths but as precepts and statutes, and prescribed them as laws of God, and hence it came to pass that he imagined (*imaginaretur*) God as a leader, legislator, king, merciful, just, and so on, though on the contrary all these are attributes of human nature only and are utterly removed from the divine nature.[45]

Spinoza concludes that

> God is described as a legislator or prince, and is called just, merciful, and so on, only out of the conception of the common people (*ex captu vulgi*) and only from a failure of thinking, and that in reality God acts and directs all things only from the necessity of his nature and perfection, and finally that his decrees and volitions are eternal truths and always involve necessity.[46]

Later, in a note attached to Chapter XVI, he says:

> We have shown that divine laws appear to us as laws or statutes so long as we are ignorant of their cause. Once that cause is known, however, they cease to be laws, and we embrace them as eternal truths, not as laws, that is to say. Obedience then passes into love, which arises from true knowledge as necessarily as light does from the sun. Therefore we can indeed love God from the leading of reason, but we cannot obey him, since we can neither embrace divine laws as divine, as long as we are ignorant of their cause, nor conceive by reason God drawing up laws like a prince.[47]

So it is very clear that in the treatise Spinoza rejects the concept of obedience to an external authority.

This fact, however, does not itself imply a simple rejection of the dogmas of faith. For the dogmas of faith do not say that God commands like a prince. On the contrary, as we have seen, the dogmas are defined in such a way as to leave the following questions about the exemplar of true life undetermined:

> (i) whether he is the exemplar of true life because he has a just and merciful disposition (*animum*), or because all things exist and act through him and consequently it is through him that we understand and see that which is true, just, and good; and (ii) whether he prescribes laws like a prince or teaches them as eternal truths.

---

[44] G 63; cf. E 63.
[45] G 64; cf. E 64.
[46] G 65; cf. E 65.
[47] G 264; cf. E 277 and Wernham, *op. cit.*, 249.

The dogmas of faith do not themselves *claim* that God has an *animus* (i.e., that his nature is intentional) or that he prescribes laws like a prince. So the fact that Spinoza's argument in the treatise includes a denial of anthropomorphic interpretations of God does not of itself imply that the dogmas of faith are false, or that they are devoid of significance.

Further, Spinoza explains with some clarity the sense in which we may properly speak of the "commands" of God. Since our highest good and our blessedness consist in knowledge and love of God,

> the means which this end of all human actions—that is, God himself inasfar as the idea of him is in us—requires can be called commands (*jussa*) of God, because they are prescribed for us as if by God himself, inasfar as he exists in our mind. And further, the way of living (*ratio vivendi*) which tends to this end is best called the divine law (*lex*).[48]

To the extent that we have a true speculative understanding of ourselves and of God, we see that obedience to God is unlike obedience to the commands of a human ruler. We see that it consists in conforming to the requirements of our own highest good, namely knowing and loving God, through whom we exist and act and understand.

Theologians, however, cannot expect everyone to have this speculative understanding, so they should not frame the dogmas of faith in such a way as to require it. Many pious people do in fact obey God with other conceptions of him in their minds. Theology, then, formulates those and only those notions which are necessarily involved in the *practice* of obedience to God.

When human beings frame for themselves a pattern of true life they necessarily think of an exemplar of true life as a guide to moral judgments and actions. This kind of thinking is not speculative thinking; it is the kind of thinking which is immediately involved in action. The task of theology is to adumbrate this imaginative idea of an exemplar of true life, and to explicate it in such a way that the actions of those who entertain it will be directed toward justice and charity.

In this way theology has no aim except obedience and piety; it does not aim at truth. This does not mean that the dogmas of faith are untrue. On the contrary, it is not right to speak of them as either true or untrue. They do not make truth-*claims*. They are imaginative ideas which are necessary for guiding action in certain ways. There is room for various interpretations of these ideas, various theories about how God exists and how he is the exemplar of true life. These theories may make truth-claims and hence may be true or untrue. But this is the domain of philosophy, not of theology.

---

[48] G 60; cf. E 60.

IV

Let us now assume that, in the way I have suggested or in some other way, the dogmas of faith can be understood as essential to "universal religion" without being truth-claims. And let us ask whether this negation about theology and truth is logically required for a defense of freedom of thought and expression.

As we noticed at the beginning, Spinoza's thesis about "freedom of philosophizing" has two prongs. He argues that freedom is necessary to piety, and that it is necessary to the welfare of a political community. Let us consider the latter prong first. In order to show that the welfare of a commonwealth requires freedom of thought, is it necessary to maintain that theology makes no truth-claims?

Spinoza's argument on this particular point is not as firm and explicit as it might be. But it depends in part on the premise that the ruler or rulers of a state must exercise authority over religious institutions. The state must regulate and control religion in a far-reaching way. He argues for this conclusion at some length in Chapter XIX, and treats the idea of a separation of church and state with contempt.[49]

> The cultus of religion and the exercise of piety ought to be adapted to the peace and welfare (*utilitati*) of the commonwealth, and consequently ought to be determined by the supreme rulers alone, who indeed ought also to be its interpreters.[50]

He distinguishes "the cultus of religion and the exercise of piety" (in outward action) from "piety itself and the internal worship of God." But this distinction is not absolute. For,

> although it is not possible for minds to be ruled in the same manner as tongues, minds are nevertheless in some way under the rule of the supreme power, who in many ways can bring it about that a very large proportion of men should believe, love, hate, and so on, whatever he wishes.[51]

Among rights belonging to the supreme power alone he lists those of supervising the daily sacred rites, choosing their ministers, defining and strengthening the fundamentals of the church and its doctrine, judging concerning

---

[49] G 234; E 251. His argument against separating sacred from civil rights and granting the former to the church assumes that the former entail civil jurisdiction. See also E 238. This, from the point of view of modern proponents of religious freedom, begs the crucial question.

[50] G 228 f.; cf. E 245.

[51] G 202; cf. E 216.

morals and acts of piety, excommunicating anyone or receiving him into the church, and even providing for the poor.[52] Speaking of the ancient Hebrews, he says that, but for the prophets, the kings would have had the same authority (*jus*) over all sacred affairs (*sacra*), without exception, as over civil affairs. Since modern rulers have no obligation to recognize prophets, they have this authority absolutely.[53] Again,

> even the divine law (*jus divinum*), that is the law concerning sacred affairs, depends absolutely on the decree of the supreme rulers, and they are its interpreters and champions. From which it follows that the ministers of the word of God are those who teach the people piety by authority of the supreme rulers, according as it has been adapted to the welfare of the commonwealth by their decree.[54]

It seems clear that one freedom for which Spinoza was *not* concerned was freedom of worship.

Spinoza does not argue for a state-church in the treatise. On the other hand, he does not argue against religious uniformity as a matter of principle,[55] though he speaks approvingly of the protection given various religions in Amsterdam,[56] and pleads in Chapter XX for toleration of religious *opinions*. And the far-reaching extent to which he would submit religion to the state, including the determination of religious doctrines, would seem to involve a state-church, though not in such a way as to entail enforcement of religious uniformity. But the premise in his argument to which I call attention is that the state should have complete control of religion, whether or not there is a state-church.

Now, assuming state control of religion, Spinoza's thought seems to run as follows. Freedom of thought, and thereby the welfare of the state, would be jeopardized if the church should make truth-claims. For then it would be

---

[52] G 234 f.; E 252.

[53] G 238; E 256.

[54] G 236; cf. E 254.

[55] Wernham, *op. cit.*, 35, cites two reasons for "Spinoza's refusal to prescribe religious uniformity in his model states." One was that the national religion of the Jews hindered trade with foreigners. But Spinoza's argument here is not against uniformity of religion; it is against a theocracy. See E 228 f., 237. The second reason, according to Wernham, was that religious uniformity would lead to turmoil where strong opposition exists. But Spinoza does not oppose religious uniformity in the passages Wernham cites. So it is going too far to speak of Spinoza's *refusal* to prescribe uniformity. Also the "reasons" he attributes to Spinoza are not matters of principle but of expediency.

In the uncompleted *Tractatus Politicus* Spinoza says that in a monarchical state there would be no temples (*templa*) at the public expense. E 326. But in an aristocratic state there would be a national religion, to which the patricians are required to belong, for which large and expensive temples would be provided. Temples of other religions would be small and scattered. E 368.

[56] E 264.

natural and perhaps necessary for the state to prescribe assent to the dogmas of the church, or at least to proscribe public contradiction of those dogmas. Thus the claim of a church to truth would open the way, at least, to repression of philosophizing. If on the contrary theology does not, and indeed cannot (logically), claim truth, then *this* danger to repression of philosophy does not exist.

It is worth noticing that Spinoza's argument for the subordination of the church to the state itself rests in part on his theory that faith has an entirely practical significance and does not involve truth-claims. Faith is that thinking about God which obedience requires, and which is present whenever obedience is present. Further, obedience consists in justice and charity. Therefore,

> since it is the function of the supreme ruler alone to determine what is necessary for the safety of the whole people and the security of the realm, and to command what he judges to be necessary, it follows that it is also the function of the supreme ruler alone to determine in what way each man ought to honor his neighbor in accord with piety, that is to say, in what way each man is required to obey God.[57]

If religion has an entirely practical significance, it becomes possible, on Spinoza's political assumptions, to subordinate religion to the state.

There is another, and perhaps less important, way in which Spinoza's view of theology contributes to his argument for freedom of thought, and this also depends on the assumption of state control of religion. If theology makes truth-claims, this opens the way to disputes and dissensions in the church. And since the government of the church is a function of the state, this increases the danger of turmoil in the commonwealth and hence the danger of tyranny, as an alternative to public disorder. So, for the sake of public order, rulers should not allow the dogmas of religion to become very numerous or to be confused with knowledge.[58] And this is possible only if theology does not make truth-claims.

I have been arguing that the positive contribution of Spinoza's view of theology to his argument for freedom of thought in the public domain depends on the premise of state control of religion. If this is true, and if we remove this premise, then his negation of truth-claims in theology is not required for a defense of freedom of thought. And a number of very good arguments, from moral principles, from past political experience, and from theological principles, can be offered against this premise.

---

[57] G 232; cf. E 249 f.
[58] G 238; E 256.

V

Now let us consider the other prong of Spinoza's argument for freedom of thought. Let us ask whether the conclusion that freedom of thought is necessary for *piety* requires the denial of truth-claims in theology. In this case his argument would seem to hang on a certain implicit conception of the authority of a church over its members.

If we consider the individual pious man, no link is apparent between (P) "freedom of thought is necessary for true piety" and (Q) "theology does not aim at truth." Spinoza speaks often, echoing the Great Commandment, of obeying God "with the whole heart,"[59] and of knowing and loving God from true liberty and a whole and constant heart.[60] Religion, he says, consists not so much in external actions as in simplicity and truthfulness of heart (*animi simplicitate & veracitate*).[61] And he argues that thinking freely is essential to loving God freely.

But this conclusion does not require Q. Indeed, we might ask, does the requirement of freedom and integrity of mind *permit* theology *not* to aim at truth? For it would seem that, in order to love God in this way, the kind of thinking about God (*de Deo sentire*) which faith requires ought to be open to the other kinds of thinking which go on in the same mind. And how could this be, if faith-thinking is not concerned with truth?

A link between P and Q in Spinoza's argument appears when we consider the pious man not by himself but in relation to a religious community. If he belongs to a religious community, then his faith is not a purely private matter. He participates in the faith of the community. Suppose now that the community requires of him, in some way or other, not only certain types of action, moral and ceremonial, but also certain beliefs. Then a threat to singleness of heart may arise. But beliefs could be required only on the ground that they are true. So if theology does not aim at truth, this threat could not arise. Also, if theology does not claim truth, theological controversies, which would tempt rulers to decide them and thus provoke schisms in the church, could not arise.[62]

But Spinoza's argument can show at most that this is a potential danger to piety, not an inevitable danger. Freedom and integrity of mind could be maintained in two ways vis-à-vis this threat. (i) In a situation of religious freedom, where churches are neither controlled by the state nor possessed of

[59] G 10 *"integro animo"*; E 9.
[60] G 62; E 62. See also E 97, 182, 188, 245.
[61] G 116; E 118.
[62] E 262, 264.

special political privileges, they cannot rely on or employ civil sanctions; the individual does not suffer loss of civic rights and privileges if he leaves the church. (ii) If a church conceives its own theology as subject to judgment, by reference to the word of God for example, it must be open in principle to the individual's own contributions to thinking out its faith. It will formulate its theology with fear and trembling (but not a paralyzing fear) and treat its members with charity and wisdom. This depends on the structure of the church and the way its authority is distributed and employed.

As Spinoza himself argued, belief *cannot* be commanded.

> Simplicity and truthfulness of heart is not infused into men by command of laws nor public authority, and no one at all can be compelled by force or laws to become blessed. For this, pious and brotherly advice, good education, and above all [use of] one's own free judgment are required. . . . the supreme right of thinking freely, even about religion, is in the possession of every man, and it cannot be conceived that anyone is able to surrender this right. . . .[63]

This is an ultimate ground of arguments for freedom of thought both in the state and in the church. But the reason why belief cannot be commanded is this: A proposal for belief is unlike a proposal for action in respect of the kind of question it poses. A proposal for action (which *can* be a command) poses the question "Shall I do it?" A proposal for belief poses the question, "Is it true?"

[63] G 116 f.; E 118 f.

Pascal's Wager Argument

ROGER HAZELTON

Dean, Professor of Theology
The Graduate School of Theology
Oberlin College
Oberlin, Ohio

I

Few writers can match Blaise Pascal in his power to fascinate and irritate the reader at once, and this strange double effect is nowhere produced more sharply than in his *pensée* called the wager, or *Pari*. William James, for example, who used the wager argument as grist for the development of his own "will to believe," could describe the *Pari* as "a last desperate snatch at a weapon against the hardness of the unbelieving heart"; but later on in the same famous essay he allowed that it "seems a regular clincher" in its stress upon the role of the will as a maker of truth.[1] Many similar testimonies and mixed reactions may be gathered from almost three centuries of discussion generated during what has well been called the posthumous life of Pascal's *Pensées*.[2]

A fragment like the *Pari* may inspire several kinds of interest and will accordingly raise different sorts of questions. As with all the *pensées,* which constitute in Ronald Knox's phrase "the ruins of a temple that was never built," we have to ask just what it was that Pascal intended to say, or would have said if his jottings had ever been reworked into the complete *Apology for the Christian Religion* which he projected. In the case of the *Pari* this question is sharpened by the fact that while we certainly have in it an argument addressed to the nonbeliever, it moves on more than one plane and by

[1] James, *The Will to Believe, and Other Essays* (New York: Longmans, Green, 1897), 6, 11.

[2] Bernard Amoudru, *La vie posthume des Pensées* (Paris: Bloud & Gay, 1936).

fits and starts, as numerous corrections and marginal additions in the original manuscript bear witness.

Another kind of inquiry is concerned with the type of person whom Pascal wished to reach through the *Pari*. There is an interlocutor, usually identified as the *libertin* or freethinker to whom much of Pascal's *Apology* seems to refer, whose questions and rejoinders move the argument along. But as Pascal conceives him, he is also something of a gambler, a mathematician of sorts, and one to whom the existence of God and a personally held faith are at least open possibilities. Yet the fact that Pascal's reader is allowed to overhear this dialogue suggests strongly that the author may have wished to draw him into it; and thus the *Pari* may rightly be interpreted in more universal terms, as its subsequent history has proved, rather than as a mere period piece designed with a given type of individual in mind.

A third line of study leads to a consideration of the logical force and value of the wager argument. How seriously must we take the fact that much of it is cast by its author *in more geometrico?* Is it meant as a conclusive demonstration of God's existence, possibly supplanting the scholastic proofs, or as an *ad hominem* appeal hitting below the belt of rational conviction in order to soften resistance and provoke consent? What does the *Pari* have to teach us concerning Pascal's understanding of infinity and probability, the faith-reason relationship, or religious truth?

These are, I think, the most significant and fruitful angles of approach to the study of the *Pari* for the reader of Pascal in our day. There are others of both narrower and broader interest, such as the effort to determine the precise place of this fragment in the plan which Pascal might have followed had he completed his *Apology,* or the bearing of the argument upon characteristic and recurring Pascalian themes like the misery and grandeur of man, the three orders, or the reasons of the heart. Such matters may be dealt with best, however, as they are suggested or implied by the lines of inquiry already indicated, and the following account of the *Pari* will therefore move within this threefold scheme.

II

If Pascal's real motives and meanings in writing this particular passage are to be determined, then a careful look at the original manuscript becomes imperative. As found on pages 3, 4, 7, and 8 of the *Recueil Original* of the *Pensées* (Bibliothèque Nationale, fonds français no. 9.202), it seems to be a veritable maze of confusing phrases and incoherent ideas. This is how Georges Brunet describes these four pages:

> A rough draft terribly scrawled, in spots hardly legible, abrupt, disorderly, overburdened with crossed-out words, corrections, and repetitions; an amalgam of mathematical reasonings, psychological observations, and sheer mystical effusions. . . . As far as form and sense go, at first glance it is a labyrinth.[3]

The impression of hurried disarray is further confirmed by Jean Orcibal:

> Scarcely a page of the *Pensées* presents graver difficulties. . . . Contradictions, at least apparent, obscurities, mistakes, improprieties of language are abundant . . . evidently it consists of no more than an *aide-mémoire* which the author has hastily drawn up for his own use.[4]

Although this impression almost disappears in the uniformity of a printed text in the major editions, and needs to be emphasized here if only for the purpose of accurate analysis, we should not despair entirely of recovering what Brunet calls the *tison de feu* or firebrand which runs throughout the *Pari.* However broken or meandering, the flow of Pascal's thought is there and it can be detected, albeit with some initial difficulty. The lack of straightforward development from beginning to end is amply compensated in the sinuous richness and existential abruptness of this celebrated fragment. When, moreover, we add to the *Pari* those other passages which are joined with it in the *Recueil Original,* we have what Jacques Chevalier regarded as "a marvelous proliferation" of diverse thoughts inserted between the many "stratifications" of the *Pari* itself.[5] Then if we further add Pascal's notes numbered 72, 194, and 242 in the Brunschvicg edition, we do not lack a substantial body of material eminently worth our interpretation and reflection. Only after this preparatory work has been done can we confront the *Pari* as it stands with a view to discovering for ourselves its authentic and historic importance.

Port-Royal, when it published the first edition of the *Pensées* in 1670, printed the *Pari* as Chapter VII with this title: "That it is more advantageous to believe than not to believe what the Christian religion teaches." After the title comes an introductory note which, when due allowance has been made for its Jansenist bias, still stands as a penetrating summary of Pascal's wager argument:

---

[3] Brunet, *Le pari de Pascal* (Paris: Desclée de Brouwer, 1956), 7; translation mine, as in all following French texts except the *Pensées.*

[4] Orcibal, "Le fragment 'infini-rien' et ses sources," in *Blaise Pascal: L'Homme et L'Oeuvre* (Paris: Les editions de minuit, 1956), 159.

[5] See Orcibal, *ibid.,* 160. The *pensées* under consideration are those in the Brunschvicg edition numbered 89, 231, 606, 477, 535, 277, 278, 604, and 542. The comment by Chevalier may be found in his essay in *Mélanges de littérature, de philologie et de l'histoire offerts à M. Louis Arnould* (Poitiers, Sté française d'imprimerie et de librairie: 1934), 69.

> Almost everything contained in this chapter concerns only certain sorts of persons who, not being convinced of the proofs of Religion, and still less by the reasonings of atheists, remain in a state of suspension between faith and faithlessness. The author claims only to show them by their own principles, and by the clear light of reason, that they should deem it advantageous to believe, and that this is the side they ought to take if this choice depended on their will alone. From which it follows that at least while waiting until they find the light necessary to convince them of the truth, they should do everything which can dispose them towards it, and break away from all the hindrances which divert them from this faith, which are chiefly the passions and vain amusements.[6]

Although this is a fine condensation of the *Pari* proper, it suffers from an evident desire on the part of the Port-Royal editors to restrict the significance of the whole *pensée* to a specific apologetic encounter, and to remove any possible misgivings as to its crass and cheapening effect with reference to the truth-claims of the Christian faith. Also, it leaves quite unaccounted for the initial portion, which in essence is a justification of the agnostic attitude toward the rational knowledge of God. Pascal, on the contrary, it seems clear, wished to prepare the way for his argument of the wager by insisting that God cannot be an object of our knowledge, either in his existence or his nature. Thus he begins, not by singling out the nonbeliever as his target, but by some general reflections on the impossibility of the finite knowing the infinite. He draws a striking parallel in this connection between the mathematical infinite and the divine infinite, which is dropped when he comes to speak of the total incomprehensibility of God.

A study of the manuscript shows clearly that Pascal, in trying to articulate his original thought more precisely, only complicated it further. The added sentence, "Thus we may be sure that there is a God without knowing what he is," based on the analogy with mathematical infinity, seems flatly contradicted by his initial assertion, "But we do not know either the existence or the nature of God."[7] The main stress of this passage, however, together with its bearing upon everything that follows, gives the strongest possible indication that Pascal meant to assert that the only knowledge of God open to man is the knowledge of faith and not of natural reason. Perhaps indeed Pascal was not contemplating the *Pari* when he began to write the fragment headed by the words *infini-rien;* but the subsequent development of the *pensée* as a whole

---

[6] This passage may be found in *Oeuvres de Blaise Pascal,* 3rd ed. (Paris: Hachette, 1925), XIII, 169.

[7] *Pascal's Pensées,* trans. with an introduction by Martin Turnell (London: Harvill, 1962), 201. All further quotations from the *Pari* are taken from this translation based on the Louis Lafuma edition, unless otherwise noted. This *pensée,* numbered 343 by Lafuma, is numbered 233 in the earlier English translations based on Brunschvicg.

is meaningless unless the point is accepted that reason cannot determine either the existence or nonexistence of God.

The words, "Let us now speak according to our natural lights," conclude the first stage of the argument. The abstract antithesis, finite-infinite, now becomes personal, we-God. And it is made clear that Christianity makes no pretense of giving what in any case cannot be had, namely, a knowledge of God by reason alone. (Orcibal remarks in passing that at this point "it is difficult not to think of the Preface to the second edition of *The Critique of Pure Reason.*)[8]

The second stage then begins in earnest: "What is your bet?" Here the nonbeliever puts in his first appearance and retorts, not unnaturally, "Why bet at all?" Pascal's response is simply that not to bet is actually to bet against God. The option, as William James declared much later, is not really "optional" at all, but live, forced, and momentous, for "you are embarked."

"But perhaps I am staking too much," objects Pascal's imaginary opponent, who is no straw man but a self-concerned human being who places a high value upon the good things of this life. In answer, Pascal argues tediously, a bit loftily, but certainly to some extent ironically, to the effect that one's own self-interest demands the leap of faith, that it would be imprudent, i.e., unreasonable, not to abandon reason in order to save one's life, when the finite must be staked in a game where chances of loss and gain are equal, and the infinite (namely, eternal life) is the prize. It is as if the merest hint of hesitation on the part of the interlocutor were enough to call forth this torrential, overpositive monologue, assuring him with intricate and solemn logicality that the risk he must take is really no risk at all since he has nothing (namely, himself in contrast to the infinite) to lose.

Not that Pascal is trying to convince himself of the truth in what he is saying; on the contrary, he is thoroughly assured of it. Yet there is more than a touch of banter in the argument which prepares for the outright raillery soon to come. (The question of the cogency of his reasoning will concern us subsequently.) Pascal believes in the superiority of the Christian faith, as truth, over any and all agnosticism and skepticism taken as final positions. But even when he is in earnest, Pascal is seldom if ever heavy-handed, and his deft sense of the dramatic (strange in one who professed such disdain for the theater) never leaves him.

The God whose existence is thus depicted as a matter of odds, stake, gain and loss is no conceptual infinite but the God of Abraham, Isaac, and Jacob, whose encounter with man is so unforgettably recorded in the author's

---

[8] Orcibal, *op. cit.*, 166.

Mémorial and the *Mystère de Jésus*. Faith, Pascal realizes, must always seem to the nonbeliever a bet placed upon the unknowable. In entering this apologetic situation Pascal does not mean to make God's existence hang upon a game of chance; he identifies himself with the nonbeliever's position only in order to make him abandon it later. Having dislodged him from the opinion that the right course is not to bet at all, Pascal then shows him that in deciding to live as if God exists he has nothing to lose and everything to gain, while in living as if God does not exist he has everything to lose and nothing to gain. It is as simple as that. Jean Steinmann in his treatment of the *Pari* calls to mind the anecdote of a conversation between a nonbeliever and a priest named Mugnier. "You will be greatly cheated after your death," says the nonbeliever, "if God does not exist." "And you, if he does exist?" replies the priest.[9]

There are some nice and plainly debatable points here, but the main thrust of Pascal's argument is clear enough. His imaginary protagonist may still complain that although he is forced to believe, he cannot; but he is unable to pick flaws in Pascal's reasoning and has to regard it as *démonstratif*. His reluctance is now seen to be lodged in his will, and Pascal therefore turns abruptly in this direction.

As the *Pari* enters its third stage all pretense of rational demonstration is left behind, since this has already accomplished its apologetic purpose. Now that the desire for faith has finally been aroused in the nonbeliever, Pascal turns upon him with a directness that is almost brutal. The way to get faith, he says, is to imitate the behavior of those who already have it: "Take holy water, have masses said." That is how they began, by going through the motions, for their faith in the first instance was also faith in someone else's faith. What Pascal wishes to emphasize at this juncture, however, is not so much that faith is a community of trust as that faith is a conditioning process which humbles the reason and acclimates the heart.

"That will naturally make you inclined to believe and will calm you." But Pascal's last word is stronger—*abêtira*. It has shocked generations of intellectuals and occasioned endless debate. Some critics, far from regarding it as the climax of the *Pari,* have seen in it the sorry collapse of Pascal's whole argument. Others, seeking to defend him against the charge of sheer irrationalism, have tried to mitigate its force, as in all the available English translations. Port-Royal did not dare or wish to print it in the 1670 edition. "Brutalize" would probably be the most literal rendering; but this will not do because it evokes today a totally different set of meanings than was in Pascal's

[9] Jean Steinmann, *Pascal* (Paris: Les éditions du Cerf, 1954), 320.

mind when he wrote down this "powerful idea expressed with a streak of humor and picturesque exaggeration."[10] Pascal was thinking instead of the instinctual, seemingly automatic level of human and animal behavior, which his great contemporary Descartes had described after the model of the machine. He was also, no doubt, trying to convey something of the Pauline conviction that "God chose what is foolish in the world to shame the wise" (I Cor. 1:27), so that faith must be largely docility and humility. It is this striking juxtaposition of the gospel stress on "lowliness" and the currently fashionable theory of the animal-machine which gives such force and resonance to Pascal's *abêtira*. Probably the best translation would be "abase" or "humble"; this at least would put the accent where Pascal most wished.[11]

Thus the third stage of the wager argument recalls the main themes of the first; man is a soul thrown into a body, and his physical existence means radical estrangement from the realm of the infinite and the divine. As Pascal says elsewhere, since man is neither angel nor animal, his attempt to play the angel results only in his becoming more of an animal. Man is "made for thought," as Pascal declared, but the last office of his reason is to acknowledge that there is an infinity of things which surpass reason. Self-abasement, then, is both the condition of becoming an *honnête homme* and the primary requirement of a life offering itself to the inspirations of grace, "that in this way strength might be given to lowliness."

It may rightly be claimed, therefore, that in the *Pari* we have, despite its unlikely method of composition, a clearly worked out progression of thought designed to lead from nonbelief to the threshold of readiness for faith.[12] As such, the *Pari* may be said to recapitulate the whole of the projected *Apology*, as well as representing an important turning-point within it.

III

A second range of problems which interests the student of the *Pari* has to do with the *libertin* to whom its argument is ordinarily supposed to be addressed. Just who were the freethinkers whose company Pascal had frequented and whom he seems to have kept in view throughout much of his work on the *Apology?* How does his own impression of the *libertin* accord with what we know from other sources about the milieu of religious discussion in the first half of the seventeenth century?

These questions have occupied the attention of *pascalisants* for many

[10] Maurice Barrès, *L'Angoisse de Pascal* (Paris, Plon-Nourrit 1923), 196.

[11] See Raymond Francis, *Les pensées de Pascal en France de 1842 à 1942* (Paris: Nizet, 1959), 463–468.

[12] Cf. Orcibal, *op. cit.,* 174.

generations. Much effort has gone into reconstructing the historical scene, particularly the context of conversations between believers and nonbelievers which occasioned such precursors of the *Pensées* as Pierre Charron's *Les Trois Veritez,* Raymond de Sebond's *Théologie Naturelle,* and others. This period in France was marked both by a renewal of church life (St. Francis de Sales and St. Vincent de Paul are conspicuous examples; the Jesuit-Jansenist controversy is another) and by the growth of an opposed tendency which would today be termed humanist or secular-liberal. The representatives of this latter movement were a mixed lot, drawing their inspiration from Montaigne and Rabelais, as from classical models of Stoicism and skepticism. They appear to have shared an outlook which was emphatically this-worldly, man-centered, and in varying degrees critical or nonconformist with regard to the inherited faith. "The great heresy of these latter days is incredulity," wrote Pascal's friend Nicole.[13]

In the *Pensées* and elsewhere Pascal refers very seldom to the *libertin* by name, but it is obvious that he has this type of person in mind as he writes. In his eyes the *libertin* is part skeptic, part hedonist, a man indifferent to his soul's salvation, uncommitted because unconvinced, yet sure of what little he knows and reluctant to abandon it for what is uncertain and perhaps unreasonable. He is pleasure-loving, calculating, yet also in some measure disenchanted and restless. His manner of thought and life alike are characterized by what Pascal calls a "curious complacence," by a vicious circle of *divertissement* and *ennui,* by self-seeking and self-despair. In short, the *libertin* is for Pascal a very special instance of the contradiction and disproportion that define the being of man himself.

Now while it would be useless to deny that Pascal had the *libertin* very much in view as he wrote the *Pari,* it is quite unwise to fix upon the *libertin* as Pascal's exclusive target. To be sure, if one were trying to bring this dialogue to life upon the stage it would be necessary to call up from the past a concrete personage, someone perhaps like Miton or the Chevalier de Méré, with whom Pascal may well have had just such a conversation as this as they rumbled along in a coach to Poitou. But when the *libertin* is taken as a sort of category of explanation, accounting for Pascal's exaggeration, excusing his improprieties, or giving to his argument a merely *ad hominem* value, the danger of possible misinterpretation of the *Pari* becomes acute and its intended thrust may only be parried.

---

[13] On the views of the *libertins* see the following: Jacques Rennes, *Pascal et le libertin* (Paris: Librairie Valois, 1950), 133–138; Jacques Chevalier, *Pascal,* trans. by Lilian A. Clare (London: Sheed & Ward, 1930), 23–29; and Julien-Eymard d'Angers, *Pascal et ses précurseurs* (Paris: Nouvelles éditions latines, 1954), 11–28.

The *libertin,* for example, is sometimes used to defend Pascal's dogmatic orthodoxy, either as a Jansenist true believer or as an essentially sound Catholic thinker. It is alleged that the very fact that Pascal talks like a free-thinker means he could not possibly have thought like one. His identification with the *libertin,* just because it seems so complete, is actually only provisional and purely strategic. The mask is dropped when Pascal writes "end of speech" following his "demonstration" of the advantages of believing. In this vein Steinmann comments: "It is evident that it is the agnostic, not the Christian, nor Pascal, who sees faith as a wager on the unknowable."[14] But if this is so, how are we to understand Pascal's own characterization of the faithful, later on in the *Pari,* as "those who now stake everything they possess" (*ceux qui parient maintenant*)? Is this too said only from the perspective of the *libertin,* or does Pascal mean to convey here his often-repeated conviction that there is an ever-present element of risk, of wagering, in the act of faith as such? And if we answer this latter question in the affirmative, as we surely must, then we are clearly not out of line in thinking that whatever may have been the biographical origin of this *pensée* its intended destination was not exclusively the *libertin,* but also perhaps the lukewarm and conventional Christian whose so-called faith had lost all semblance of "laboring for tomorrow and the uncertain."[15]

Or, again, the *libertin* may be concentrated upon as a means of refuting Pascal's argument. This is the line followed in Jacques Rennes' otherwise valuable study *Pascal et le libertin,* where it is asserted that the would-be apologist, "blinded already by a very narrow faith, then carried away by the ardent wish of persuading, and finally too confident of his own methods, misconceived the *libertin.*"[16] According to Rennes, Pascal underestimated the powers of his adversary; he sadly lacked the freethinker's feeling for nature and respect for reason; and the latter, having heard Pascal out, would be bound to go his own way unconvinced and not a little nettled.

This may or may not be the case, but it is obviously a rather oblique and hypothetical way of approaching the study of the *Pari.* Quite possibly the true *libertin* is unlike Pascal's image of him, finding it repugnant to submit God's existence to the probability-calculus, feeling that the *Pari* tends to subjugate the conscience, and so refusing the argument as "ineffective and in some measure degrading."[17] However, the real point, as Rennes himself admits, is not what an imaginary interlocutor might have thought of the argument but

[14] Steinmann, *op. cit.,* 318.
[15] *Pensée* 346 (Laf.), 234 (Br.).
[16] Rennes, *op. cit.,* 138.
[17] The whole of this sentence summarizes the passage in Jacques Rennes, *op. cit.,* 207–209.

what in fact Pascal's actual reader does think of it. No matter how intriguing historical speculation may be, any significant judgment as to the true worth of Pascal's argument can only come from *une méditation solitaire, nue et libre.*[18] It is not the hypothetical freethinker who is justified as over against Pascal, but the freedom of every actual thinker who confronts the *Pari*—a freedom which is signally respected throughout the substance of the *Pensées* and is guaranteed by their very style as well.

Hence the figure of the *libertin,* regardless of how much it may add to the *Pari* in dramatic or dialogic resonance, cannot legitimately be employed either to defend Pascal's argument (as the sort of thing he had to say whether he personally believed it or not) or to discredit it (as much too limited to be presently useful, wide of the mark, or rationally distasteful).

There have been some commentators who recognized the difficulties and disadvantages of singling out the *libertin* as the sole intended target of the *Pari,* and who have therefore made alternative suggestions. These range all the way from Chevalier's specific mention of gambler-mathematicians like Miton and Méré[19] to Vinet's opinion that Pascal was writing for a man instinctively favorable toward the gospel yet at the same time "halted at the threshold by invincible doubts,"[20] or that of Dugas and Riquier that this fragment deals "exclusively with one who already admits the vanity of earthly happiness in line with original sin and the fall of man, at least the weakness of reason, and all that pessimistic philosophy which Pascal took from Christian dogma."[21] The problem here of course is that as the target becomes broader it ceases to be a target at all; if the *Pari* can be taken to prove something to everybody then we begin to suspect that it proves nothing to anybody. Some, indeed, have made just this assertion, adding that the *Pari* suggests "the bargain counter, shocking, cynically self-interested,"[22] that it could only have come into Pascal's head on account of his mental infirmity,[23] or that it deserves to be disregarded because of its "logical monstrosity and moral enormity."[24]

Must we then give up all effort to locate precisely Pascal's apologetic object in writing the *Pari,* if indeed he can be said to have had such an object? The question is complicated by the fact that the *Pari* does not figure

---

[18] Rennes, *ibid.,* 210.

[19] Chevalier, "La methode de connaître d'après Pascal," in *Études sur Pascal,* published by *Revue de Métaphysique et de Morale,* XXX (1923), 181–214.

[20] Alexandre Vinet, *Études sur Blaise Pascal* (Paris: Payot, 1936), 138.

[21] "Le pari de Pascal," *Revue Philosophique,* CXL (Sept., 1950), 245.

[22] Rene F. A. Sulley-Prudhomme, *La vraie religion selon Pascal* (Paris, 1905), 270 f.

[23] A. Regnard, "Génie et folie," *Annales Médico-Psychologiques* (janv.-fevr., 1899), 41.

[24] Dugas and Riquier, *op. cit.,* 245.

in the lecture which Pascal gave to his friends at Port-Royal telling them of the plan and purpose of the *Apology* on which he was working.[25] At the same time, however, this fragment is included in both the *Recueil Original* of the *Pensées* and the *Première Copie* (the latter antedates the appearance of the former, surprisingly, by half a century); also, it is printed as a chapter in the 1670 edition despite the lack of reference to it in the Preface; and its concordance with a dozen or more *pensées* of similar bent indicates that it must have had some genuine importance in relation to the projected *Apology*. We shall not go wrong, I believe, if we follow Strowski,[26] Brunschvicg,[27] and Lafuma[28] in placing the *Pari* before the midpoint of Pascal's planned outline, though we can naturally never be entirely sure of this. The best conjecture is that which puts the *Pari* somewhere after the *pensées* describing the condition of man and before those which advance the "proofs" that the Christian faith is true.

If we are unable to single out a special target for the *Pari* or to know for certain just what use Pascal would have made of it in the completed *Apology,* how then shall we acount for the strange and moving power of this fragment? Only, I believe, by concluding that it was written "for every man conscious of his condition and implicitly also for Pascal himself."[29] Pascal understood the nuances and pitfalls of his task better than most apologists. He knew that the defense of the faith was not a matter of presenting an open-and-shut case in a take-it-or-leave-it manner which could only harden and fix the distance between himself and his reader. Pascal sought instead to engage the reader in a common venture by appealing to him on his own ground, and by striking through his defensive poses to hit directly at his "heart." And Pascal was well aware that this could not be done without exposing himself as being in some sense a fellow seeker and fellow sufferer, "embarked" in finitude yet willing to gamble on the infinite.

Seen in this light, the *Pari* is a prime example of apologetic finesse in the history of Christian thought. It belongs to a genre of writings designed to dispose the nonbeliever favorably toward faith, from Arnobius through Augustine and Anselm to our own day. Yet Pascal surpasses all or most of these in his unique ability to disclose and disturb the slumbering self of Everyman,

[25] It is not mentioned in the record of this lecture which is included in the Preface to the 1670 edition of the *Pensées* written by Filleau de la Chaise, who was present at the time.

[26] Fortunat Strowski, *Pascal et son temps* (Paris: Plon, 1922), III, 281.

[27] Léon Brunschvicg, *Descartes et Pascal, lecteurs de Montaigne* (Neuchàtel, Edit. de La Baconnière: 1945), 171.

[28] See Blaise Pascal, *Pensées,* ed. Louis Lafuma (Paris: Delmas, 1960), 3rd ed., 17.

[29] Lucien Goldmann, "Le pari est-il écrit pour le libertin?" *Blaise Pascal, L' Homme et L'Oeuvre,* 121.

for his own good and for God's glory, as he puts it in the concluding sentence of the *Pari*.

IV

But what is the *Pari* worth as an argument? That, after all, is the form in which Pascal cast it and to which the reader's response should properly be made. Whatever may have been its original intention and destination, and whether one refuses to be drawn into the debate or professes to find it "delightful" and "ravishing," sooner or later a judgment must be rendered by any serious reader as to the logical value of the argument itself.

What makes it difficult to arrive at such a judgment is that Pascal has utilized two kinds of language, the mathematical and the moral, without carefully distinguishing them; and he has also taken two sorts of human action, betting and choosing, as a single mode of behavior. This compounding of perspectives has invited much misunderstanding on the part of Pascal's devotees and critics alike. For Lanson, the *Pari* is simply "an application of the calculus of probabilities to the problem of believing."[30] To Strowski, on the other hand, "those commentators who have studied the *Pari* as a calculus of probabilities have utterly falsified its meaning."[31] These are honest differences of judgment and something may be said on both sides; but the disagreement arises almost inevitably out of the fact that Pascal, having adopted for his purposes both the form of mathematical demonstration and the force of moral persuasion, moves freely and without warning from one to the other.

But can there be any real doubt as to which accent is finally the stronger? The man who has analyzed the wager argument most minutely and thoroughly, Jules Lachelier, summed up his view of the matter by saying, "What is at stake in the *Pari,* for us as for Pascal, is the sacrifice of the *moi.*"[32] It is toward the securing of that *abêtissement* on the part of the nonbeliever that Pascal's whole argument is directed; an unbroken, if hardly straight, line of thought leads from the first antithesis, *infini-rien,* to the last, *force-bassesse.*

From this point of view the integrity of this fragment becomes evident and its relationship to the entire book of the *Pensées* can be made clear. Whatever might have been the place of the *Pari* in a completed *Apology,* it now stands as a real epitome of Pascal's whole effort "to save us from our indifference," as Mauriac has written.[33]

---

[30] G. Lanson, article "Pascal," in *La Grande Encyclopédie* (Paris, 1898), XXVI, 29b.

[31] Strowski, *Les pensées de Pascal* (Paris: Mellottée, 1930), 104, n. 1.

[32] In "Notes on Pascal's Wager," *The Philosophy of Jules Lachelier,* trans. by Edward G. Ballard (The Hague: Nijhoff, 1960), 97.

[33] François Mauriac, "La rencontre avec Pascal," *La Revue Hebdomadaire,* numéro du Tricentenaire, 1923, 97.

Thus to acknowledge the morally pragmatic aim of the *Pari* does not however land us in the same camp with Voltaire, who found it "a bit indecent and childish: this notion of a game, of gain and loss, does not at all suit the gravity of the subject."[34] Pascal appeals to the highest as well as the lowest forms of our self-interest, to reason as well as to instinct, which does not mean that he tries to satisfy the demands of both but only that he accepts them and calls them into play. In the words of Ernest Havet, Pascal's argument is "one of those strokes of logic that seizes the opponent, not by his weak side, but by the one which seems the strongest."[35]

The fact that so much of the *Pari* is given the form of rational argument should not be discounted, despite this recognition of Pascal's admittedly moral purpose. Its logical apparatus is not windowdressing intended to throw the nonbeliever off his rational guard while a low blow is being launched at his will. But neither is the *Pari* to be taken as a simple demonstration *in more geometrico* which gets fouled up in an *ad hominem* atmosphere. Taken as it stands, it *is* an argument and deserves to be judged by the appropriate principles of logical adequacy, even though its thrust is undoubtedly "existential."

Pascal's line of reasoning, as I have indicated earlier, moves on three distinct yet continuous stages. The first concerns infinity, the second probability, the third the practicability of the Christian option. It can be shown without much difficulty that the argument is generally tight and cogent, that it merits rational respect, not to say admiration, whether one happens to like it or not, and that its logical structure and development are with minor exceptions harmonious.

At the head of the first stage there might well be written that other *pensée,* "Reason's last step is the recognition that there are an infinity of things beyond it; it is merely feeble if it does not go so far as to grasp that."[36] Pascal's purpose is not to use reason to destroy reason, to "rationalize irrationality" as Unamuno indignantly supposed,[37] but to push reason by its own methods to the recognition of its own limits. For his purpose he employs the example of mathematical infinity, to show that it is possible to know the existence of something without knowing what it is. This general possibility of reason leads Pascal to distinguish three kinds of things in terms of their knowability; his implicit assumption is that only like can know like. Being limited and extended in space, we know both the existence and the

---

[34] Voltaire, *Lettres Philosophiques,* ed. Taylor (Oxford: Blackwell, 1943), 98.
[35] Cited by Raymond Francis, *op. cit.,* 224, n. 242.
[36] *Pensée* 373 (Laf.), 267 (Br.).
[37] Miguel de Unamuno, *The Agony of Christianity* (New York: Ungar, 1960), 109.

nature of finite space. Having one of the qualities of spatial infinity, extension, but not its other quality, infinity, we know therefore its existence but not its nature. Having neither of the attributes of God, infinity and nonextension, we know neither his existence nor his nature. Hence the general possibility applies in the case of spatial infinity, but not in that of God.

By faith, not reason, we can know God's existence, just as by reason we know that of finite space. The cases are analogous, but not identical or even parallel. If we speak only according to our natural (i.e., rational) lights, we cannot solve the problem of God's existence and nature, and we must not blame men of faith for not giving us the kind of proof they never claimed to possess. Faith, though not itself a rational possibility, is nevertheless open to reason and hence reasonable.[38]

The second stage, introduced by the first appearance of Pascal's adversary, moves the argument from the plane of rational knowledge to that of reasonable surmise. In a manner suggestive of Kierkegaard, Pascal poses his alternative: "Either God exists or he does not exist. . . . What is your bet?" And when Pascal says "God" he means, of course, the promise of infinite happiness beyond death and the necessity of renouncing self-love and its satisfactions in this present life. The first is the prize to be gained, the second is the stake to be put up, according to the rules of this particular game. It is not a game that can be avoided; there is no third possibility alongside the existence and nonexistence of God.

Not to bet that God exists, according to Pascal, is to bet that he does not exist. Léon Jeantet insists, on the contrary, that "to bet against is *not* to bet, since there is no stake involved except in betting for" God.[39] But this is hardly an objection to be taken seriously, as it could be made of any bet at all, where the option is always that between taking a chance and staying as one is. Another criticism, put forward by Tsanoff[40] and Walter Kaufmann[41] among others, is that there really are other alternatives than those presented by Pascal. A Muslim, for instance, might employ the same sort of argument to encourage belief in Allah; or God might actually reward honest doubt instead of the make-believe which Pascal seems to be approving in God's name. True, but the question is not how many other versions of the wager argument can

---

[38] The foregoing summary I have adapted from Jeanne Russier, "Une interpretation possible pour un texte important et obscur de Pascal," *Revue Philosophique,* CXLI (avr.–juin, 1951), 302–306.

[39] Jeantet, "Le pari de Pascal est-il un veritable pari?" *Revue Philosophique,* CXXX (mars–avr., 1940), 233 f.

[40] R. A. Tsanoff, "Pascal's Despair of Reason," *Rice Institute Pamphlet,* IX (Oct., 1922), No. 4, 208–209.

[41] Kaufmann, *Critique of Religion and Philosophy* (New York: Harper, 1958), 122.

be imagined, but what we are to think of this one. The alternative which Pascal poses *is* unavoidable; either God, however conceived, is or is not. And for Pascal this means the choice between eternal life and nothingness—a choice which is *involontaire* because the self is never neutral with respect to its own interest.

For Pascal, the stake to be put up is always the same—the pleasures of this present life. They may be slight or even "nothing" in comparison with the prize to be won, but they are certain, while the prize is uncertain. May it not then be the case that an infinite good which I may never gain is worth no more than the finite good which I am asked to give up once and for all? This possible objection occurs to Pascal, after he asserts, "If you win, you win everything; if you lose, you lose nothing." So he argues that if the intrinsic value of the prize is infinite, it will always infinitely exceed the finite value of the stake, whatever may be the number of chances for and against getting the prize. He buttresses this position by a calculus of probabilities designed to show simply that it would be unreasonable not to bet a finite stake, with a finite number of chances to lose, against even one possibility of securing an infinite prize.[42]

The prize Pascal envisages is described in two ways, as "an eternity of life and happiness" and "an infinity of infinitely happy life." Does he strengthen his case or weaken it by this revised definition of the prize, by multiplying two infinities, one of duration and one of degree? He means to say, I think, following Lachelier's interpretation, that in the first instance we may safely bet, while in the second we really ought to do so.

In a recent treatment of the wager argument, Jean Guitton has again made the familiar charge that in it Pascal seeks to diminish the margin of unfavorable chances, to cut down the amount of risk. Pascal's gambler, says Guitton, "has the absolute certitude that even if he is mistaken he will lose nothing. He bets on a sure thing, which is to say that at bottom he doesn't bet at all."[43] I do not believe that this charge can be sustained. What Pascal is attempting to do throughout the entire argument is to show that it is not unreasonable to stake a certain thing in order to gain an uncertain one; his point is not that we are to stake nothing but to stake everything, even if what we stake seems like nothing when compared with the prize. The element of risk is always present and recognized, whether the chances of gain and loss are

---

[42] Cf. Lachelier, *op. cit.*, 102–103.

[43] In *Génie de Pascal* (Paris: Aubier, 1962), 80; see the whole section beginning at p. 76.

equal or unequal. Faith, just as much as or more than sea voyages, business enterprises or battles,[44] is an *uncertain certitude;* we work as if tomorrow were a certainty when we cannot know that it is so.

As Pascal's argument enters its third and last stage, introduced by the interlocutor's question, "What do you expect me to do?" we reach the point where the giving of reasons for believing (betting, choosing) must give way to the arousal of the will to believe. The reasonableness of the wager having been demonstrated, the time has come for making it. "If the hope of future happiness is based only on a logical possibility, then we must discard Pascal's wager," writes Lachelier;[45] and Strowski adds, "the *pari* of Paschal will not give us one ounce of faith."[46] Pascal himself would have been the first to agree with them; hence the final part of his open-ended argument.

For Pascal knows perfectly well that no argument can produce faith, even an argument which turns, as his does, from the probable to the practical. "Reason would never submit unless it considered that there were occasions on which it must submit," writes Pascal elsewhere; "it is therefore right that reason should submit when it decides that it ought to submit."[47] That time having arrived, the *Pari* presses for a decision: the will, which finds its reasons for justifying its choice and which therefore alone can dispose a man toward faith, must be arrested and engaged. After the decision, but not before, understanding will come; its cost is that submission of reason which itself is fully reasonable. "The wager is the discipline of faith, it leads to it through humility," as Chevalier observes.[48]

What Pascal is trying to accomplish in the last stage of his argument is something which all "existential communication" must attempt—the conveying of a moment of truth in which, to use Canon Ramsey's favorite phrases, "the penny drops," "the light dawns." And so Pascal leads us to the very edge of his argument, having, as Canon Ramsey says religious language ought to do, evoked the discernment from which the commitment follows as a response.[49] Whether Pascal succeeds, no one can say but the reader himself in his *méditation solitaire, nue et libre*. It can rightly be claimed, however, that Pascal, by using language that is "appropriately odd" in Ramsey's words, has brought the matter of belief in God home, has cleared the way for the reasons of the heart.

---

[44] *Pensée* 346 (Laf.), 270 (Br.).
[45] *Op. cit.,* 108.
[46] Strowski, *Pascal et son temps, op. cit.,* III, 279.
[47] *Pensée* 359 (Laf.), 270 (Br.).
[48] *Pascal,* 251.
[49] Ian T. Ramsey, *Religious Language* (New York: Macmillan, 1957), 41.

V

It remains to indicate, now, something of the bearing of the *Pari* in the history of Christian thought. Certainly this curious fragment has its own illustrious ancestry: we might begin with Plato's *Phaedo* (114D) where it is said, "If there be any risk in believing that the state of the soul will be such after death, this is a risk which it is good to run." Arnobius' *Adversus Nationes* definitely belongs in the same line: "But Christ does not prove the truth of his promises. That is true; there is no proof possible of that which is to come." Arnobius continues:

> But if the condition of things future is such that they cannot be reached or grasped by any anticipated apprehension, the most reasonable course, between two doubtful opinions and while waiting for an uncertain outcome, is to adopt that which gives hope, is it not, instead of that which gives none? On one side, in effect, [there is] no risk, if what is shown to us as future does not eventuate and we are found to be in error; on the other, the damage is enormous, for it is the loss of salvation, if when the time arrives we have not been misled (II, 4).[50]

In the Augustine corpus there are several passages which bespeak the same lineage, such as those in the short work *De Utilitate Credendi* (X, 24; XVI, 34), or the *De Vera Religione*.[51] One may also find echoes of Lactantius and Tertullian in the *Pari,* though no evidence of their influence on Pascal's formulation.

It is in the seventeenth century, however, that the use of a wager argument abounds and conscious borrowing by Pascal becomes clear. Julien-Eymard d'Angers has turned up no less than nine French versions of the wager in this period, to prove either the existence of God or the immortality of the soul (Mersenne, Antione Sirmond, Yves de Paris are representative of this trend).[52] But it is to the works of Raymond de Sebonde and Pierre Charron that we must turn to discover actual models for Pascal's own argument, which as we have seen is far from being a proof in the traditional apologetic sense.[53] In each case the parallelism is striking, but Pascal's originality in adapting the argument is equally impressive.

---

[50] Translation mine. Cf. *Ancient Christian Writers,* VII (Westminster, Md.: Newman, 1949), I, 116–117.

[51] Sister Marie Hubert claims a direct influence of the latter work on Pascal; see her *Pascal's Unfinished Apology* (New Haven: Yale, 1952), 85–91.

[52] D'Angers, *op. cit.,* 206–213.

[53] On the influence of Sebonde, see Hubert, *op. cit.,* pp. 95 f.; on that of Charron, see Orcibal, *op. cit.,* 168–172.

One may also trace something like the posterity of the *Pari,* though without assurance of definite dependence upon Pascal in every instance. The line would go through English thinkers such as Locke,[54] Butler,[55] Newman,[56] possibly Feuerbach and Ritschl, certainly the French philosophers Renouvier, Bergson, and Blondel, to William James and such present-day apologists as Father Martin D'Arcy.[57] Without doubt, Pascal's wager is representative of a strain in Christian thought which keeps reasserting itself in many fertile mutations.

How shall this strain be identified? The words which leap to mind most quickly are negative ones: antisystematic, nonmetaphysical, antirationalist. Yet it may also be described more positively: empirical (in the sense of experiential), dialectical, voluntarist. Since it comes to expression in many different periods and within a variety of contrasting perspectives, there are few if any objective markings by which it can easily be detected. Rather, its signature is to be found in a sense of the contingency of human being, a conviction that truth is hard to come by because self-knowledge is inextricably bound up with every form of knowledge, and consequently an approach which is deliberately and artfully *ad hominem* since it is concerned to reach the thinker in the depths of his thought.

An argument *ad hominem,* the dictionary informs us, is "an irrelevant or malicious appeal to personal circumstances; it consists in diverting an argument from sound facts and reasons to the personality of one's opponent, competitor or critic."[58] This accusation has frequently been leveled against Pascal's wager; but those who make it seem unwilling or unable to understand that the communicating of Christian truth is necessarily personal in form and purpose. Hence there exists a whole genre of writings such as the *Pari* which aim beyond exposition or demonstration at persuasion; they take most often the form of letters of dialogues rather than that of formal disputations of treatises; and they follow more or less faithfully a principle enunciated by Léon Bloy: "Always be sure to aim at the head, in order not to hit lower than the heart."

Such writings may not carry in themselves the full thrust of the development of doctrine and may therefore be regarded as of secondary importance

---

[54] John Locke, *Essay Concerning Human Understanding,* Bk. II, chap. XXI, sec. 70, contains a version of the wager argument.

[55] William Butler, *The Analogy of Religion,* Pt. II, chap. vii, end; "probability is the very guide of life."

[56] Cardinal Newman's doctrine of the "illative sense" in particular; but he did not approve of Pascal's wager.

[57] D'Arcy, *Mirage and Truth* (New York: Macmillan, 1935), 69–82.

[58] Ralph B. Winn in *The Dictionary of Philosophy,* ed. by Dagobert D. Runes (New York: Philosophical Library, 1942), 19.

by the historian. This is to be regretted, since every constructive theological thinker is a man of his time, either immersed in or reacting to those currents and modes of thought which are available to him. Moreover, his own doctrinal formulations cannot actually be understood except in terms of such involvement, no matter how reluctant or hesitant. The case of Pascal affords a signal instance of the type of Christian thinker whose contribution may be all the more important because he sits so loosely to the preoccupations of theology in the technical sense, a contribution which for that very reason has ramifications and reverberations of great consequence for many fields, and especially for the interrelationship between these fields.

Pascal, to borrow Nietzsche's description of himself, was a "posthumous man." His work, just because it was unfinished, asked and needed to be completed by others, but by that same token it was profoundly creative of their collaboration and correction. It may be too much to find in the *Pari,* as Lucien Goldmann does, "the capital instant, the decisive turning-point in the history of modern thought: the passage of individualistic philosophers, whether rationalist and dogmatic or empiricist and skeptical," to dialectical and tragic thought.[59] But we shall not be wrong in recognizing in the *Pari* a doubly fruitful source for modern reflection which can fairly be claimed for Pascal. The first is his critique of scientific and philosophical reason; the second is his complementary stress upon intuition and instinct as the undeniable matrix of all believing and thinking.[60] Both of these anticipatory views are found in embryo in the *Pari,* as in the whole and not inconsiderable body of Pascal's writings. Difficult though it may be to "place" him in the history which belongs to him, the *Pari* will long assure his germinal importance for modern philosophy and theology.

Yet it is not in these repeated themes and modulations that the most basic influence of Pascal's argument may be discovered. If he chooses to speak *ad hominem* that is because he speaks *de homine;* his figure of the man at the gambling table, betting for or against God, will not cease to irritate and fascinate us. In all its ironic triviality and deceptive simplicity, it stands for the fact that whether we believe or disbelieve, "in either case we *act,* taking our life in our hands."[61]

---

[59] Goldmann, *op. cit.,* 128.

[60] See D. Nedelkovitch, *La Pensée philosophique créatrice de Pascal* (Paris: Alcan, 1925), 49–50.

[61] James, *op. cit.,* p. 30.

The Hermeneutics of Holiness in Wesley

CARL MICHALSON
Andrew V. Stout Professor of Systematic Theology
The Theological School
Drew University
Madison, New Jersey

Preaching and not theology was the main concern of John Wesley. Lord Shaftesbury had established for the eighteenth century that "the most ingenious way of becoming foolish is by a system,"[1] and Wesley declined to be that kind of fool for theology's sake. The first principle of Methodism was "wholly and solely" the foolishness of preaching.[2] Not that there were no other ministries besides preaching. On the one side, the sacrament of the Lord's Supper was regarded as more powerful than preaching.[3] For that reason, if forced to choose, Wesley would have preferred the service of the Church of England with its sacramental life to the service of a Methodist society with its kerygmatic edification.[4] On the other side, instruction and discipline were regarded as more durable than preaching, so that without them preaching merely prepared lambs for the world's slaughter.[5]

Notwithstanding the limitations of preaching, at the rise of the Methodist movement a single virtue was made of twin necessities: Methodists were licensed only to preach, and the established sacramental community almost everywhere refused its pulpit to Methodist preachers. Thus, "field preaching" or "preaching abroad" became the Methodist mode. Preaching was "speaking

---

[1] Anthony Earl of Shaftesbury, *Characteristics,* ed. by John M. Robertson (London: Grant Richards, 1900), I, 189.

[2] *Sermon* CXV, 12, *The Works of John Wesley* (Grand Rapids: Zondervan, a reprint of the authorized edition published by the Methodist Conference, London, 1872), VII, 277. Except as otherwise indicated, the Zondervan edition is referred to throughout. To facilitate the use of other editions, references to the *Journals* will include the date, and, to the *Sermons,* the official number of sermon and paragraph.

[3] *Jour.,* Nov. 13, 1763 (III, 156).

[4] *Jour.,* Jan. 2, 1787 (IV, 357).

[5] *Jour.,* Aug. 25, 1763 (III, 144).

before a congregation" wherever assembled.[6] And if it were only the reading of the Word by a layman in the congregation, that also was preaching.[7] Out of "this strange way of preaching"[8] the Methodist movement was born.

One of the responsibilities of a theologian within the communion which Wesley's preaching inspired is to illuminate the doctrinal import of that influence. Specifically, my purpose here is to show how Wesley, in sharpening the focus of his preaching, has contributed suggestions which have yet fully to seize the mind of the Church. These distinctive elements classify as a hermeneutics, and they are distinctive primarily for the way in which they emerge from the Wesleyan emphasis on holiness.

Hermeneutics is the science of interpretation, especially the interpretation of texts, and in the case of the theologian, particularly the text of the Bible, but involving a theory of language and of understanding. In his preface to the *Notes on the New Testament* Wesley is discernibly conscious of hermeneutics in his program. It is there he associates himself with Bengel's methods, discusses the sense in which human words communicate God's word, and cites Luther as had Bengel to the effect that the proper study of theology is "a grammar of the language of the Holy Ghost."[9]

The suggestions about to be proposed here will not seem too forced if one recalls how the concept of hermeneutics shifted in the very epoch in which Wesley thought and preached. With the rise of the historical consciousness which followed upon the dawn of experimental science, the concept of the science was qualified to include methodologies more congenial and distinctive to human studies, such as history, law, religion, and art. Within this development John Locke gave hermeneutics an impulse when he attempted to interpret Paul's letters on the basis of the apostle's own use of language. Inspired by Locke's effort, a Dutch Remonstrant, Wetstein, developed what Wilhelm Dilthey has called "the seed of subsequent grammatico-historical method."[10] At the same time, the emerging German pietism emphasized that interpretation was never complete when it had simply determined the meaning of a text. Application of the meaning was expected. To interpret thus meant to read the text in such a way that the reader's own existence was given meaning.

In Bengel's *Gnomon,* which appeared in England in 1742, the preface expressed his principles of interpretation. Among them was the new view of

---

[6] *Sermon* XXXV, 9 (V, 451).
[7] *A Father Appeal to Men of Reason and Religion,* Part III, iii, 13 (VIII, 222 f.).
[8] *Jour.,* Apr. 21, 1775 (IV, 41).
[9] *Explanatory Notes upon the New Testament* (London: Epworth, 1952), 9. Hereinafter simply *Notes.*
[10] Dilthey, *Gesammelte Schriften* (Leipzig and Berlin: Teubner, 1914), II, 135, n. 2.

applicatio. "I have not thought it necessary," he said, "to subjoin *Practical application, 'usus,'* as they are termed, to each chapter; for he who submits himself to the constraining influence of divine Love in the search after divine Truth, imbibes from the divine Words, when he has once perceived their meaning, all things profitable for salvation as without labour, and without stimulus."[11] In England in the early part of the seventeenth century *applicatio* was already held to be one facet of the procedure for preparing oneself to hear the word of God with understanding. In the treatise of Robert Bolton, "Concerning the Word of God," which Wesley included in his *Christian Library,* Bolton comments: "No plaster can do the patient good, unless it be applied; no meat be able to do us good, be it dressed ever so curiously, unless it be eaten and digested." This is not the startling item in Bolton's discussion, however. I refer rather to the three classes of rules given for "hearing": rules governing what to do before hearing, after hearing, and "in hearing." The startling thing is that *applicatio* is included not under the rules for what to do after hearing but for what to do "in hearing." Application in hermeneutics is not something one does after he has understood. It is inseparable from the process of understanding.[12]

Now Wesley was a supernaturalist in a traditional sense. That fact is reflected convincingly in his understanding of the work of the Holy Spirit in the communication of the word. Only the Holy Spirit can teach, he said. "We can do nothing."[13] "I spoke," he said of his encounter with an "unconcerned" congregation. "But it is only the voice of the Son of God which is able to wake the dead."[14] In the letter of the Scripture when read there is "no inherent power . . . the whole power is of" God.[15] God can even give understanding where there is no understanding.[16] On some occasions after preaching, Wesley reports that he felt himself free of all further responsibility for the souls of his auditors. "God answers for himself," he would say; "I am clear of their blood."[17] On one occasion however, he began to say the same thing, then changed his course. "I am clear," he said, then interrupted himself: No—let God judge.[18] Or, earlier, "God answered for himself to all candid hearers."[19]

[11] Johann Albrecht Bengel, *Gnomon of the New Testament,* ed. Andrew R. Fausset (Edinburgh: Clark, 1859), I, 65.

[12] John Wesley, *A Christian Library* (London: Cordeaux, 1819), V, 185. The texts referred to in this connection are John 5:47, Rom. 15:4, but especially Isa. 55:2.

[13] *Jour.,* Feb. 14, 1736 (I, 25).

[14] *Jour.,* Sept. 10, 1739 (I, 224).

[15] *Sermon* XVI, ii, 3 (V, 188).

[16] *Jour.,* Nov. 5, 1746 (II, 34).

[17] *Jour.,* Apr. 15 and May 4, 1788 (IV, 413, 416).

[18] *Ibid.,* June 8, 1788 (IV, 423).

[19] *Jour.,* Apr. 14, 1788 (IV, 413; italics mine).

Such moments of tentativeness toward his customary supernaturalist attitude about preaching may be evidence of his own explicit hermeneutical understanding. "Though it is God only changeth hearts," he said, "yet he generally doeth it by man."[20] When Wesley appeals to "the right of private judgment,"[21] he is not merely conditioned by the age of toleration. He is participating in the rise of the hermeneutical method in which human understanding and the divine word are brought into correspondence. Concern is said to precede enlightenment.[22] Importance to man is thereafter held to be instrumental to understanding.[23] It is not just any kind of importance, such as that prompted by "curiosity," that would be adequate for proper understanding. Yet one is led to believe that an understanding impelled by curiosity is more sensible than an understanding which does not have even curiosity to stimulate the "desire to know."[24]

Attention to Wesley's reflections, as recorded in his *Journals,* on the attitudes of the congregations to which he has preached reveals a man at times seriously aware of the hermeneutical implications of his responsibility as preacher. At the outset of his career he despaired of preaching to the American Indians because he found in them no desire for instruction. After Aldersgate the Holy Spirit seemed a more powerful and autonomous agent in the communication of God's message. For many years Wesley's view of how the Holy Spirit works was illustrated by the device of breaking open the Bible for a passage which would speak to the situation at hand. Two things are notable in the eventual disappearance from Wesley's *Journals* of recourse to this practice. First, on one occasion he failed repeatedly to break the Bible open to a suitable text, so he cast lots instead.[25] Second, and dating almost from that lot-casting incident with its exposé of his bibliomancy, Wesley began to find scriptural solutions being suggested to him from within his own interrogative situations. At length, it became a matter of policy with Wesley that preaching, which includes the interpretation of the text, was related for its effectiveness to the situation in which the hearer existed. "What hold can you have upon a people who neither know books, nor men; neither themselves, nor the Bible; neither natural nor scriptural things?"[26] All hear the preaching. Some hear it in vain. When the word sent does not return empty, when the hearing ear and the understanding heart are found to be in some rapport, interpretation has occurred. Some sermons, like Italian opera, lack the

---

[20] *Sermon* XXIV, Discourse IV, iii, 7 (V, 307).
[21] *An Earnest Appeal to Men of Reason and Religion,* 17 (VIII, 7).
[22] *Sermon* XLVI, iii, 5 (VI, 87 f.).
[23] *Jour.,* May 1, 1779 (IV, 151).
[24] *Jour.,* Apr. 1, 1748 (II, 90).
[25] *Jour.,* Mar. 28, 1739 (I, 176).
[26] *Jour.,* Nov. 5, 1770 (III, 420).

capacity to awaken the soul.[27] Why did Wesley find the Scottish people the "best hearers"?[28] Why, when speaking to dissenters, did he expect very little good to result?[29] Why were the laboring men regarded as the most susceptible to the Gospel and the rich the least?[30] Why do some scriptures "commend themselves" to our conscience before others?[31] Why are those who mourn the absence of God called blessed?[32] Because hearing without understanding is as futile as eating without digesting.[33] Because "no man can be justified and not know it!"[34] Because the foundation of religion "stands on the nature of God and the nature of man, together with their mutual relations. . . . for it begins in a man's knowing himself. . . . it finishes all, by restoring the due relations between God and man."[35]

I. Holiness Augments the Hermeneutical Circle

What Wesley calls "concern," "desire," "importance to man," "mourning," and the like are known to current hermeneutics as a form of pre-understanding for the Gospel and participate in a "hermeneutical circle." Such pre-understanding is the ground in man on which the word of God, when it falls, grows up, even though it is no credit to the ground that the seed grows. The relation between man's pre-understanding and God's word has the likeness of a circle because the circuit of understanding is never complete where either functions in independence of the other. Pre-understanding (*Vorverständnis*) was not unknown to Wesley. Probably it was known to him, technically, in German before it was in English, even though Locke and Shaftesbury gave the notion its earliest philosophical development. It was Oetinger, however, who gave to the experience of "presentiment" and "taste" the German translation *Vorempfindungen.*[36]

---

[27] *Jour.*, May 15, 1774; Apr. 8, 1787 (IV, 13, 367).

[28] *Jour.*, May 13, 1788 (IV, 418).

[29] *Jour.*, Oct. 12, 1780 (IV, 192).

[30] *Jour.*, Sept. 19, 1788 (IV, 437), May 30, 1756 (II, 363); Yet cf. Oct. 18, 1757 (II, 429).

[31] *Sermon* XCI, Introduction (VII, 45 f.).

[32] *Sermon* XXI, Discourse I, ii, 3 (V, 258 f.).

[33] *Jour.*, Apr. 11, 1748 (II, 92).

[34] *Minutes of Some Late Conversations,* I, Question 5 (VIII, 276). Shaftesbury's aversion to system illuminates Wesley's hermeneutic. This seventeenth-century philosopher had no objection to scientific systems. One does not expect to advance "in wisdom or the knowledge of himself or mankind" through natural science. But when a philosophy which professes to enlarge human understanding develops systems in which "nothing we can truly call our interest or concern" is expressed, it manifests "ignorance or idiotism," which is to say, foolishness (*Characteristics* I, 188 f.).

[35] *An Earnest Appeal to Men of Reason and Religion,* 28, 29 (VIII, 12).

[36] Hans-Georg Gadamer, *Wahrheit und Methode* (Tübingen: Mohr, 1960), 25. Cf. also Carl August Auberlen, *Die Theosophie F. C. Oetinger's* (Basel, Bahnmaier: 1869), 69 ff. Wesley refers to his reading of Oetinger's *de sensu Communi et Ratione* as a dis-

Wesley expressed the hermeneutical function of pre-sentiment or pre-understanding in two forms. One was in his general definition of faith as evidence, a *sensus communis* in man of a spiritual sort which yearns for something invisible that it cannot of itself supply. The other was in his use of the Law as a schoolmaster to Christ, traditionally referred to as the *usus theologicus*. A living faith, Wesley believed, must be preceded by a sense of sin.[37] The chronology of pre-understanding seems actually quite irrelevant to Wesley's case, for it is as conceivable that one believe in Christ first as it is that one be convinced of sin first, so long as the sense of need and the sense of gratification of the need correspond.[38] The strategy of preaching the Law as a preparation for the Gospel is based on the assumption that one ought not to offer Christ to sinners. Not that they do not deserve him but that they cannot discern him. Only one in a thousand is apt to be awakened by the Gospel message, so that to preach the Gospel to sinners does not serve a properly hermeneutical function.[39] The model of proper procedure is Paul's sermon at Lystra where Christ is not even mentioned. The same was the case with Paul's witness before Felix. It is true that Paul and Silas speak of Christ to the jailor, but, as Wesley comments, he was already convinced of sin.[40] Prior to faith the Law is preached to render men poor in spirit, giving them a knowledge of themselves.[41] When pardon is gained, the Law continues to be preached as a rule for believers. There are not, however, two laws but two uses of the one Law. One who preaches Christ will necessarily preach the Law because "to preach Christ, is to preach all things that Christ hath spoken," which include his commands as well as his promises.[42] But God unites Law and Gospel in the preaching of Jesus. Therefore in the preaching of the Church, what God hath joined let not the preacher put asunder, otherwise "he cannot be said to preach the whole gospel."[43]

---

appointment. "When I had with huge labor read fifty or sixty pages, finding the sense did by no means make amends for the time and pains bestowed in searching it out, I took my leave of him forever" (*Jour.*, Jan. 27, 1759 [II, 467]). While I am not claiming direct influence upon Wesley for Oetinger's view, it is not inconceivable even from this reference.

[37] *Sermon* XVIII, 3 (V, 214).

[38] *Sermon* VI, iii, 3; *Sermon* XIV, iii, 3 (V, 75, 169). Instances where "deep conviction of our *demerit* after we are accepted" is "absolutely necessary in order to our seeing the true value of the atoning blood."

[39] *Sermon* XXV, i, 3 (V, 449).

[40] *Sermon* XXXV, i, 8 (V, 451).

[41] *Sermon* XXI, Discourse I, i, 4 (V, 253). In Vol. V of his *Christian Library* Wesley includes Robert Bolton's *Instructions for Confronting Afflicted Consciences* in which he says, "Were it not absurd in surgery, to pour a most sovereign balsam upon a sound part? It is far more senseless, to proffer the blood of Christ, and promises of life to an unwounded conscience." The procedure recommended: "First, to wound by the Law, and then to heal by the Gospel," 17 f.

[42] *Sermon* XXXV, i, II (V, 452).

[43] *Jour.*, June 2, 1742 (I, 375, the words of Mrs. Holmes's sister, reported approvingly

The hermeneutical circle, in which man's concerned questions are addressed by God's word, is also strikingly illustrated in Wesley's view of conscience. Conscience relates to pre-understanding. Here the *sensus communis* of Shaftesbury perhaps foreshadows Wesley's "conscience." In every man there is a "common humanity," Wesley affirmed.[44] In his account of Hutcheson's *Essay on the Passions* Wesley explains what this common humanity means. It embraces a *public sense,* which is sensitive to the misery of the fellow man, and a *moral sense,* which endorses benevolence and condemns cruelty both in others and in one's self.[45] Thus, conscience as an instrument of understanding is a form of pre-understanding in so far as it is a capacity for "knowing with another." Its understanding has a social character.[46] So, indeed, Wesley defines *con-scientia,* and it takes place for the Christian in correlation with the written word of God. Thus, conscience is man's "agreement" with God's word. It can be said to function when it is "duly enlightened by the word and Spirit of God, and comparing all our thoughts, words, and works with that word, pronounce that they agree therewith."[47] The Law condemns the conscience. But the conscience finds the word of Christ "agreeable."

A really curious element in Wesley's position, however, is not the fairly standard view of the hermeneutical circle. The startling thing is how his understanding of the Christian faith as a life of holiness[48] seems to call for an augmentation of the pre-understanding, supplied by the Law in its *usus theologicus,* with another form of pre-understanding suitable to the Christian in his life of "faith working by love." It is as if the *circular* strategy of hermenutics were pushed by Wesley into a cyclical strategy.

The pre-understanding of man antecedent to faith, which the preaching of the Law is designed to clarify, operates at a quite different level of understanding from the pre-understanding of the Christian man. Actually, a spiraling transcendence is what is meant by hermeneutical circle, for questions which are open to answers, as the circle proposes, stand to be transformed by the answers. I specify cyclical rather than circular here to accentuate this

---

by Wesley). There is a notable exception in Wesley to the preaching of the Law as preparation for the Gospel and that is the circumstance in which consolation seems to be called for. Cf. July 4, 1788 (IV, 429). In the same *Instructions* (Cf. n. 41) Bolton says of this "high and heavenly art," were it well known and practised, what a world of tortured and troubled minds would it prevent."

[44] *A Farther Appeal,* I, vii, 5 (VIII, 123).

[45] *Sermon* CV, i, 7 ff. (VII, 188 f.). Wesley's only objection to this analysis was that these powers are no longer completely intact in man, considering sin.

[46] *Ibid.,* i, 1.

[47] *Notes* (I *John* 3:21), 913.

[48] *A Short Method of Converting All the Roman Catholics in the Kingdom of Ireland,* 8 (X, 131).

factor in Wesley's hermeneutical circle in which attention is being called more emphatically to the answer than to the question. A man who is grasped by God's grace is asking about what he must do to go on to perfection. He is, as Wesley describes him, "groaning for full redemption,"[49] desiring to "endure to the end,"[50] "agonizing to be altogether" Christian,[51] "now more ashamed of [his] best duties than formerly of [his] worst sins,"[52] "zealous . . . to attain the whole mind that was in Christ."[53] In sum, unlike the pre-faith pre-understanding, the holiness pre-understanding is the dimension of expectation which keeps believers from growing cold. Its role as pre-understanding for the newer and higher stage of the Christian life is reinforced by Wesley in his refusal to concede that perfection is only realizable at death, beyond history. "I say an hourly expectation; for to expect it at death, or some time hence, is much the same as not expecting it at all."[54]

The man who lives "under law" lives under a sense of condemnation and has the pre-understanding appropriate to that mode of existence. The man who lives "under grace" is "going on to perfection" and has the pre-understanding appropriate to that status. The former is characterized more by concerns oriented to fear and frustration, the latter to concerns prompted by love and exhilaration. Wesley cites John Locke as asking, "What is it moves desire?" Locke's answer is twofold in much the same sense in which Wesley's hermeneutical pre-understanding is twofold. Desire is moved both by "uneasiness" and by "happiness." These two *Vorempfindungen* correspond almost precisely to Wesley's existence "under law" and "existence under grace" or to his uses of the Law as *usus theologicus* and *tertius usus*.[55]

To the heart whose pre-understanding has been elevated from "uneasiness" to "happiness" our Lord must speak a second time.[56] The content of his speech will be the same as before: the Gospel with its Law. But this time the Law will sound different. Even though it is the same Law,[57] the preacher's use of it will be different, because the hearer's pre-understanding will be different. The manner of preaching the Law to "those pressing on to the mark," holding up the love of Christ, will surely differ from the manner of preaching

[49] *Jour.*, Mar. 30, 1764 (III, 165).
[50] *A Dialogue Between an Antinomian and His Friend* (X, 267).
[51] *Jour.*, Mar. 12, 1767 (III, 274).
[52] *Sermon* XLIII, iii, 7 (VI, 50).
[53] *Sermon* LXXXIX, 5 (VII, 28).
[54] *Jour.*, Sept. 15, 1762 (III, 113).
[55] *Remarks upon Mr. Locke's 'Essay on Human Understanding'* (XIII, 456). While this comment on Locke was written in 1781, the work from which it is derived was referred to by Wesley as early as 1745 and had been in print since 1690.
[56] *Sermon* XIV, 20 (V, 165).
[57] *Notes* (Rom. 3:20), 529 f.

to the "careless."[58] One need never preach to the "accepted" the terrors of God, such as the Law before faith inspires. "Love is . . . the strongest of all motives, . . . always drawing, rather than driving."[59]

II. Holiness Is a Type of Demythologizing

A science of hermeneutics is not exhausted in the exercise of interpreting human existence in the light of a text. Also provided in hermeneutics is a critical procedure for assessing the immediate as well as the ultimate context and purpose of a text. No one is surprised to see Wesley making the customary orthodox statements about the inspiration of the text and its authority for faith. To find him setting up a basis upon which the text can be analyzed, notwithstanding its authority, is less usual, however.

What basis can a man find for assessing God's word? Surely nothing outside God's word will qualify. However, if the word of God is essentially and fundamentally concerned with "holiness," then anything in the text which deviates from that concern is subject to the judgment of greater or less worth. The text is allowed to judge itself, but not according to the more obvious canons of interpretation which Wesley learned from Bengel. It is true, as he said, that one must let a text derive its meaning from its context, and it is true that if texts seem to contradict each other, one must be patient in determining whether the larger context helps to resolve that contradiction. But beyond this, Wesley is contending that not every statement in the Bible has the same status for faith.

References to faith in the New Testament, for instance, need not all be harmonized, for not all the forms of faith referred to are equally valid. The Gospel talks of a faith that removes mountains. Hankering for that faith is openly criticized by Wesley, not because he entertains doubt concerning what is possible with God but because New Testament faith is the "faith which worketh by love." That faith is "saving" faith. The faith which removes mountains may be had of devils. "It is only a super-natural persuasion given a man, that God will work thus by him at that hour. Now, 'though I have all' this 'faith, so as to remove mountains,' yet, if I have not the 'faith which worketh by love,' I am nothing."[60]

One can refer to this sort of practice as "demythologizing" without too great a risk of *vaticinium ex eventu,* because demythologizing is a form of

[58] *The Letters of the Rev. John Wesley, M.A.*, ed. by John Telford (London: Epworth, 1931), III, 80 f.

[59] *Minutes of Some Late Conversations,* II, Aug. 2, Question 18; Question 8 (VIII, 284 and 286).

[60] *Notes* (Matt. 17:20), 86.

hermeneutic in which the text is criticized by the text in order that the kerygma may manifest itself to human understanding. Wesley's critique takes the form of reinterpretation rather than annihilation of the passages which are, on the surface, deficient in scriptural holiness. Deficient passages are usually those which rely excessively on the first century world view and its presuppositions. Notwithstanding his avowed adoption of the Copernican world view and his avid pursuit of an experimental knowledge of nature, Wesley seems to be completely at home in the world of the first century. This suggests that his few efforts to reinterpret the biblical text are not apologetic appeals to a scientific age or a retreat in the face of advancing science, even though he did say that Methodism desires to be as free from superstition as from heresy.[61] Rather, Wesley is eager to let the biblical message become important to human concerns without biblical impediments. Thus hermeneutics rather than apologetics seems to be Wesley's motivating principle. In a sermon on the text of Mark 9:38, having to do with "casting out devils," he affirms that "every minister of Christ does cast them out." This exorcism is, however, bringing sinners to repentance, which is both an inward and an outward change in man. This is, in a sound sense, to cast out devils. And how does repentance come about? "This change was wrought by his hearing this man preach."[62]

In the sermon "The Signs of the Times," the customary messianic signs are listed: the deaf hear, the lame walk, and lepers are cleansed. Nevertheless, Wesley repeatedly insists that the text be allowed to declare its "plain meaning." Plain meaning excludes imaginative play with the text[63] and includes encouragement to remain faithful to its "childlike simplicity" and openness.[64] Wesley's use of the word "historical" is a synonym, or perhaps a surrogate, for "plain." Thus, in his note on "the foolishness of preaching" Wesley says, "*we* go on to *preach,* in a plain and historical, not rhetorical or philosophical, manner."[65] That this may indicate some dependency upon Locke's use of the identical parallelism in the previous century—"the historical, plain method"—is strongly suggested.

To return to "The Signs of the Times," we may ask more narrowly how Wesley illustrates his historical method, that of plain interpretation? The deaf who hear are those who were deaf to the outward and inward call of God. The lame who walk are now running the race that is set before them. The lepers who are healed are those inflicted with "the deadly leprosy of sin."[66]

---

[61] *Sermon* CXXXII, 8 (VII, 426).
[62] *Sermon* XXXVIII, i, 13 and iii, 3 (V, 483 and 487).
[63] *Sermon* LXXII, ii, 7 (VI, 387).
[64] *A Farther Appeal,* Part II, iii, 5 (VIII, 185).
[65] *Notes* (I Cor. 1:23), 588.
[66] *Sermon* LXVI, ii, 4 (VI, 308).

Likewise, in his sermon "On the Trinity" Wesley poses the mystery of the Incarnation, how the word was made flesh. He concludes "there is no mystery in it." The mystery does not inhere in the "how," the "manner" of the Incarnation. "I know nothing about it; I believe nothing about it: It is no more the object of my faith, than it is of my understanding. . . . I believe just so much as God has revealed, and no more."[67]

In his treatise, *A Farther Appeal to Men of Reason and Religion,* Wesley allows that the miracles of the apostolic age are no longer required of the Church. They were "outward miracles." The Church is called to nurture the inward miracle.[68] The very desire for miracle is the sign not of piety but of infidelity. Miracles, indeed, may be wrought in support of falsehood, whereas "the proper topics of Scripture and reason" are sufficient without miracles, but "miracles without these are not."[69] And, in the same treatise, the prospect of heaven and hell is raised with the strong reminder that Christian salvation is concerned with the present restoration of the soul to health. "Holiness . . . is the thing itself."[70] "Myself am hell," he later said,[71] and holiness delivers a man from himself! "I will not now shock the easiness of your temper by talking about a future state; but suffer me to ask you a question about present things: Are you now happy?"[72]

III. Holiness Secularizes the World

The hermeneutics of holiness, as a method of scriptural interpretation, relates the biblical text in such a way that the text "interprets" the reader, effecting a significant change in his situation. While the language of holiness resembles that of piety and religiousness, this does not mean that holiness needs to support a species of otherworldiness. In practice it did so, and Wesley's otherworldliness is evident enough as it was, indeed, with most churchmen in the eighteenth century. That is why it is illuminating to see the extent to which, when the Bible is allowed to express its intention, the result for the world is transforming. The world is brought to maturity. From the faith of a servant believers are elevated to the faith of a son.[73] Sonship in the New Testament faith involves responsibility for God's world.

One who understands existence in the light of scriptural holiness antici-

---

[67] *Sermon* LV, 14, 15 (VI, 204).

[68] *A Farther Appeal,* Part III, iii, 9 (VIII, 220). This is not unlike the position of John Locke on miracle to the effect that in Christianity the power of the outward miracle has been lodged with the state.

[69] *Ibid.,* III, 29 (VIII, 234 f.).

[70] *Ibid.,* Part I, i, 3 (VIII, 47).

[71] *Ibid.,* Part II, iii, 17 (VIII, 195).

[72] *An Earnest Appeal,* 42 (VIII, 16).

[73] *Jour.,* Sept. 3, 1741 (I, 326 f.).

pates "this strange sight; a *Christian world.*" "The time will come," said Wesley, "when Christianity will prevail over all and cover the earth."[74] Wesley's several and violent repudiations of Constantinian Christianity[75] are evidence that he had nothing like that kind of acculturation in mind in presaging the triumph of Christianity. Chiliasm would be closer to his understanding when he rejoiced in the sign of "God's arising to maintain his own cause, and set up his kingdom over the earth."[76] Actually, the extent to which Wesley saw biblical holiness as a call for a new worldliness is negligible. He required of holiness what could not be secured either empirically or exegetically. He assumed that a man who loved God and his neighbor with his whole heart would and could manifest it in a way that would distinguish him from other men. Ever since that position was expressed it has been under attack for its built-in temptation to pride. The more formidable objection, one would think, would be its sheer misapprehension of the Christian view.

Prior to faith the Law is used as a schoolmaster unto Christ, that is, as a means of quickening a pre-understanding for the Gospel. The resulting question was, "Why can't I do what I ought?" For those in faith, Wesley's hermeneutical circle spiraled to a new level with the question, "What do ye more than others?" By Wesley's own account this message was branded "a damnable doctrine."[77] Presumably, this was because it violated the Protestant principle of justification by faith alone. It did not in fact do so; nor was it damnable for requiring Christians to "exteriorize" what is, in the first place, an interior reality. It is, however, damnable because it has miscalculated the extent to which human history, both within and without the Christian arena, has arrived at the capacity to assume responsibility for the world, to love one's neighbor, and to manifest fruits indistinguishable from "the fruits of the spirit." In requiring the Christian to do what distinguishes him from the world, Wesley put himself in the graceless position of depreciating the very world which was already assuming its responsibility without explicit faith.

As long as Wesley was working with acknowledged drunks, thieves, and adulterers, holiness on his terms had an appeal. With responsible citizens he tended to invent and accent distinctions in order to fortify his case. One cannot be a true friend, he claimed, if he is false to God.[78] Occasionally in his contacts with Christian congregations he would confess to his diary that he preferred an "honest heathen" to a Christian. But repenting thereof, he would

[74] *Sermon* IV, iii, 1 (V, 45).

[75] *Sermon* LXI, 27 (VI, 261 f.).

[76] *Sermon* LXVI, ii, 4 (VI, 308), although Wesley's omission from his *Notes* of the heavy apocalypticism of Bengel's *Gnomon* is noteworthy.

[77] *Jour.*, Sept. 3, 1774 (IV, 28). Wesley has even been accused of basing his view upon texts in the New Testament which were redactions of early Catholicism.

[78] *Jour.*, Oct. 30, 1763 (III, 155).

add that while it is true that the "honest heathen" would condemn gluttony and drunkenness, would he condemn "a regular, reputable kind of sensuality, an elegant epicurism?"[79]

The least attractive aspect of the Wesleyan view is the way in which he persistently depreciates the world. When he is tempted to admire the poise and success of a British statesman, he interrupts his reverie to say, "What is a Lord, but a sinner, born to die?"[80] In a moment in which he seems thoroughly to relish the beauty of the Irish landscape, he checks himself by saying, "The eye is not satisfied with seeing! It never can, till we see God."[81] Toward his seventieth year he remarks about an acquaintance: "He is the greatest genius in little things, that ever fell under my notice. . . . I really believe, were he seriously to set about it, he could invent the best mousetrap that ever was in the world."[82] When young people fall in love, he insinuates that the Holy Spirit has left them.[83] Observing the talents of a blind artisan, he muses, "What is he the better for all this, if 'without God in the world'?"[84] Beholding evidences of benevolence between people about him, he observes, "Benevolence itself is no virtue at all, unless it spring from the love of God!"[85] He approves the parent who explains to his child his fondness by saying, "It is God that makes me love you."[86] Through it all runs his uncompromising admonition to all men, "Let nothing satisfy thee but the power of godliness," with its corollary, "Canst thou hope to dig happiness out of the earth?"[87] His understanding of godliness became so alienated from worldliness that it no longer seemed odd to him why a man should prefer death to life in the world.[88]

At the outset of his ministry Wesley ruled out joy as a fruit of faith in the face of the obvious biblical inclusion of it.[89] Later he hesitantly endorsed it.[90] In his developed position he finally regarded joy—or happiness—as a criterion of the love of God.[91] "He who is not happy is not a Christian," he ultimately said.[92] How then shall one account for the evident good fun in the world around one, notwithstanding its apparent indifference to Christian faith?

---

[79] *Sermon* L, ii, 2 (VI, 131).
[80] *Jour.*, Jan. 25, 1785 (IV, 296).
[81] *Jour.*, July 29, 1765 (III, 231).
[82] *Jour.*, Jan. 14, 1772 (III, 451).
[83] *Jour.*, June 12, 1774 (IV, 18).
[84] *Jour.*, May 6, 1776 (IV, 73).
[85] *Sermon* XC, 2 (VII, 38).
[86] *Sermon* XCIV, iii, 7 (VII, 82).
[87] *Sermon* XXII, Discourse II, ii, 6 (V, 269).
[88] *An Earnest Appeal,* 43 (VIII, 17).
[89] *Jour.*, May 15, 1738 (I, 103).
[90] *Jour.*, Dec. 11, 1739; Dec. 28, 1740 (I, 253, 292).
[91] *An Earnest Appeal,* 48 (VIII, 19).
[92] *Sermon* LXXXVII, iii, 6 (VI, 433).

They are only "merry," Wesley explained, introducing one of his fine terminological distinctions. Christians are "happy."[93]

In the face of this evident and conventional otherworldliness, what is striking in Wesley are the scattered signs of a kind of Christian worldliness. His intention is not really otherworldliness but attack upon the corruption of the world as it is. Worldliness is defined by him as loving the world, where that love competes with the love of God.[94] There is no final question about the usefulness of the world but only about how, when one seeks the ultimate source of his happiness there, the world becomes his idol.[95] By nature—sinful nature, that is—man loves the world and worships the creature.[96] That is why the big question at the last judgment will be: How did you use your worldly goods?[97] It is fairly clear that the kind of worldliness which idolizes the world weakens the chances for a holiness which is oriented to the love of God.[98] The question being raised here is the same question Wesley himself once raised: "Would not one who was . . . sanctified be incapable of worldly business?" The answer Wesley gave: "He would be far more capable of it than ever, as going through all without distraction." Question: "Would he be capable of marriage?" Answer: "Why should he not?"[99]

Which is to say, the problem is the same, and so is the solution: When you buy, you will hold what you possess as if not possessing, when you marry, as if not married. Christian worldliness removes the distraction of idolatry and thus liberates a man to assume responsibility for the world. Without that liberation, a man may turn the world into an idol *to* which he feels responsible. Just so, he may lose his capacity to be responsible *for* it.

How, then, can you tell a Christian from one who is not? After undergoing this dialectic, it is no longer so easy for Wesley to get a rule of thumb by which to rebuke and discipline his religious societies. He once admitted that he was unable to distinguish the good from the bad in his societies without the help of informers.[100] He provided long descriptions of the empirical, observable traits of those who live under the covenant of works and those who live under the covenant of grace, but the lists were almost indistinguishable.[101] Noting this, he agreed that the difference was not to be found in the

[93] *Ibid.*, iii, 5 (VI, 432). "Happy" was Wesley's translation of *makarioi* in the Beatitudes.
[94] *An Earnest Appeal*, 48 (VIII, 19).
[95] *Sermon* LXXVIII, i, 14 (VI, 440).
[96] *Sermon* XCV, 8 (VII, 89).
[97] *Sermon* LI, ii, 5 (VI, 146).
[98] *Sermon* LXXXVII, ii, 11 (VII, 11).
[99] *Minutes of Some Late Conversations,* Questions 5–6 (VIII, 285 f.).
[100] *Jour.*, Mar. 9–12, 1747 (II, 48).
[101] *Sermon* IV, i, 5 ff., VI, ii, 1 ff. (V, 40 ff., 71 f.).

visibility but in the God-relation, in the "whole soul now sensible to God."[102]

The question raised by the pre-understanding of a holiness that is mature enough to embrace worldliness is then no longer, "What do we more than others?" It is simply, "How long can we love our neighbors without bringing that love under subjection to the love of God?" Responsibility *for* the world can easily become responsibility *to* the world, for to "love the world" is, as Wesley said, an "almost insuperable temptation." Or, to say it in the way he did, more rigorously, "From Atheism there is an easy transition to idolatry; from the worship of no god to the worship of false gods."[103] Holiness, without disparaging the world, is committed to orienting the world to God in order not to turn the world into the very idol, exclusive devotion to which obstructs the sense of responsibility for it.

In this understanding the pre-understanding of the Law as *usus theologicus* would give way, and the hermeneutical circle would be restored at the new level to which it had spiraled through holiness. A man to whom responsibility *for* the world comes naturally is as immune to the condemnation of the Law as Wesley found the wife of William Penn to be.[104] But why, then, any longer classify the responsible man of the world with the Pharisee who has "the form of religion but not its power"? The case of the Pharisee had to do with his efforts to justify himself in the eyes of God by ceremonial and moral practices which had lost their capacity to mediate God's power. The modern man, already in Wesley's time, is no longer religious in form. In his new-found secular freedom he can be responsible for the world without exploiting the world on behalf of his own salvation. One ought not, therefore, expect to succeed in subjecting modern man to the dialectic of a law which is contrived to produce repentance, if the religious dynamics of the Law have been eliminated.

Wesley's holiness pre-understanding, "What do ye more than others?", when stripped of its futile implications of empirical comparison, would sound like this: "How shall we assume responsibility *for* the world without turning it into a new object of devotion?" The Gospel answer would be, "Ye shall be perfect!" which is to say, "Love the Lord thy God with all thy heart, and thy neighbor." This signifies the new law of life which is a word of promise and permission: "Receive the world from God!"

---

[102] *Sermon* II, iii, 9; XIX, i, 8 (V, 24, 226).
[103] *Sermon* XVIII, ii, 2 (VII, 218).
[104] *Jour.*, Jan. 9, 1786 (IV, 325).

Original Sin and the Enlightenment

CLYDE A. HOLBROOK
Chairman of the Department of Religion,
Danforth Professor of Religion
Oberlin College
Oberlin, Ohio

Few doctrines have enjoyed so controverted a history as that of original sin. From Augustine's spirited controversy with the Pelagians to the late seventeenth century battles flared and subsided, with victory more than once seemingly assured to the affirmers. In the eighteenth century, however, the doctrine met its severest challenge at the hands of the Enlightenment.[1] In the English-speaking world original sin, with its companion problem of theodicy, was to meet an ethos which repudiated its depressing implications and strenuously attempted to show the beneficent rationality of a world in which evil took its proper place.

From a contemporary perspective the controversies waged over these issues have appeared irrelevant, but in fact they were struggles which largely settled the direction in which Western man would conceive himself, his society, and his religious aspirations for nearly two centuries. Not only was Protestant doctrine decisively reshaped in regard to man, but his image was so convincingly fashioned that succeeding generations accepted as beyond dispute what the eighteenth century tirelessly labored to establish. To trace part of the history of the doctrine in the crucial age of Enlightenment carries us back to religious conditions and thought in England. Thence we are brought to the American colonies, where Jonathan Edwards desperately fought off the encroachments of the Enlightenment as interpreted in the writings of John Taylor of Norwich. Until the revival of interest in the doctrine in mid-twentieth century no treatment comparable to his in depth and thorough-

[1] See Ernst Cassirer, *The Philosophy of Enlightenment* (Princeton: Princeton University Press, 1951), 141; Paul Tillich, *Systematic Theology* (Chicago: University of Chicago Press, 1957), II, 38; Reinhold Niebuhr, *The Nature and Destiny of Man* (New York: Scribner's, 1943), I, 93.

ness appeared. In this sense his work marked the close of an era and the opening of another in which a more flattering view of mankind flourished. However, it remains a question as to whether in his convictions and insights, if not in his arguments, Edwards' conception of man's predicament comes closer to the mark today than do pronouncements which draw upon the perspectives of the Enlightenment.

I

The principal opposition in eighteenth-century England to the doctrine of original sin came from a group known by the notoriously inaccurate title of "Arminian." This term included a variety of theological opinions which were in acute disaffection with aspects of Calvinism. Moderate Arminianism sought an authentic Christianity which could outflank two of the most troublesome contentions of Calvinism: predestination as opposed to a measure of free will, and total depravity as opposed to some capacity for moral virtue. In its more extreme forms it tended to Pelagianism, Arianism, and Socinianism. With skeptical rationalism of the Enlightenment to its left and moderate latitudinarianism and genial rationalism stemming from the Cambridge Platonists on the right, a formidable array was opposed to Calvinism.[2] Whatever differences separated these movements, they nevertheless marched under one banner, announcing their cordial dislike of Calvinism both as a system of divinity and as politics.

The troubles of orthodox Calvinism were magnified by political implications which from the beginnings of Puritanism had been intertwined with doctrinal controversies. Dr. Samuel Brooke had expressed his opinion to Archbishop Laud that "Predestination is the root of Puritanism, and Puritanism the root of all rebellion and disobedient intractableness and all schism and sauciness in the country, nay in the Church itself."[3] Brooke's diagnosis proved largely correct, since the army which overthrew the Royalists in the civil wars numbered many Puritans. Since the Royalists were often identified as Arminians, the success of Parliamentary arms and the establishment of the Commonwealth decisively retarded the prospects of that party. However, among the sects which spawned during the wars and under the Commonwealth, Arminian ideas prospered, much to the discomfiture of the Presbyterian wing

[2] "If the Cambridge men were looked upon by the advocates of the Enlightenment as religious reactionaries, by the Puritan controversialists they were considered religious indifferentists." Ernst Cassirer, *The Platonic Renaissance in England* (tr. by James P. Pettegrove; Austin: University of Texas Press, 1953), 37.

[3] Quoted by Gerald R. Cragg, *From Puritanism to the Age of Reason* (Cambridge: Cambridge University Press, 1950), 16.

which had hoped for an established church reformed along Genevan and Scottish lines. Its efforts to unite church and state under Calvinistic auspices contrasted strongly with the relative religious toleration under Cromwell and reflected adversely upon the Calvinist cause. Furthermore, the often unfair identification of Calvinism with the suppression of innocent pleasures cast an additional stigma upon its fortunes. Calvinistic thought of course flourished, as did Arminianism, among the sects, but by the late seventeenth century it no longer played a significant role in shaping the fortunes of either the established church or state. At the Restoration the brief sway of Calvinism ended. As G. R. Cragg puts it:

> The ascendancy of Calvinism ended as abruptly as did the rule of the saints . . . the Restoration definitely marked the end of an era in English religious thought. It drove from power the exponents of Calvinism, and by the same token it restored to positions of influence men who on the whole were favorable to Arminianism.[4]

During the eighteenth century the Arminian influence increased in church, state, and sect. Even among the nonconformist and dissenting groups, who had maintained Calvinistic principles in the seventeenth century, enthusiasm for the doctrines of the Genevan waned, until as with the English Presbyterians "a veritable landslide from orthodoxy into what later became known as Unitarianism" set in.[5] What Stanley Gower, one of the Westminster divines, had excoriated in the mid-sixteenth century now bade fair to become the new orthodoxy of the eighteenth. He had said, "There are two rotten pillars on which the fabric of late Arminianism (an egg of the old Pelagianism which we had well hoped had been long since chilled, but is sit upon and brooded by the wanton wits of our degenerate and apostate spirits) doth principally stand." These he identified as "that God loveth all alike" and "that God giveth . . . Christ, the great gift of his eternal love, to all alike to work out their redemption . . . if they please to make right use of that which is so put into their power."[6] In the eyes of the orthodox no one could expect from such notions other than the calamities which had come to pass—bad manners, vitiated morals, and a continuing declension in vital piety.

The picture of eighteenth-century England as a land far gone in heterodoxy and ebbing religious vitality and morals has often been overdrawn. To be sure, the Bible's authority and divine origin were severely overhauled by sophisticates; miracles and other "superstitious nonsense" were ridiculed; and

---

[4] *Ibid.*, 18.

[5] Norman Sykes, *The English Religious Tradition* (London: S.C.M. Press, 1953), 62.

[6] John Owen, *The Death of Death in the Death of Christ* (London: The Banner of Truth Trust, 1959), 35.

doctrines once held to be the unshakable foundation of the Christian faith were rigorously assailed and radically modified. Societies for moral reform were common, and protests against the vulgarities and cynicism of the age were heard, thus indicating both the conditions which evoked these remedies and the vitality of a moral, if not a deeply religious spirit which combated the decadence.[7] Up to the time of the Methodist revival undoubtedly religious fervor flagged, but it is also true that the vigor and success of that movement cast a distorting light upon religious conditions of preceding decades.

Innumerable estimates have been offered concerning the religious conditions of the first half of the eighteenth century. J. H. Colligan called the years between 1730 and 1750 "the most depressing twenty years in English Christianity in the eighteenth century."[8] Another author claims that "the years 1700 to 1750 were a period of dead weight in religion . . . if men discussed it seriously at all, they discussed it in much the same way as a geologist discusses fossils."[9] Bishop Butler characterized the vice of his age as "an avowed scorn of religion in some and a growing disregard of it in the generality," while Addison claimed that there was "less appearance of religion in England than in any neighboring state or kingdom."[10] However, these somber estimates must be received with caution.

Much of the skeptical thought of the period simply passed over the heads of common folk, and deism, widely heralded as a feature of the age, was largely a surface phenomenon. Stromberg notes that free thinking and atheism were not popular. "Blasphemy or radical free-thought were the last things the Augustans wanted to hear," although they did hear them! It is likely that the drawing rooms of the town more than the countryside heard talk which endangered Christian doctrine. As Philip Doddridge explained in 1726, "An atheist or a deist is a monstrous kind of creature which in the country we only know by report."[11] Sykes offers a balanced estimate of the century's religious climate when he states, "An age which numbered Isaac Watts and Philip Doddridge amongst dissenters cannot be accused of lack of piety, hymnody, pastoral zeal, or theological learning; nor can the names of Butler, Gibson, Wake, and Secker in the established church be considered synonymous with

---

[7] Dudley W. R. Bahlman, *The Moral Revolution of 1688* (New Haven: Yale University Press, 1957), ch. 1.

[8] Ernest A. Payne, *The Free Church Tradition in the Life of England* (London: S.C.M. Press, 1951), 78.

[9] A. T. S. James, "Philip Doddridge: His Influence on Personal Religion," in *Philip Doddridge,* ed. by Geoffrey F. Nutall (London: Independent Press, 1951), 33.

[10] W. E. H. Lecky, *History of England in the Eighteenth Century* (London: Longmans, Green, 1913), 13.

[11] Roland N. Stromberg, *Religious Liberalism in Eighteenth-Century England* (Oxford: Oxford University Press, 1954), 4–5.

lethargy and worldliness." He admits, nevertheless, that a temper of pessimism was abroad in religious circles, and that moral conduct was in serious decline.[12]

Alert Arminian and Calvinist leaders were alarmed by this drift. They disputed vigorously among themselves concerning the doctrines of predestination, free will, atonement, depravity, and the origins of sin, but they also turned their attention to a common remedy for the listless estate of Christianity. They agreed that a heart-warming evangelical faith must be stirred in the populace, and although cool heads damned the practices of Wesley and Whitefield with the fateful term "enthusiasm," revivalism began to turn the tide by mid-century.

II

The practical task of renovating morals and the spiritual life accompanied efforts to explain how in God's world evils of all kinds could exist. Theodicy became a preoccupation of the intelligentsia, in and out of the church. While some constructed world views in which a divinely appointed place for evils was found, others industriously subverted these exalted schemes by insisting on an ancient dilemma. If God is good, then evil argues to his lack of omnipotence, and if he is all-powerful, evil denies his beneficence.

One of the most influential efforts to make divine wisdom and beneficence comport with concrete evils was that of William King in his *De Origine Mali.*[13] King, operating with the neo-Platonic conception of the plenitude of being, attempted to demonstrate that "all evil was not only consistent with infinite wisdom, goodness, and power, but necessarily resulting from them."[14] He argued that the universe is a marvelously constructed, purposeful whole, constituted of degrees of being, stretching from the infinite wisdom and goodness of God down to the minutest entities and activities. As he put it:

> If we thoroughly understand the connection, subordination and mutual relation of things, the mutual assistance which they offered each other; and lastly, the whole series and order of them; it would appear that the world is as well as it could be; and that no evil in it could be avoided which would not occasion a greater by its absence.[15]

---

[12] Sykes, *op. cit.,* 63.

[13] This work was published in Latin in 1702 and reappeared with the English title, *An Essay on the Origin of Evil: added Two Sermons,* in 1731. Edmund Law corrected and translated the book. I have used the third edition of 1739. [Spelling and capitalization modernized by the editors in quotations from this and other sources.]

[14] *Ibid.,* 213.

[15] *Ibid.,* 219.

God's goodness and reason make necessary the actualization of all essences, each according to type. Anything less than the operation of this principle would suggest limitations upon deity. "God would neither have been infinitely powerful nor good if he could not have made anything which we call evil."[16] Abundance and variety of existents rather than sheer peaceful coexistence among his creatures or the absence of pain seem to have been the aim of God's creative goodness.

Moral evil King regarded as "those inconveniences of life and condition which befall ourselves and others through wrong elections," a doctrine which was a stock in trade of many Arminians. To substantiate his position he passed on to a subtle defense of a doctrine of indifference. Freedom of the will is not sheer spontaneity; it is the will determining itself out of a state of indifference. Surely men make unhappy choices owing to error, ignorance, levity, habit, or appetites, he suggested, but these are not coercive determinants, but only occasional causes or opportunities. "It is not at all necessary for anyone knowingly and willingly to pursue the worse," but if these misuses of freedom occur in God's world, should not God have refused freedom of the will to man? Not at all. God, given the alternatives of withdrawing or restraining free will of man's misuse of his freedom of choice, wisely chose the lesser evil, that of allowing men freedom. If one wished to quibble with divine reason and goodness for not removing the possibility of the will's misuse with its dire consequences, King offered the cold comfort that God's "goodness chose the benefit of the universe rather than that of yourself."[17] He admitted that "an almost universal deviation from a way to happiness" occurs, but in the end "God will procure the good of the whole by our folly no less than by our wisdom."[18]

In 1757 Soame Jenyns published *A Free Inquiry into the Nature and Origin of Evil.* Herein he echoed similar views in crasser terms. Jenyns baldly announced that evils are "in truth no evils at all; but only the absence of comparative good, resulting wholly from the necessary inferiority of some beings with regard to others," which cannot be prevented in a system of "creation, whose very essence consists in a chain of subordination descending from infinite perfection to absolute nothing."[19] Of course, if evils are no evil, then it was incumbent upon Jenyns to show in particular how even moral evils redound both to the glory of God and the benefit of mankind. In a manner calculated to earn the ridicule of Dr. Johnson, Jenyns explained

[16] *Ibid.*, 489.
[17] *Ibid.*, 225–236, 373–414.
[18] *Ibid.*, 451, 462–463.
[19] Pp. 6–7 (London).

that acts commonly supposed to be outrageously immoral served the total good.

> Thus for instance robbery may disperse useless hoards to the benefit of the public; adultery may bring heirs and good humor too into many families where they would otherwise have been wanting. . . . Luxury maintains its thousands and vanity its ten thousands, superstition and arbitrary power contribute to the grandeur of many notions, and the liberties of others are preserved by the contentions of avarice, knavery, selfishness and ambition.[20]

On this insipid controversion of moral values, Jenyns piled the equally unpalatable notion that "there is something in the abstract nature of pain conducive to pleasures: that the sufferings of individuals are absolutely necessary to universal happiness."[21] Little wonder then that Dr. Johnson satirized Jenyns' joyous acceptance of pain and disease.

> Many a merry bout have these frolick beings at the vicissitudes of an ague, and good sport it is to see a man tumble with an epilepsy, and revive and tumble again and all this he knows not why . . . we have no way of procuring any sport so brisk and so lasting, as the paroxysms of the gout and stone, which undoubtedly must make high mirth, especially if the play be a little diversified with the blunders and puzzles of the blind and deaf.[22]

The cosmic perspectives of a King or Jenyns did little to persuade the tougher minds of the age. Their efforts to reconcile the patent evils, natural and moral, of this world with the wisdom and beneficence of deity, could only build a structure of hopelessness and despair on the foundations of credulous optimism. Calvinists repudiated the notion that evil was not evil, that sin was not sin, and they fought off indignantly the blasphemous supposition, to which their own views of divine sovereignty threatened to lead them, that God was the author of sin. Arminians of course could not accept God's authorship of sin. Neither could their incessant praise of "reason" be allowed to degenerate into a view which, however rational its proponents might insist it was, turned out to be a cosmic strait jacket for free men. Paradoxically, the more coercively rational the world appeared, the less opportunity there seemed to be for Arminian free will. Rationalism moving toward determinism threatened moral responsibility and the reality of the moral life itself. To go down that path, one would be caught in the strangely mixed company of Calvinists and free thinkers. Nor would some free thinkers

20 *Ibid.*, 85.
21 *Ibid.*, 67–68.
22 Quoted in Basil Willey, *The Eighteenth Century Background* (London: Chatto and Windus, 1946), 53.

accept the palliatives offered by a King or a Jenyns. Evils provided too good a tool with which to embarrass liberal and orthodox Christians alike.[23] Better to insist on the reality of evils and press them home as counting heavily against Christian orthodoxy!

God's reputation was not measurably enhanced by the maladroit essays of King and Jenyns, but more importantly man's dignity was seriously impaired when it turned out that God was pledged to original sin for the benefit of a cosmic plan. King with his talk of "an almost universal deviation from the way to happiness" came close to affirming original sin, and in his sermon on the "Fall of Man" went all the way. Jenyns too floundered into the quagmire of original sin, but he blandly explained that his own doctrine of original sin obviated those erroneous conceptions of the doctrine which regarded man as having been made by God with "depraved dispositions"—a doctrine, incidentally, few if any Calvinists ever thought of holding. The term "original sin," Jenyns explained, was a contradiction in terms, since "original" meant "innate," and "sin" referred to the "act of an accountable being." Original sin therefore cannot mean original or innate guilt "for that is absolute nonsense," but it can only mean "original depravity or an innate disposition to sin."[24] Having stripped away the notion of guilt from original sin and having allowed for a minimal degree of freedom—just enough to permit the word "accountable" to make some sense—Jenyns nevertheless had to face up to his basic principle. Sin was ingressive in God's cosmic plan as a necessary manifestation of God's power, wisdom, and goodness. And, he concluded lamely, even the evildoers in their "just punishment may probably . . . remotely contribute to universal happiness."[25]

Clearly neither Arminian nor Calvinist found these conclusions acceptable. The doctrine of original sin needed a candid examination which would free God of complicity in causing it, and free Adam's descendants from a guilt which was in no way theirs. Calvinists and Arminians agreed on the former aim, but disagreed violently with each other on the second.

III

A precipitous decline of English Presbyterianism into Arminian and Pelagian views engulfed John Taylor of Norwich. Eventually he was to be hailed as a leading Unitarian, but it is unlikely that he was so far inclined when he published *The Scripture-Doctrine of Original Sin, Proposed to Free*

---

[23] Cf. Anthony Collins, *A Vindication of the Divine Attributes* (London, 1710).
[24] Jenyns, *op. cit.*, 108.
[25] *Ibid.*, 171–173.

and Candid Examination in 1740.[26] His book appears to have quickly won both notoriety and acclaim for its destruction of the doctrine. Isaac Watts hastened to pen with his *Ruin and Recovery of Mankind,* and David Jennings followed with *The Vindication of the Scripture-Doctrine of Original Sin.* These two worthies were given a sharp drubbing in the Supplement to Taylor's second edition of 1741, and in 1746 another edition of his work appeared. It was this edition which Jonathan Edwards used in preparing what he hoped would be a crushing reply. In 1757 John Wesley, who felt that Taylor had undercut the faith itself, wrote against him, but failed to make an impressive case.

Taylor's treatise was undoubtedly a tract for the time. Its extravagant show of amiable reasonableness, its appeal to refined moral sensibilities, and its marks of sound learning, attracted the moderate rationalists of England and New England. Its anguished reception by Calvinists and the more conservative Arminians proved that it had hit the mark with precision. A Calvinist divine of northern Ireland warned his flock against its pernicious doctrines, calling it "a bad book, and a dangerous book, and a heretical book," but he was forced to concede woefully that it was unanswerable.[27] The book, with other writings of Taylor, found its way across the Atlantic, where it provided encouragement for those in rebellion against traditional ways of interpreting Scripture and Calvinism. Lemuel Briant recommended its reading to parishioners, but under cross-examination by fellow clergy dissociated himself from its conclusions. Charles Chauncy in his later works paid his respects to Taylor, and specifically referred to his treatise on original sin. Samuel Webster helped himself from it liberally for his *A Winter Evening's Conversation upon the Doctrine of Original Sin* (1757). Whether or not the book was "immediately popular" or "became the rage," as two modern scholars have suggested, it certainly evoked controversy on original sin, and several American divines hastened to answer it.[28]

Samuel Niles went to press with *The True Scripture-Doctrine of Original Sin Stated and Defended* in which he claimed that this doctrine was the one "most eagerly struck at and virulently opposed by many in the present age."[29]

---

[26] See H. Shelton Smith, *Changing Conceptions of Original Sin* (New York: Scribner's, 1955), 13, n. 10. The date usually given for Taylor's volume is 1738.

[27] Earl M. Wilbur, *A History of Unitarianism in Transylvania, England, and America* (Cambridge, Mass.: Harvard University Press, 1952), 267, n. 55. The original story appeared in a note in Taylor's *History of the Octagon Church, Norwich* (London, 1848), 27.

[28] Thomas A. Schafer, "Jonathan Edwards and Justification by Faith," *Church History,* XX (1951) No. 4, 64, n. 4; Perry Miller, *Jonathan Edwards* (New York: Sloane, 1949), 110.

[29] P. 40 (Boston, 1757).

Peter Clark attempted to fend off Webster's *Conversation* with *A Summer Morning's Conversation* (1758). By the time he brought out *A Defense of the Doctrine of Original Sin Further Vindicated* (n.d.), he could refer Webster to Edwards' demolition of Taylor, wherein "he might have found all or most of his arguings and objections anticipated and finally and forever silenced."[30] Joseph Bellamy in an open letter to Webster also suggested that he examine Edwards' book "now in press . . . wherein all these points are fully considered and every objection of any moment answered."[31] And Sereno Dwight retails the story, probably apocryphal, that Taylor "had indiscreetly boasted that his book would never be answered, but that his days were shortened by mortification upon learning of Edwards' reply to it."[32]

Edwards did not waste his efforts upon such lesser lights as Webster, who had for the most part parroted Taylor. Although he perhaps knew of the hot dispute raging in eastern Massachusetts, he saved his ammunition for Taylor himself. He had long known of the decay of piety and morals in England and on the Continent, which, as he saw it, went hand in hand with the declension in pure doctrine. As he began work on his *History of Redemption* in 1739, he noted sadly that the "principles on which the power of godliness depends are in great measure exploded," and those who support vital piety are "commonly looked upon to be crack-brained and beside their right mind." Never before had there been such apostasy, such scoffing and ridiculing of the Gospel, as was now taking place in England, "the principal Kingdom of the Reformation." Arminianism had not only superseded Calvinism in the established church, but was rife among dissenters as well, and now this lamentable state of affairs had been transported to New England.[33]

Edwards knew of Taylor's books and influence some time before he worked out his rejoinder. It is barely possible that as early as 1743 he had read Taylor's *Key to the Apostolic Writings with a Paraphrase and Notes on the Epistle to the Romans*. On a sheet of newsprint bearing that date Edwards had scribbled some ideas on the subject of original sin, in the course of which he refers to Taylor's *Key*.[34] In his letter to John Erskine, dated August 31, 1748, Edwards not only thanked the Scottish divine for his gift of Taylor on original sin and the *Key*, but he specifically stated that he has not heard of the *Paraphrase*, which normally circulated as part of the *Key*. "I am ex-

[30] *A Defense of the Doctrine* . . . , 4, 69, 128.

[31] Bellamy's letter is bound with the writings of Webster, Clark, and Chauncy in a volume bearing Webster's title as given above, Yale University Library, 14.

[32] *Works of President Edwards* (1829), I, 613.

[33] See *Works of Edwards* (Worcester ed., 1808), II, 304–306, 311–312.

[34] *Princeton University Chronicle*, XV (Winter, 1954), No. 2, 76–77. I am indebted to Professor Thomas A. Schafer for calling this item to my attention.

ceedingly glad of these two books of Taylor's." Had he known of the latter, he owned, "I should not have been easy till I had seen and been possessed of it." By this time he had borrowed and read Taylor's book on original sin, and now expresses his gratitude at possessing a copy of his own.[35] In a letter of July 7, 1752, Edwards thanked Erskine "for the account you give me of Mr. Taylor's writings and of the things which he is doing to propagate his opinion." Erskine's melancholy report on Taylor's success abroad moved Edwards to conclude gloomily that "things are going down hill so fast and truth in religion both of heart and practice are departing by such swift steps that I think it must needs be that a crisis is not very far off."[36]

The nemesis of Taylor also appeared in the course of Edwards' quarrel with Solomon Williams over qualifications for communion. To his *Misrepresentations Corrected and Truth Vindicated* Edwards appended a letter to his former flock at Northampton in which he pointed out that Williams' views coincided in several ways with Taylor, whose scheme of religion "seems scarcely so agreeable to the Christian scheme as the doctrine of many of the wiser heathen." If his former parishioners accept the false ideas of Williams, he warned, they will have fallen in with "the strange opinions of Mr. Taylor," whose conception of Christianity "utterly explodes the doctrines you have been formerly taught." He went on to recall that even before his departure "Arminianism and other loose notions of religion and Mr. Taylor's in particular began to get some footing among you."[37] In the preface to his own work on original sin, he observed that "no one book has done so much toward rooting out of these western parts of New England the principles and scheme of religion maintained by our pious and excellent fore-fathers."[38]

Taylor's influence having spread abroad for some fifteen years, it was high time an effective antidote was administered. During the year 1756 Edwards assembled his notes into *The Great Christian Doctrine of Original Sin Defended; Evidences of its Truth produced and Arguments to the Contrary Answered.* By May 26, 1757, the writing was completed, and later in the same year it went to press. Edwards was to see a few of the first printed pages, but he died before the first edition appeared in 1758.

IV

Edwards determined that Taylor's *Original Sin* should be thoroughly nullified. Not without reason he claimed to have "closely attended to that piece in

---

[35] *Works* (1829), 251, 265.

[36] *Ibid.*, 497.

[37] *Ibid.*, 495; IV, 546 ff., 601.

[38] Edwards, *The Great Christian Doctrine of Original Sin . . .* (Boston, 1758), XI. All quotations in the text are taken from the first edition.

all its parts and endeavoured that no one thing there said . . . should pass unnoticed."[39] Yet this was not simply to be a quarrel between himself and Taylor. He made clear at the outset that his treatise was a general defense of the doctrine, rather than "merely as an answer to any particular book." Taylor had conveniently provided a broad target for Edwards' comprehensive purpose, because his works brought together the most representative viewpoints of the liberals. To crush Taylor, therefore, was to confound the mind of an age whose romanticized conception of man was being accepted as sober truth.

Edwards' treatise showed few marks of literary excellence. It was rather a methodical crunching of his opponent's position, to prove that all men do sin and have done so since the beginning of time. Strictly considered without any interposition of divine grace, human nature shows its true inclination by expressing itself in a variety of circumstances in profligate evil. Universal history, Scripture, and even Taylor's admission that wickedness had widely prevailed among heathens and Christians furnished evidence for Edwards' doleful thesis. Even when compared to savage animal life, humankind comes off badly: "No creature can be found any where so destructive of its own kind, as mankind are."[40] The enormous effort which has been expended by God and men to control vice, and the apparent futility of these labors show that the stark fact of human depravity cannot be blinked.

Taylor had never denied that sin was a prevalent and vile affair, but he raised an embarrassing question concerning evidence for the universality of sin. Generalizations about all mankind, past and present, he maintained, went beyond proof. If one has not counted heads, how can one be sure that all men are or have been sinful? Furthermore, how can one ever delve into the secret recesses of the human heart, where sin resides, and bring forth convincing evidence? Taylor's point was not that these investigations had not been carried out, but rather that in principle they could not be carried out.

Edwards was not at his best in meeting this gambit. He allowed, for example, that although he had not seen a thousandth part of the Indians of North America, or ever looked into their minds and hearts, he had sufficient reason to judge that there "were not many good philosophers" among them. And since Taylor had delivered universal judgments about mankind, the argument could be turned back upon himself. Furthermore, if men be "not sufficient judges" of this whole matter, yet "God is sufficient, and his judgment . . . determines the matter."[41] Whereupon Edwards spattered his pages with quotations and references from Scripture to settle the point.

---

[39] *Ibid.*, XII.
[40] *Ibid.*, 75.
[41] *Ibid.*, 66.

If Taylor wished to dispute further about the evidence for the universality of sin, let him consider the universal fact of death, the divine punishment for sin. As no one has escaped or will escape death, it follows that all have been and are sinners. Although Taylor had not overlooked the problem of death, his optimism surmounted the grim fact by discovering great benefits in it. God had thereby effectually weaned men from vanity, excited them to sober reflections, and induced moderation of appetite.[42] Ever looking to the bright side, Taylor suggested that by abbreviating life, God had reduced the time and opportunity for sinning![43] Edwards scoffed at this tenderhearted, unscriptural way of reading the evidence. Perhaps, as Taylor had maintained, afflictions and death are beneficial to training up humanity, but, Edwards asked, when men need such "sharp medicines," how can one escape the conclusion that they are diseased of spirit?

> If any thing can be a proof of a perverse and vile disposition, this must be a proof of it, that men should be most apt to forget and despise God when his providence is most kind, and they should need to have God chastise them with great severity, and even to kill them, to keep them in order.[44]

For Edwards, the decisive argument for the universality of sin lay in his conviction that a savior was needed in the Christian plan of salvation. If men were as innocent or as capable of doing the will of God as Taylor held, what need would there be for Christ's coming? If men are not sinners deep in their hearts, why are they called to a thoroughgoing repentance, rather than summoned to increased exercises of their free wills? If men do bring themselves into a bondage too strong to be overcome by their own efforts—and Taylor admitted they do—then this evil must be accounted as "necessary." But since, as Taylor had argued, "necessary evil can be no moral evil," it followed that there was no evil from which to be saved, and no savior was needed![45]

In meeting the charge of the universality of sin, a favorite response of the liberal was to suggest a tally-keeping procedure by which men's good deeds were balanced by his evil deeds. This way of reasoning, it was urged, gave fair place to notable virtues among men, and eliminated the dark views of Calvinists. A fair estimate of human nature, Turnbull contended, acknowledged "the prevailing innocency, good nature, industry, felicity, and cheerfulness of the greater part of mankind at all times."[46] And Taylor argued that

[42] *Ibid.,* 125, 126, 171 f.
[43] Taylor, *op. cit.,* 67 f., 237.
[44] Edwards, *op. cit.,* 126.
[45] *Ibid.,* 296.
[46] *Ibid.,* 3.

"we must not take the measure of our health and enjoyments from a lazar-house, nor of our understandings from Bedlam, nor of our morals from a Gaol, nor of this passion from harlots and debauches."[47] Nothing seemed fairer.

Edwards, however, was not content to rest his case on a moralizing arithmetic, since he refused to identify sin simply with actual deeds. Deeds certainly are evidences of the sin that courses through humankind, but its nature lies deeper in the very core of the self, where a relish and taste for the divine is lacking. Sin was not simply a certain quantity of evil deeds strung along the neutral strand of the personality, among which were interspersed about an equal number of good deeds. Sin is a persistent failure to enjoy and cleave to the glory of God for its own sake. Sin is a propensity or condition of personality, and therefore operates in a different dimension from that of good or bad deeds. To suppose the addition or subtraction of good and evil acts gives a true indication of man's state is as ridiculous as to suppose that a ship which sails more hours on the water than it takes to sink is accounted a serviceable vessel.[48]

To make perfectly clear the enormous disproportion between specific good or evil deeds, on the one hand, and sin on the other, Edwards reached back to an argument developed by Anselm, and one which he himself had used extensively in his imprecatory sermons.[49] The true nature of sin is not to be estimated by comparing man with man, but by recognizing that man the finite has acted disobediently and hatefully against God, the Infinite Being. Man has thereby contracted an infinite debt which he as a finite being cannot recompense by any number of good deeds. His punishment must also be infinite to fit the magnitude of his demerit. An infinite sin incurs an infinite debt, and, an infinite debt, an infinite punishment. The excellency of the object, God, against which sin is committed, not the nature of the subject, man, determines the enormity of sin. If this be the case, all talk of man's good deeds is prattle; they are simply disproportionate to the infinitely distressing state in which man is placed before deity.[50] Or as Edwards put it in a homely analogy, to continue to insist on the value of one's good works is like the wife who "though she committed adultery, and that with the slaves and scoundrels some times, yet she did not do this so often as she did the duties of a wife."[51]

Now if all men do indeed unfailingly fall into an abyss of corruption, there

---

[47] Taylor, *op. cit.*, 77.

[48] Edwards, *op. cit.*, 28.

[49] *Cur Deus Homo,* I, 21, in *St. Anselm* (tr. by Sidney N. Deane, La Salle, Ill.: Open Court, 1951).

[50] Edwards, *op. cit.*, 29 f.

[51] *Ibid.*, 33.

must be an adequate cause. "A steady effect argues a steady cause," says Edwards, and this theme he continued to rehearse throughout his treatise.[52] Taylor, of course, had never denied the presence of sin, and at times his language sounded quite Calvinistic. "The degeneracy of mankind," he admitted, "is a point never denied or doubted by any that I know of."[53] What he could not abide were total depravity, imputation of guilt, and predestinarian determinism. Therefore, he was forced to find another way than that of the Calvinists to explain the degeneracy of mankind. The favorite device of Arminians was to insist upon some form of freedom of choice which would at one blow get rid of all three of the offensive doctrines.

Taylor accordingly intoned repeatedly what was soon to be regarded as the common-sense view. Men are free to choose good or evil, but they have misused this God-given capacity by repeatedly surrendering to baser drives and appetites. For this misuse of freedom and its consequences, each man was singly responsible, and therefore each man's guilt was his own, just as Adam and Eve's guilt was properly theirs. On the other hand, "If we come into the world infected, and depraved with sinful dispositions, then sin is natural to us; and if natural, then necessary; and if necessary, then no sin."[54] If I am not free, I am not responsible, and all is of necessity; if I am free, no one except myself can corrupt me, and all talk of imputation of guilt goes by the board. Similarly, it is of no avail to talk of original righteousness, for righteousness, like moral evil, must also be the outcome of free choice.[55]

Edwards had laid the ax to this way of thinking in his *Treatise on the Will* in which he had demonstrated moral necessity to his own satisfaction and the dismay of the Arminians. Holding to his conception that the universality of sin pointed to a prevailing cause and propensity for it, Edwards now inquired as to how such universal exercise of sinfulness could be explained on the grounds of sheer freedom. "If the cause is indifferent, why is not the effect in some measure indifferent?" Since free will implies contingency in its most radical sense, no previous inclination affects a particular choice and nothing could be "more unfixed than that." And if this be so, how then can Taylor account for that universal and unswerving expression of sin, which he himself has admitted exists, and to which Scripture, experience, and reason clearly attest?

Taylor's free-wheeling interpretation of sin and virtue showed that he had little of Edwards' knack for metaphysical subtleties. Taylor supposed that

---

[52] *Ibid.*, 2 f., 17–21, 51, 101–105.

[53] Taylor, *The Scripture-Doctrine of Original Sin* . . . (3rd ed., 1746), *Supplement*, 30.

[54] Taylor, *op. cit.*, 20, 125, and *Supplement*, 144.

[55] Taylor, *Supplement*, 161–167.

virtue and vice, to be chargeable as such, proceeded from a free act of will. Edwards set forth the alternative thesis. Before a good choice occurs, there must be an antecedent "good disposition, temper, or affection of mind, from whence proceeds that good choice." And if this be the case, and Edwards was very full on the point, then there can be virtue antecedent to choice, and "therefore it is not necessary that there should first be thought, reflection, and choice before there can be any virtuous disposition." The essential principle is "not that principles derive their goodness from actions, but that actions derive their goodness from the principles whence they proceed."[56]

Once Edwards had Taylor caught in the cause-effect pattern of choices, the field was his. He needed only to refer to his *Treatise on the Will* to demolish thoroughly the Arminian position. Since the first choice is by definition first in a chain of choices, and a retreat to prior free choices is thereby ruled out, it must be that this first choice is necessary and, in the case at issue, also sinful. Moral evil or sin is then logically as well as experientially founded not on free choice but on a nature or underlying tendency which operates by necessity.[57]

Edwards was still confronted with the problem of the origin of Adam's fall. The Arminian-Pelagian view, he believed, persisted in misunderstanding the relation between the creation and the fall. It assumed, erroneously, that human nature was despoiled at the outset by God's having implanted some positive evil in men. But "there is not the least need of supposing an evil quality infused, implanted or wrought into the nature of man by any positive cause or influence whatsoever, either from God or the creature."[58] Mankind, Edwards argued consistently with Aquinas, was originally created with natural principles, appetites, and instincts, as well as conscience and reason, and in the case of Adam, with superior principles of "a spiritual holy and divine character," the exercise of which constituted righteousness, summarily identified as love to God. These supernatural principles were intended to exercise government over the natural principles. When Adam fell, these controlling principles were withdrawn, thus releasing the natural principles in an orgy of self-love, from which source confusion and evil stemmed.[59]

Sin thus originated from a privative cause. The essential thing, however, Edwards neglected to mention. The withdrawal of the supernatural principles followed the fall; it could not serve as an explanation of the fall. If there must be a cause for every event, if there is an inclination preceding every act of

---

[56] Taylor, *op. cit.*, 140 f.

[57] *The Works of Jonathan Edwards* (New Haven: Yale University Press, 1957), I, 340 f.; *The Great Christian Doctrine of Original Sin . . .*, 314 f.

[58] *Ibid.*, 317.

[59] *Ibid.*, 319.

will, how does it happen that natural principles left to themselves have been so created as to break out in a disorderly manner? Edwards finally fled to the shelter of sheer mystery.

> The first arising or existing of that evil disposition in the heart of Adam was by God's permission; who could have prevented it if he had pleased by giving such influences of his spirit as would have been absolutely effectual to hinder it; and whatever mystery may be supposed in the affair, yet no Christian will presume to say that it was not in perfect consistence with God's holiness and righteousness, notwithstanding Adam had been guilty of no offense before.[60]

The role of deity in the origin and continuation of sin was a serious problem, since God's moral as well as his metaphysical attributes were now at stake. Edwards repeatedly insisted that no positive influence of God had corrupted men, but was he not the author of sin, since he was the creator of all? Taylor and the reader were referred to his full treatment of this charge in the *Freedom of the Will.* There his answer was as straightforward as could be asked.

> If by "the author of sin," be meant the sinner, the agent, or actor of sin or the *doer* of a wicked thing . . . I utterly deny God to be the author of sin. . . . But if by "the author of sin," is meant the permitter or not a hinderer of sin; at the same time, a disposer of the state of events . . . for wise, holy and most excellent ends and purposes . . . I don't deny that God is the author of sin.

With a defiant flourish he added:

> I don't deny, that God's being thus the author of sin, follows from what I have laid down; and I assert, that it equally follows from the doctrine which is maintained by most of the Arminian divines.[61]

After all, the Arminians admit that sin continues to flourish, so it must be God permits sin, and yet is not the author of it in any positive way.[62]

The doctrine of original sin was especially distasteful to Enlightenment views because it appeared that both Adam's sin and guilt had been passed on to succeeding generations. Taylor incessantly pounded home the irrationality and monstrous implications of this view. Sin and guilt are nontransferable attributes of individual persons, he claimed. Adam's sin and guilt cannot be imputed, since they belong only to him and to no one else. Nothing could be more intolerable to clear reason and moral sense than the idea that a man living centuries ago could implicate in his evil unborn persons of the eighteenth century. Adam does not stand for the human race, and to be punished

---

[60] *Ibid.*, 330–332.

[61] *The Works of Jonathan Edwards* (New Haven: Yale University Press, 1957), I, 399.

[62] *The Great Christian Doctrine of Original Sin* . . . , 321.

for his failure, in the performance of which posterity had no responsibility, and of which it had no knowledge, is a hideous perversion of justice.

From Scripture, the authority to which Taylor himself appealed, Edwards showed that God had dealt with Adam as a "public person, and as the head of the human species, and had respect to his posterity as included in him."[63] Humanity—all the humanity there was at the time—was compressed into Adam, so in his sin all sinned, argued Edwards, but he went further to explain patiently to the outraged Taylor in what respects mankind was constituted in identity with Adam, and why, as he put it succinctly, "The sin of the apostasy is not theirs merely because God imputes it to them; but it is truly and properly theirs, and on that ground God imputes it to them."[64]

Some things in certain respects are "entirely distinct and very diverse," but in other views they may be seen as "united by the established principles of God." Locke had suggested that identity largely consisted in sameness or continuity of consciousness in a person, but Edwards, after thinking over Locke's helpful idea, decided that the British empiricist had not told the whole story.[65] Memory, after all, does not operate by itself; it is constituted by God like all finite, dependent being, to function in accordance with his will. Memory is part of self-identity, but lest an Arminian beg off from sin and guilt on the grounds that he has no memory of Adam's sin, Edwards delved to a deeper metaphysical explanation of identity.

A created object is dependent for its existence on some antecedent cause. Its cause must lie either in an "antecedent existence" of its substance or in the power of its creator. It cannot be due to its own antecedent state, because what existed a moment before is only a passive entity and not an active power. Nor can any cause produce effects in a time or place where it does not exist. "In point of time what is past entirely ceases when present existence begins; otherwise it would not be past."[66] Coexistence in time or space is impossible as an explanation of cause-and-effect relations. "The prior existence can no more be the proper cause of the new existence in the next moment or next part of space than if it had been in an age before . . . without any existence to fill up the intermediate time or space." Only one conclusion remains. "The existence of created substances in each successive moment must be the effect of the immediate agency, will, and power of God."[67]

---

[63] *Ibid.*, 184, 327.
[64] *Ibid.*, 350.
[65] *Works of President Edwards* (1829), I, 680 f.
[66] *The Great Christian Doctrine of Original Sin* . . . , 341.
[67] *Ibid.*, 341. The similarity of Edwards' argument to that of Malebranche and even Whitehead is noteworthy, but his reworking of the argument in the manuscript shows dependence only on Locke.

What bearing does this metaphysical excursion have upon Edwards' interpretation of imputation? The world and all that is therein depend from moment to moment upon God's creative powers, and whatever oneness or identity is found in that world is the immediate production of the divine will, whereby "these successive new effects" are made to be one, because he communicates to them "like properties, relations, and circumstances"; and this arrangement Edwards called an arbitrary constitution, wherein all depends on nothing but the divine will. "In this sense the whole course of nature, with all that belongs to it, all its laws and methods and constancy and regularity, continuance and proceeding is an arbitrary constitution."[68] Identity depends, then, upon God's sovereign constitution, and the sheer fact of this ordering of affairs is what "makes truth in affairs of this nature."[69]

Whereas Taylor had assumed that causation at a distance, from Adam to posterity, was an unintelligible idea, Edwards had skillfully shown that if one takes seriously God's sovereignty as a perpetual creation of each moment, then there was no need to assume that Adam caused sin and guilt in his posterity. He and they were identical by divine constitution. When he fell, they fell, and man's present vile state is nothing more than a recapitulation, an extension of the first fall.[70] Sin and guilt are theirs, and therefore rightfully imputed to them.

Edwards might establish the unity of Adam and his descendants on sophisticated metaphysical grounds, but there remained a troublesome ethical problem. The kinds of arrangements which Edwards and the less ingenious schemes of Calvinists had argued for, in Taylor's opinion were not fair to men, who had thereby been penalized before they ever began the race of life. But Edwards calmly pointed out that God's scheme was not only just, but in fact, originally held possibilities for the greatest benefits to mankind. Everything at the outset had been in favor of a happy outcome. Adam knew that the eternal welfare of his progeny depended upon him, that he possessed the full powers of manhood, and the promise of an eternal, happy life. Nevertheless, he spoiled it all by disobedience. Thus the same plan by which God purposed to pour unimaginable blessings upon mankind had now become the vehicle by which sin continued to course through the human race. One might regret the results, but it was incomprehensible to Edwards that anyone should impugn God's righteousness for having established the system.

What of the disastrous ethical consequences presumed to follow upon acceptance of a doctrine so defamatory of human dignity and discouraging to

---

[68] *Ibid.,* 345.
[69] *Ibid.,* 346.
[70] *Ibid.,* 328 f.

all moral effort? On this Taylor rehearsed nearly all the arguments against original sin with which contemporary defenders of the doctrine have had to cope.[71] In sum he contended that belief in original sin encourages "all manner of iniquity"; it negates men's efforts for their own reformation and that of the world; it discourages a proper humiliation, cheerful obedience and love to God, and prompts men to treat one another with contempt and hatred. With this vilification of human nature, human dignity is surrendered, and immorality is left to abound.[72]

Opinions like these Edwards scored as childish. He remarked sarcastically that there are some "who are so very delicate (to say no worse) that they can bear nothing but compliment and flattery," and pointed out that it is a poor demonstration of friendship for one's fellow men to gloss over the extreme peril in which they stand. In fact, to disown sin and guilt, instead of leading to benign feelings for one's fellows, leads in the opposite direction, to pride and ill will. Understood correctly, the doctrine begets humility and compassion, for it "teaches us to think no worse of others than of ourselves."[73] Nor can there be any denial of human dignity. "No contempt is by this doctrine cast upon the noble faculties and capacity of man's nature or the exalted business and divine and immortal happiness he is made capable of."[74] True, as he elsewhere stated, "We are the highest species with the lowest excellencies,"[75] but when viewed against the background of divine grace and mercy, man may hope for a glorious fulfillment and a transcendent dignity, beside which the paltry virtues of the Pelagians pale.

V

Edwards' faithful supporters granted him the laurels of victory for having routed Taylor and his ilk. However, judged by the waning enthusiasm for Calvinistic perspectives in the remainder of the eighteenth century, and the proportional rise in acceptance of liberal views, Edwards' treatises on the will and original sin had failed. Religious and ethical opinion continued to swing away from what were regarded as depressing and unworthy estimates of human nature. Some who had read Locke on government were brashly talking of political "rights" and "freedoms" rather than "duties" and "responsi-

---

[71] Cf. Emil Brunner, *Man in Revolt* (tr. by Olive Wyon; Philadelphia: Westminster, 1947), 273–276.

[72] Taylor, *The Scripture-Doctrine of Original Sin . . .* (3rd ed., 1746), 139, 169, 258, *Supplement,* 75.

[73] *The Great Christian Doctrine of Original Sin . . .* , 370.

[74] *Ibid.,* 369.

[75] Harvey G. Townsend, ed., *The Philosophy of Jonathan Edwards* (Eugene, Ore.: University of Oregon, 1955), 241.

bilities." And Locke on the mind, on whom Edwards had drawn, was now no match for Locke on the rights of man. Edwards had been speaking to generations who had begun to learn that human determination, self-confidence, and native acquisitiveness could thrust the American frontier westward. He was debating with a colonial clergy who had managed to identify themselves intellectually with that urbane clerical group in England whose study windows looked out upon pleasant gardens as "rationally" laid out as they dreamed themselves to be, and whose view was seldom darkened by a vision of the bloody edge of an expanding British empire, where precious little of the sweet reasonableness and generous virtue they had lavishly attributed to mankind was discernible in the horrors of border warfare. The calm, rational posture adopted by men of this stripe owed as much to their distance from such sights as to their superior wisdom. In Edwards' opinion, men like Taylor would neither bear to look at the evidence for a depraved human estate, nor follow the arguments built thereon wherever they led. The conclusion reached, they simply denied the evidence or repudiated the logic on the grounds that the conclusion offended the sensibilities of an enlightened generation.

The terms "human dignity," "moral freedom," "reason," and "virtue" never were successfully woven together into a tight logical combination by the liberals, but they provided effective rallying cries for the battle against Calvinism. Human dignity was supposed to depend upon virtue, and virtue in turn upon responsibility; responsibility could rest upon no other foundation than that of moral freedom. If this be the case, there could be no place in an enlightened man's philosophy for moral necessity or an inevitably corrupted human nature. But for Edwards, this rendering was simply off the mark. The dignity of man was not to be identified with the achievement of moral virtue. Dignity was grounded on God's constitution, whereby even as a sinner man was honored and given dignity by virtue of the deep and significant business he had with his Creator. It was not a dignity to be bargained for with deity by accepting human responsibility on condition of freedom of choice; nor was it a dignity contingent upon the virtuous decisions of certain individuals, while others who failed to choose virtue were to be held in contempt. Humanity was one in both sin and dignity. Surely, as Edwards saw it, human dignity rested on more solid grounds than those found in the fumbling and transient moral and spiritual achievements of a mankind which in spite of its undeviating self-exaltation continued to hate, lust, and deceive, and which failed to honor God for his own glorious nature. He pointed to a self-deception characteristic of men, in which they mistakenly supposed their approval of the ideals of freedom and virtue and reason was tantamount to the achievement or possession of these values, but whose conduct proved instead that freedom was lost by the enslavement to the finite, their virtue contradicted by their immoralities, and their reasons securely bound to the interests of a prideful self.

Although the controversy over original sin sputtered on through the nineteenth century, by the early twentieth century it was out of vogue. It came to the center of the theological stage again in the mid-twentieth century, in the renaissance of Protestant theology. Reinhold Niebuhr could even say that the sinfulness of man "is one of the best attested and empirically verified facts of human existence."[76] However, none of the moderns wishes to state the doctrine in the form in which Augustine, Calvin, or Edwards left it. As represented by Niebuhr and Brunner, the modern case for original sin is a less tightly reasoned case than that offered by Edwards. Rather it is an uneasy compromise between anti-Pelagian and semi-Arminian views. It is insisted that sin is universal; all men sin; they are in "permanent revolt."[77] Furthermore, "the whole person is sinful"; there is no aspect of the person, define him as we will, that is exempted from sin.[78] Accordingly, sin is inevitable, although neither Brunner nor Niebuhr admits it is necessary.[79] Man is responsible for his sin; there is no being or condition "outside of man" upon which responsibility can be placed.[80] But responsibility is unthinkable without freedom. Without it there could be no sin, for sin is posited by personal acts which by definition are grounded in freedom.[81]

Stated in this bald fashion, without additional qualifications, the position obviously lacks coherence. Taylor would doubtless be gratified to learn that freedom is once more linked with responsibility, thus turning aside Edwards' hard-won arguments on causality, for as Niebuhr puts it, "The whole crux of the doctrine of original sin lies in the seeming absurdity of the conception of free-will which underlies it."[82] For Edwards, however, the word "seeming" could well be omitted, precisely because neither Brunner nor Niebuhr can make clear what kind of freedom is consistent with men's universal, total, and inevitable sin, which at the same time permits free decisions to be made between sin and no sin. Some capacity of man must be exempt from bondage

---

[76] *Handbook of Christian Theology* (New York: Meridian Books, 1958), 349.
[77] Brunner, *op. cit.*, 169.
[78] *Ibid.*, 150; Niebuhr, *op. cit.*, I, 183.
[79] Niebuhr, *ibid.*, I, 242, 251 ff.; "To-day our slogan must be: No determinism, on any account!" Brunner, *op. cit.*, 257.
[80] Brunner, *ibid.*, 116; Niebuhr, *op. cit.*, 251, 255.
[81] Brunner, *op. cit.*, 258; "Man is most free in the discovery that he is not free. . . . The final paradox is that the discovery of the inevitability of sin is man's highest assertion of freedom." Niebuhr, *op. cit.*, 260, 263; cf. also 96, 124, 134, 164, 185, 197 f., 251.
[82] *Ibid.*, 243.

to sin! In Edwards' terminology, a "steady and universal propensity," operating as moral necessity established by God, can alone explain how men universally in fact do sin. Such an effect cannot be due to what Perry Miller has called a "discontinuous series of private decisions,"[83] and the logician asks: If there is freedom, where are the negative instances which show some human beings have chosen not to sin, and whence comes that freedom to turn to God, which in a state of sin Brunner counts an impossibility?[84] In fact, how can responsibility be justified unless there is a unity between the self and its willing known as moral necessity? Moral necessity is not identical with fate or some form of compulsion operating from outside the human frame. As F. J. E. Woodbridge commented on Edwards' doctrine of the will, "We should recognize . . . that necessity is not some exterior fate compelling events, but the actual linkage which the events disclose in their existence, and that they do disclose such linkage wherein they exist in the mind as well as in nature. . . . The causes of volition, whatever they may be, do not affect its voluntary aspect or destroy the function of the will any more than the causes of life destroy the functions of life."[85] Man is in the willing, and for that reason alone can be held responsible. Nor can he find freedom by postulating a realm of "freedom of spirit" which transcends God's order of things in nature and reason, Niebuhr to the contrary notwithstanding.[86] Attempts to escape moral necessity by appeals to remorseful feelings for evil done or to the knowledge of the inevitability of sin do not in the slightest budge men off the grounds of moral necessity, since necessity also is experienceable, and recognition of inevitability cannot be equated with freedom from that same inevitability. Mere recognition of a state of affairs does not establish freedom from the state of affairs itself.

Brunner and Niebuhr may have made the doctrine of original sin more palatable than did their forerunners, but it is doubtful that they have made it more convincing intellectually than did Edwards, working with the tools at his disposal. Those who hold to the sovereignty of God seldom have been able to make an airtight case for original sin, which did not at last reflect upon the moral attributes of deity.

The recurrence of the doctrine in contemporary theology admittedly owes little to Edwards' treatise. Niebuhr, for example, writes extensively upon the subject without a single reference to the Stockbridge theologian. Yet original sin and sinfulness come to the foreground in theology and modern literature

---

[83] Miller, *op. cit.*, 278.
[84] Brunner, *op. cit.*, 274.
[85] *Edwards Bicentenary Volume* (Andover: Andover Press, 1904), 55.
[86] Niebuhr, *op. cit.*, I, 96.

because they express a profound dimension of human experience. Doctrinal niceties may not fully capture that experience, but as Perry Miller remarks, "The doctrines of original sin, of the depravity of man, and of irresistible grace, were not embraced for their logic, but out of the hunger of the human spirit and anxiety of the soul."[87] Perhaps because of its very nature, sin can never be placed within any coherent scheme, or as Brunner puts it in his cryptic way, "Only he who understands that sin is inexplicable knows what it is."[88] In this light Edwards did no better nor worse than our contemporaries.

[87] Miller, *The New England Mind: The 17th Century* (New York: Macmillan, 1939), 22.
[88] Brunner, *op. cit.*, 132.

The Christology of Paul Tillich

ROBERT E. CUSHMAN
Dean, Professor of Systematic Theology
The Divinity School
Duke University
Durham, North Carolina

I. Tillich and Schleiermacher

The Christology of Paul Tillich is implied in much of his writing but is fully articulated in the Second Volume of his *Systematic Theology*. Indulging a judgment of appreciation, I would venture the view that what is offered in this volume, in respect to both the predicament of man and his restoration in Jesus as the Christ, is in dialectical acumen, boldness of conception, and comprehensive cogency worthy to be compared with the massive dogmatic achievement of Schleiermacher's *Der christliche Glaube*. Indeed, I would judge that the performance rivals Schleiermacher's Christological *tour de force* as it also, in some important respects, recalls it.

It is well understood that Schleiermacher made the uniqueness of Jesus rest upon the fact that, unlike all other men, the God-consciousness in him developed with such unvarying and constant vitality that the "sensible self-consciousness" was, at every moment of his experience, subordinated to the "higher self-consciousness." This unexampled attainment in the life of Jesus, understood as the actualization of potentiality inherent in "the original perfection of the world" but unattained apart from Jesus Christ, made him the historical agent of redemption for those who were prompted to participate with him in the quality of his God-consciousness. Thus, while Jesus Christ "is not removed from the circle of our humanity" by natural endowment, he is removed by *attainment,* that is by actualization of potentiality, however astonishing and inexplicable that actualization may appear in view of the universal domination of the sensible self-consciousness in the experience of all other men.

Tillich's Christology is reminiscent of Schleiermacher's, yet with significant differences. It is like Schleiermacher's in its pivotal and fundamental assertion "that in *one* personal life essential manhood has appeared under the conditions of existence without being conquered by them."[1] Here is the same emphasis upon uniqueness and the uniqueness of victory. Here is a comparable emphasis upon the actualization of potentiality, that is, "essential manhood." Here also is implied a similar insistence upon the true humanity of Jesus who is, at the same time, known by faith, and only by faith, as the Christ. Here is, furthermore, an acknowledgment that the peculiar significance and dignity of "Jesus as the Christ" rests upon his reversal of the universal human condition, called "estrangement." And, finally, here is a like recognition that this "actualization" is not a normal expectancy but the contrary of all "opinion derived from man's existential predicament and all expectations imaginable on the basis of this predicament."[2]

On this last point, Tillich is emphatic in a way that goes beyond Schleiermacher. And yet the domination of the sensible self-consciousness, as described by Scheiermacher, is so invariable and universal as to make the triumph of the God-consciousness in Jesus an extremely improbable expectation when conceived as progressive actualization of essence.

This difficulty suggests that Schleiermacher, like Tillich, and in Tillich's own terminology, should be regarded as "existentialist" rather than as "essentialist" in standpoint. Yet this can hardly be credited, for Schleiermacher most certainly stood firmly within the metaphysical tradition of Hellenic-Christian culture. Unknown to him was the existentialist phenomenology that renders essence discontinuous with existence or, as in Heidegger, banishes it altogether. In Schleiermacher's tradition, existence participates in essence as the condition of its being and is possessed of the permanent potentiality of manifesting ever more fully its supervening essence. And, while essence remains ultimately transcendent, it is, nevertheless, residually immanent by participation. Thus Schleiermacher, for all his radical analysis of the human plight, remained ontologically an "essentialist," if an ambiguous one, in his Christology. This is undoubtedly what constitutes both an element of difference and an element of advance, if one will, of Tillich over Schleiermacher. Certainly this is so in Tillich's intention. For, when Tillich states that it is "the basic Christian assertion that essential God-Manhood has appeared

[1] Paul Tillich, *Systematic Theology,* Volume II: *Existence and the Christ* (Chicago: University of Chicago Press, 1957), 94. Cf. pp. 98, 126, 159, 169. The present paper aims to be a critical analysis of its subject in the style and manner learned by the author under the guidance of Robert Lowry Calhoun, who portrayed his method not only in lectures but in the guidance of the author's doctoral dissertation. The present study is a revision of a paper presented for the reply of Professor Tillich at the 1959 Annual Meeting of the American Theological Society.

[2] *Systematic Theology* II, 92; hereafter noted as ST II.

within existence and subjected itself to the conditions of existence without being conquered by them," he is to be credited with something like faithful representation of the *scandalon* of the Gospel. Faith's assertion that Jesus is the Christ is veritable paradox, signifying a "new reality" which is contrary to, and offends, all creditable human expectation in view of man's predicament "under the conditions of existence."[3] On this, it may be conceded, and owing to his "essentialism," Schleiermacher was not equally emphatic.

II. The Way from Essence to Existence

As a basic motif running through all of Professor Tillich's work, and especially Volume Two of the *Systematic Theology,* is the important distinction between existence and essence and the undeviating view—taken to be at once Christian and Platonic—that man's existence entails defect of essence. This standpoint is contrasted with both the Enlightenment and the Romantic contention that existence is "the progressive actualization of essence."[4] Tillich adopts as his own what he describes as a common view entertained by modern existentialist interpretations of man's existential situation: man is in "a state of estrangement from his essential nature."[5] This is taken to be fully comparable with the Christian symbol of the Fall; indeed, existence and fallenness are coincident.[6] Existence is estrangement; it is "falling away from what man essentially is." Yet the loss is not complete, for Tillich would agree with Plato that, though fallen, man "still stands in his potential or essential being."[7]

This universal state of humanity under the conditions of existence is regarded by Tillich as "an original fact" to be apprehended and acknowledged through proper self-knowledge and existentialist analysis. It is not, however, rationally explicable nor logically necessary as it would be in essentialist ontology. Thus Tillich declares: "the way from essence to existence is 'irrational.' . . ."[8]

Whatever may be the total import of this dictum, its immediate implication seems to be at least threefold. In the first place, it opposes the fundamental error of "essentialism," the sort of ontology for which existence—whether nature or history—is understood as the logically necessary and progressive actualization of essence. In this view, "essence actualizes itself in existence,"[9]

---

[3] ST II, 98, 92.
[4] ST II, 23.
[5] ST II, 25.
[6] ST II, 44.
[7] ST II, 22.
[8] ST II, 3.
[9] ST II, 24.

with two consequences—a loss of divine transcendence (naturalism) and a perverse inability to acknowledge the actuality of defect, evil, and estrangement in existence. Secondly, the assertion that "the way from essence to existence is 'irrational' " enables Tillich to separate himself, in ontology, in a decisive way from his otherwise close association with Spinozistic monism. The defect of that monism was twofold. It was deterministic and therefore had no place for "finite freedom." It was illogical because, while it affirmed *reality* and *perfection* to be one and the same thing, it had to acknowledge that, in the spectacular case of man, there was reality but at the same time manifest deficiency of perfection. Spinoza's monism was deductive and therefore rigid. In it, essentialism and existentialism were in unresolved conflict. In the third place, the proposition that the way from essence to existence is irrational is offered as a necessary alternative to Biblical theistic personalism which derives existence from the divine fiat, the Word.

This last goes against Tillich's grain on several counts: First, it encounters the perennially troublesome fact of the "coincidence of creation and the Fall." Tillich is convinced and says that "actualized creation and estranged existence are identical."[10] In such a case, on the ground of Biblical personalism, God would be to blame. Secondly, Biblical personalism "places the created outside the creative ground" and so "denies any participation of the creature in the creative substance out of which it comes." "The doctrine of creation through the word denies any substantial participation of man in God. It replaces substantial identity by personal distance."[11] Herein is a basic issue beween Christian theism and Tillich's ontological monism. Tillich's preference for monism is, in the last analysis, a judgment of the larger significance of Being over Value in ontology. In Biblical theism, the way from essence to existence is rational in so far as it is mediated by the eternal Word, although it is irrational in so far as it is grounded in the absolute and sovereign gratuity of Grace.

Creation by way of the gratuity of Grace would perhaps commend itself to Tillich were it not that he has committed himself to ontological monism and therefore to a radically symbolic view of all personalistic Biblical language. His monism, furthermore, prompts him to come at the absolute gratuity of Grace by way of the "ground of Being" rather than by way of a personal Creator. For a personal God is disqualified as Deity, in any case, in virtue of standing over against his world as *a* being, with respect to whom all relations must be external and transitive rather than immanent and who himself could

---

[10] ST II, 44.

[11] *Biblical Religion and the Search for Ultimate Reality* (Chicago: University of Chicago Press, 1955), 36.

not be conceived save as under "the conditions of existence." Furthermore, it should be remembered that, despite the apparent reach of "ontological reason"—a reach which seems considerably shortened in Volume Two—this reason does not attain to a standpoint exceeding the proposition that God is "power of Being" which is "eternally creative."[12]

Epistemologically speaking, the resulting issue seems to be that the knowledge of God is severely limited, not by the traditional gap between the finite and the Infinite, but by virtue of a residual phenomenalism in epistemology which, while not eluding the influence of Kant, owes most to phenomenalism of the Husserlian and Heideggerian type. The fundamental standpoint of existentialist phenomenalism seems to be a "phenomenological analysis," sometimes styled "ontological," of the categorical schema congenitally belonging to man-and-his-world.

The beginning and, perhaps, the end of ontology in this context is human self-understanding. It is what may perhaps be called *Menschanschauung* as contrasted with *Weltanschauung*. Now this is not only residually Kantian, but, in Tillich's usage, it means that the jumping-off point of philosophical and theological reflection is something called existence—man's existence (i.e., history, *Geschichte,* as distinguished from nature, *Natur*). And this existence is immediately knowable as fallen or estranged existence, albeit the acknowledgment of its estrangement also carries with it, as its obverse side, an immediate awareness of essential Being from which "existence" is presently estranged. And this latter awareness is a function of "ontological reason" apperceiving its Ground. From the convergence of these two forms of consciousness ensue, on the one hand, guilt and anxiety, and, on the other, "ultimate concern." Accordingly, the way to conceive the Ground of ontological reason is not as *a* Being over against but as Being *in* which, although I am estranged from it, I nevertheless participate on pain of being nothing at all.

In such a conception of things two results follow: The first is that any "transcendence" of the ground of Being will not be definable by way of external relations but by way of something we may call *abstraction.* And this abstraction or attenuation of Being is precisely the Fall or the estrangement of existence from its Ground, or of man from the eternally creative power of Being. Thus Tillich says: "The freedom of the creature to act against its essential unity with God makes God transcendent to the world."[13]

So we come at last to the explanation of the proposition that the way from essence to existence is "irrational." This means that the outcome (i.e., exist-

[12] ST II, 174.
[13] *Biblical Religion and the Search for Ultimate Reality,* 74 f.

ence or finite freedom) is never deducible from a prior known principle, that is, from what we may call the side of essence. Existence or finite freedom is acknowledgeable as an "original fact" that confronts honest phenomenological analysis of the human situation under the conditions of existence.[14] If we are asked to specify its ground, we are obliged to locate it in what we *know,* thus, not in God but in man. We locate its exactly in man's estrangement as the exercise of his finite freedom. So, says Tillich, "we can answer the question of how the transition from essence to existence is possible in terms of 'freedom,' which is always in polar unity with destiny." Nature, says Tillich, "is finite necessity, God is infinite freedom, man is finite freedom."[15] And later he declares: "Man is responsible for the transition from essence to existence because he has finite freedom and because all dimensions of reality are united in him."[16]

This last is really amazing. Phenomenological analysis now apparently permits us to assert that man *as* finite freedom is the cause or occasion of creation, even of nature; for not only does the world participate in man's estrangement and fall, but Tillich never, seemingly, unlearned the teaching of Schelling that man is always with a world, perhaps *his* world.[17] Again and again, throughout his writings, Tillich reminds us that the centered self is always together with its world.[18] This seems innocuous enough until one recognizes the provenance of the doctrine and begins to suspect that *Natur* is swallowed up in *Geschichte,* that is, man's estranged existence.

Tillich's hypothetical phenomenological analysis of man's fall into existence from essence is, nevertheless, most instructive.[19] As a fertile interpretation of the Biblical creation images it has permanent value. The main point for us here is that the exercise of finite freedom issues in estrangement in so far as centered personal being makes itself—in its exercise of power through freedom—its own center rather than the infinite Freedom (God) of which it is an "image."[20] This introversion issues in "unbelief," "concupiscence," and "*hubris.*" "But the freedom of turning away from God is a quality of the structure of freedom as such."[21] The resistibility of Grace, to use traditional language, is then the possibility of transition from essence to existence; but *why* it is resisted is insoluble mystery. It is irrational. Not unlike Kant's "radical evil," it is as much a surd as it is a palpable fact. "Only he who is

[14] ST II, 44.
[15] ST II, 31.
[16] ST II, 40.
[17] ST II, 41–44.
[18] ST II, 36, 49.
[19] Cf. ST II, 33–39.
[20] ST II, 33.
[21] ST II, 32.

the image of God has the power of separating himself from God."[22] For Tillich, we must leave the matter there.

The second consequence of the above epistemological analysis is that estrangement entails both ultimate concern and the universal and everlasting quest for reconciliation with essence or with the ground of Being. Together, these are the universal questing for the Christ. The Christ is the New Being and is "the expectation of a transformed reality."[23] The New Being is "essential manhood" appearing under the conditions of existence, or estrangement, without being conquered by them. This is the possible impossibility; and, therefore, it is *the* paradox of Christian faith, since it affirms that, in and with Jesus, "essential God-Manhood has appeared within existence and subjected itself to the conditions of existence without being conquered by them."[24]

III. Paradox: The Way from Existence to Essence

We are now in position to give direct attention to Tillich's Christology. It is masterful in its handling of contemporary problems relating to the historical Jesus. It is magisterial in its basic simplicity of structure. It is remarkably coherent with its own presuppositions in its treatment of the two-nature theory. And it approximates the truth, I believe, in its theory of atonement. At this point I would strongly concur with Tillich's basic insistence that the person of Christ cannot be separated from his work and vice versa. One may agree that his person, or being, is manifest through his work, and that his work is an "expression" of his being.

A. The Paradox: The Divinity

But now what of paradox? It is this: it is the assertion of Christian faith that Jesus of Nazareth who is called "the Christ" is actually the Christ.[25] It is the assertion that the New Being is really manifest with him, i.e., the New Being is "a historical fact," contrary to all other facticity. In *one* personal life it is *uniquely* true that essential manhood has appeared under the conditions of existence without being conquered by them. It comes to this: "The paradoxical character of his being consists in the fact that, although he has only finite freedom under the conditions of time and space, he is not estranged from the ground of his being."[26] So Tillich affirms the true humanity, and so

[22] ST II, 33.
[23] ST II, 88.
[24] ST II, 98.
[25] ST II, 97.
[26] ST II, 126.

he accents the *scandalon* and the paradox. But there is also the "deity," for *the Christ* is also uniquely participant in essential being. In Jesus, the gap between essence and existence is overcome.[27] In him, there is also essential God-Manhood—existence no more estranged from essence.[28] Essential manhood represents not only true man to man but God to man.[29] Moreover, as man is responsible for the transition from essence to existence, so "essential manhood" makes transition from existence to essence by the power of the eternal Spirit within him, although it is true that "the divine Spirit is nothing other than God dynamically present in us."[30] Reconciliation, then, is of grace in some sense, although it is a sort of resident grace, perhaps, that somehow expresses itself in free affirmation of God rather than in self-affirmation. And, while it is "essentially" possible, it is also "existentially" so impossible as to be paradoxical in its manifest actualization. For finite freedom is otherwise always exercised for estrangement. Thus, as the Fall remains a mystery, so also does restoration as represented in Jesus as the Christ. And, since reconciliation remains a mystery impenetrable, we are relieved of the alternatives of either attributing it to man (Pelagianism and humanism) or to God (theistic determinism). Once more Tillich's ontological monism evades an impasse both ancient and vexing!

While *existentially* Jesus as the Christ is "impossible," that is, paradoxical, *essentially* Jesus as the Christ is the actualization of "potentiality." "Potentiality is the power of being which, metaphorically speaking, has not yet realized its power."[31] But it is the "destiny" of the power of Being to realize its power, and the symbol of this destiny, the aspiration of the ages, is "the Christ." It is the character of existentialist thought to affirm that there is no rational way from essence to existence or from existence to essence. There is only an abyss, a "leap" over the "gap."[32] Here, perhaps, is Tillich's version of "the infinite qualitative difference" of Kierkegaard. And, since we view Jesus as the Christ only from our side, "under the conditions of existence," we can only properly say that he is an impossibility.

This would suggest a very "high" Christology, indeed, since—to use Schleiermacher's language—Jesus as the Christ cannot be *derived* from the sphere and potentialities of our humanity; only, with Tillich, this is emphatically so whereas Schleiermacher's residual "essentialism" does not exclude the likelihood that Jesus as the Christ is the finite resultant of the

[27] ST II, 118 f.
[28] ST II, 100.
[29] ST II, 94, 159.
[30] *Biblical Religion and the Search for Ultimate Reality*, 69.
[31] ST II, 20.
[32] ST II, 24.

progressive realization of essence without leap or gap. However, the Achilles' heel of Tillich's existentialism is his ontological monism from which vantage point it is possible, despite all assertion of "leap," "gap," and "risk," to view Jesus as the Christ from the *other side,* that is, from the side of essence and as the actualization of essence. Admittedly, this actualization is not logically necessary nor ever predictable because of the stark reality of finite freedom. Yet this is always a matter of perspective; and, since finite being exists by participation in essence, from the standpoint of essence it is the "destiny" of finite being to participate fully in essence. That this outcome is both assertable and not assertable stems from the fact that men stand always in existence under the conditions of existence so that the privileged *assertion* is that Jesus as the Christ is, for all they can know (the philosopher who knows better is an exception), simply and plainly a paradox.

But paradox is what is contrary to opinion (*doxa*), not what is contrary to knowledge (*episteme*).[33] From the standpoint of knowledge, Jesus as the Christ is actualization of essence through freedom. This to be sure does not wholly banish the mystery. It is, however, relocated on the boundary between eternity and time, between essence and existence. Somehow, in Jesus, finite freedom so concurred with the power of Being, dynamically present with him as the Spirit, that he *was* Jesus as the Christ. It is from the existential standpoint as such—a standpoint which Tillich's ontological monism does not permit him in the final analysis to hold unambiguously—that Tillich's Christology appears now higher and then, again, lower. Very reminiscent of Schleiermacher's formula for Jesus the Christ are Tillich's words concerning Jesus as the Christ: "He has man's existential nature as a real possibility, but in such a way that temptation, which is the possibility, is always taken up into the unity with God."[34]

B. The Event: the Humanity

It is wholly evident that Tillich intends to shun docetism and to maintain the Chalcedonian balance of humanity and deity respecting Jesus as the Christ. For him "the doctrine of the two natures raises the right question but uses wrong conceptual tools."[35] Tillich is emphatic that Christianity is based upon the affirmation that "in *one* personal life essential manhood has appeared under the conditions of existence without being conquered by them."[36] So crucial is this statement that it deserves repeated notice. Tillich intends to

[33] ST II, 92.
[34] ST II, 147.
[35] ST II, 142.
[36] ST II, 94.

take the historic fact seriously. We do not have to do with "the Christ" but with "Jesus *as* the Christ," it would seem.

Does this mean, then, that Christology is dependent upon the historical Jesus? The well-known answer is no, and it is fortunate that this is so, since Tillich pronounces the quest of the historical Jesus to be a "failure." The effort to find the facts about Jesus, "the reality behind the coloring and covering traditions," to find "the empirical truth about Jesus of Nazareth," all this proved finally futile. It was a failure because it issued in "more or less probable results" which are the limit to which scientific historical criticism can attain.[37] Secondly, it was a failure in that, while it undertook to provide a minimum of reliable fact as a safe foundation for Christian faith, authentic Christian faith does not rest upon determinable empirical facts as such but upon "ecstatic" appropriation of fact which *involves* the receiver quite as much as the fact. Thus, so far forth, Tillich adopts a view similar to that of Bultmann in the famous Preface to the latter's book *Jesus*—a view, however, which Tillich holds with even greater consistency and rigor. The mere probability in every "conjectural-constructive" picture of Jesus of Nazareth as formulated by historical criticism is no real deterrent of faith; and, like John Knox in his *Criticism and Faith,* Tillich declares reassuringly that "historical research can neither give nor take away the foundation of the Christian faith."[38]

Nevertheless, Tillich asserts that "if the factual element in the Christian event were denied, the foundation of Christianity would be denied." And he avers, moreover, that "methodological skepticism about the work of historical research does not deny this element."[39] How so? It is really quite simple and virtually identical with Knox's solution. Tillich redefines "the Christian event." It is, he declares, "the fact which is called 'Jesus of Nazareth,' and the reception of this fact by those who received him as the Christ." The receptive side, he says, is "as important as the factual side; and only their unity creates the event upon which Christianity is based."[40] The truth is that the receptive side is more important. Meanwhile, the fact upon which Christian faith is based has not been denied but redefined, yet redefined in such a way as to render its factuality radically ambiguous.

On such a definition of "the Christian event," it is at once obvious why the historico-critical effort to recover the empirical man Jesus is a matter mainly of indifference to faith. The empirical man Jesus, as such, was never

[37] ST II, 101 ff.

[38] ST II, 113. Rudolf Bultmann, *Jesus* (Tübingen: J. C. B. Mohr, 1926); John Knox, *Criticism and Faith* (New York and Nashville: Abingdon, 1957), 21.

[39] ST II, 107.

[40] ST II, 97, 99.

the basis of faith. From the beginning, the basis of faith was a certain fruitful confluence of fact and mode of appropriation of fact—interpretation, and appropriative appreciation. Thus, Tillich says, "Christianity was born, not with the birth of the man who is called 'Jesus,' but in the moment in which one of his followers was driven to say to him, 'Thou art the Christ.' "[41] Here we have something like the strict correlation of "sign-event" and *"ecstasis"* of Volume One. It is, indeed, an instance. Fact-and-reception are, in indissoluble unity, "the Christian event."

This position has many important entailments. One is, as Tillich asserts, that Christ and his Church are "necessarily interdependent."[42] This phrase means what it implies: Christ and his Church are indissolubly united in such a way as to be mutually constitutive through reciprocal "participation."[43] There is, therefore, no possible discontinuity between Jesus as the Christ and those who participate in him as the power of the New Being. Thus, the problem of the knowledge of Jesus as the Christ is solved not theoretically but existentially. It is solved in the moment of appropriating faith.

But when we examine this knowledge, just exactly what is it knowledge of? Careful analysis of Tillich's words on page 114 of Volume Two provides the answer and with it, for the first time, I think, the meaning of the cryptic formula, "Jesus *as* the Christ," also becomes plain: The answer is that faith, the faith of the community which participates in the power of the New Being, is the sole datum of knowledge we have of Jesus as the Christ.

Now, we are in a position to take in the full import of Tillich's assertion that "faith cannot even guarantee the name 'Jesus' in respect to him who was the Christ."[44] That alone which faith is able to guarantee is the New Being (i.e., the community of faith), and why? Because "its own existence is identical with the presence of the New Being." Tillich continues: "Faith itself is the immediate (not mediated by conclusions) evidence of the New Being within and under the conditions of existence." And so he concludes, "No historical criticism can question the immediate awareness of those who find themselves transformed into the state of faith."[45] Manifestly not—but skepticism about the historical Jesus is overcome by a monistic idealism in epistemology, that is, by the subject of knowledge swallowing the object. Object ("fact") and subject ("reception") have indeed become a "unity"; and the

[41] ST II, 97.
[42] ST II, 99.
[43] ST II, 114.
[44] ST II, 107.
[45] ST II, 114. Cf. also the related statement: "The appearance of the Christ in an individual person presupposes the community out of which he came and the community which he creates." ST II, 136.

new unity is, it would seem, Jesus *as* the Christ, but that is, seemingly, a mode of transformed existence possessed in the Church. In faith, the community of the New Being has become its own object. The problem of the knowledge of Jesus-Christ has not been solved but "transcended." We are offered not Jesus-Christ, but the faithful community, i.e., "Jesus *as* the Christ." And, in a manner of speaking, ecclesiology has swallowed up Christology.[46]

Admittedly, Tillich seems disposed to retain a modicum of epistemological realism in his very use of the concept *analogia imaginis*. This is an analogy of likeness between the faith "picture" of Jesus and the actual-original personal life.[47] But this, I think, is a surviving gesture of deference to a realism which has scanty basis in the determinative logic of his argument. If Tillich's words are to be credited as meaning what they say, and they usually are, then he means to indicate that "the Christian event"—while it may perchance presuppose an indeterminable "X" called "Jesus"—is really indistinguishable from the *event of faith,* the New Being in Christ, and that it is with this alone that we have to deal in "Christology." It appears, moreover, that this event of faith is what Tillich has called all along "Jesus *as* the Christ."

We arrive at a result, Christologically speaking, not unlike that of Bultmann and Knox. The problem of the knowledge of Jesus Christ is solved by a *tour de force,* namely, by relocating and, therewith, redefining the object. It becomes, with Bultmann, "the resurrection faith," with Knox, "a new kind of life" in the Church. The latter is very close to Tillich's meaning when he speaks of participation in the power of the New Being. The relocation mentioned above might also be called the relocation of the miracle. We shall shortly turn to the point that the miracle for Tillich, like Bultmann, is taken from the sphere of *nature* and located in "existential" *history*. This is, in the sphere of freedom and destiny, *ecstasis* and "sign-event," and of individual man-and-world.

Meanwhile we can hardly avoid the conclusion that, despite Tillich's contention that "in *one* personal life essential manhood has appeared," he has given no *evidence* of it. The "unique" is always a particular and never a universal, but he has not only been unable to identify the particular; he has in principle foreclosed upon this line of investigation and pointed us to the reality of transformed existence in, presumably, the Church. He has, moreover, adopted an idealistic or phenomenological standpoint in epistemology

---

[46] For a quite similar outcome in critical analysis of the Christology of Professor John Knox, see "Christology or Ecclesiology? A Critical Examination of the Christology of John Knox," by the author, in *Religion in Life* (Autumn, 1958), XXVII, No. 4, 515–526.

[47] ST II, 115.

that approximates to the view that reality is what it is known as. In such a view, the suspicion can never be put down that the subject determines and is constitutive of the object. Ontological monism and epistemological idealism were always twins.

In Christology, the result can hardly be other than what, indeed, I think it is in Tillich's thought: Tillich's doctrine of "the Christian event" is, if not an ontological, at the least a methodological, docetism. The reason is simple: under his guidance we have been finally deprived of the *particular,* even assuredly of the name "Jesus," and we have been offered in its place "the power of the New Being," by participation in which the Church, or the individuals who constitute it, live under the conditions of existence without being wholly conquered by them. Tillich, for all his efforts, has been able to show us only "the Christ," the universal, and the Church as the participating particular. "Methodological skepticism" seems to entail methodological docetism! Tillich can assert the true humanity, but apparently he cannot, on his own principles, vindicate it. So it appears also that the way from existence to essence cannot locate, distressing as it might be to some, a valid instance. Tillich may say, as he does, that "Jesus is the Christ for us, namely, for those who participate in the historical continuum which he determines in its meaning."[48] But the grounds upon which it may be said that Jesus *determines* its meaning have most surely not been provided. Rather they seem to have been dissolved methodologically.

C. The Incarnation: Location of the Miracle

The hard point of any Christian theology is the point at which the theologian determines to locate the mystery, that is, the miracle of the divine act of redemption—where Grace restores nature, to use an earlier terminology. It is, I suppose, not erroneous to say that the bulk of classical theology located the mystery in something called the Incarnation, signifying thereby a divine incursion that evokes the response of both nature and history. By way of contrast, it is worthy of observation that contemporary existentialism in theology avoids the concept of Incarnation generally or, as with Tillich, favors the view that the "flesh" which received the Logos signifies not material substance "but stands for historical existence."[49]

Bultmann is well-known for his contention that the Incarnation is "an eschatological event and not a datable event of the past."[50] He also declares

[48] ST II, 101.
[49] ST II, 95.
[50] Bultmann, in *Kerygma and Myth,* Vol. I, ed. by Hans W. Bartsch. Trans. by Reginald H. Fuller (London: S.P.C.K., 1953), 209.

that "we cannot speak of an act of God without speaking simultaneously of our own existence."[51] The latter dictum—regarded as revolutionary in some circles and fundamental, no doubt, to the somewhat pretentious program self-styled as "the new hermeneutic"—is scarcely more than a truism within classical Greco-Christian epistemology. While this is fully understood by Tillich, his own view shows some little accommodation to Bultmann's position. Accordingly, Tillich indicates that Christianity did not *begin* with a natural event. Rather, presupposing the highly probable facticity of Jesus, the origin of Christianity requires the ecstatic appropriation of this fact.[52] In other words, the originative event involves and invokes our existence in *ecstasis*. The invocation of existence, in the case of Jesus, was an unpredictable and irrational ecstatic event through which other men participate through him in the power of the New Being that he manifests. Thus, in some measure, reconciliation with the power of Being replaces estrangement and reverses the direction of existential being and history toward its diviner Ground.

For Tillich, Incarnation considered as incursion and evocation of nature is both absurd and irrelevant. It is absurd because the Divine Being is not over against nature, but is the very power of Being, if we may say so, of the universe. Therefore, "God's presence and power should not be sought in the supranatural interference in the ordinary course of events but in the power of the New Being to overcome the self-destructive consequences of existential estrangement in and through the created structures of reality."[53] But, secondly, Incarnation, as incursion into nature, is irrelevant because it does not touch the world at the root point of its fallenness. That point is man who *is* finite freedom and who, enigmatically, has so exercised his freedom as to incur for himself estrangement from the ground of Being. The world as "finite necessity" is fallen only in so far as it participates in man's estrangement.[54] And it does participate because *man* is never without a world! With Tillich, the priority of man to the world is certainly at least a methodological priority. It is not clear whether it is also an "ontological" priority; it is clear that world has ambiguous status in Tillich's thought especially if we take at face value Tillich's assertion: "Actualized creation and estranged existence are identical."[55] On such a view, and with the express teaching that "man is responsible for the transition from essence to existence because he has finite freedom,"[56] it is hard to resist the impression that "world" is so dependent

---

[51] *Ibid.*, 199.
[52] ST II, 97.
[53] ST II, 161.
[54] ST II, 39–41.
[55] ST II, 44.
[56] ST II, 40.

upon man as to possess, in the traditional meaning of the words, no independent ontological status.

With such a "'phenomenological" dissolution of the "world," it is hardly necessary to give credence to the older categories of *ousia* and *substantia* with their denotations; and it is not to be expected that Incarnation would any longer need to be regarded as evocation of "substance" or incursion into nature. Such incursion would be both irrelevant and perhaps even pointless. Instead, Incarnation must pertain to "historical existence" which is human existence under the conditions of existence, namely, estrangement.[57] Incarnation will mean the establishment of "the essential unity between God and man under the conditions of existence. . . ."[58] And, further, it will mean, reminiscent of Hegelianism, that "in Jesus as the Christ the eternal unity of God and man has become historical reality."[59] Any interpretation of the Word *becoming* flesh which entails a transformation of nature or seeks to find in connection with the manifestation of the New Being a constellation of natural factors exceptional to "the ordinary course of events," or as concomitant with the New Being, is untenable "supranaturalism." This, "Protestantism" is said to reject in favor of Incarnation as *actualized essence* as over against mere *potentiality*.[60]

There are a few final words to put. It has been shown that Tillich has been unable to establish the claim that "the eternal unity of God and man" has in fact become a historical reality because he has not been able to identify the historical and unique instance in which this is so. His "methodological skepticism," coupled with his indifference toward the empirical man Jesus, has blocked the way. At most, he has been able to point to a tradition and a community that lives by faith in the New Being. In the *ecstasis* of that community, the New Being may have a habitation and a home, but this is the only discernible locus of the Incarnation I find him able securely to identify.

And now I would suggest that there is no other possible alternative open to Tillich in view of his "existentialist" interpretation of "world." World is ontologically ambiguous and is, on close examination, a rather insubstantial bridgehead for the Incarnation. But if the Incarnation is not in the objective order of nature but only in "existential" history, as the sphere of existential estrangement, then there is no possibility of identifying its point of approach or manifestation. Identification would be possible only if history is, in fact, so grounded in nature that the shock of the divine incursion could, extending its

---

[57] ST II, 95.
[58] ST II, 110.
[59] ST II, 148.
[60] ST II, 149–150.

traumatic influence, leave traces and evidences in the nature in which Jesus' personal history is embedded. In short, the Incarnation remains a spiritual (i.e., ecstatic) event in the life of the community and hardly more unless the divine initiative entails a transformation of nature and the realm of objectifiable history embedded in it.

History, it seems, has no *place* and therefore no identity unless it is grounded in nature. Likewise, without nature, the Incarnation hovers insubstantially in the air without actualization because it can have no particularity. And, without particularity, uniqueness is impossible and unthinkable. And Christianity once more, as in times past, verges upon Gnosticism. Thus, classical Christian theology was not content to locate the mystery merely in history—certainly not in subjective individual "existential" history as such. The location of the mystery entailed nature as its temporal matrix—the condition *sine qua non* of its actuality, identifiability, and efficacy. Thus, the Incarnation was not a "sign event"; it was miracle attributed, not to the irrationality of the divine act, but to the unsearchable riches of the sovereign gracious divine Will. In it, the incursion of the divine power evoked the response of both nature and history or of *history as embedded in nature,* and, accordingly, the transformation of history entailed *eo ipso* some discernible alteration of nature.

Tillich's alternative to this proves to be the nonidentifiability of "the New Being" that, as "essential manhood," appeared under the conditions of existence. Tillich's Christology is, thus, inherently docetic and tendentiously gnostic.

Two Models of Transcendence: An Inquiry into the Problem of Theological Meaning

GORDON D. KAUFMAN
Professor of Theology
The Divinity School
Harvard University
Cambridge, Massachusetts

The philosophical challenge to Christian theology used to be put as a question of truth: Does God exist? Can God's existence be demonstrated? Both parties to this dispute agreed that the question itself was meaningful and important, both seeing that significant consequences followed for human affairs depending on which alternative was taken to be true. There never was, of course, agreement as to whether philosophical proofs and disproofs on this matter were conclusive, and some took them to be irrelevant, but no one doubted that the actual point at issue—the existence or reality of God—was of great moment.

There is, however, a philosophical question which, because it is logically prior, is more fundamental than this one. This is the question whether words like "God" or "transcendent" or "wholly other" in fact have any specifiable meaning at all. Though formerly the theologian could ignore, if he chose to do so, the philosophical quandary about God's existence on the ground that for him the knowledge of God was rooted elsewhere than in natural knowledge, he dare not today ignore the philosophical question about the meaning of theological terms and statements. For in this case the words and sentences being called into question are precisely his own. It is not about some *philosophical* concept of God that the question of meaning is asked: it is whether *any* concept of a "transcendent" reality has any intelligible meaning.[1]

[1] Alfred J. Ayer long since made the point that the contemporary linguistic challenge to theology is far more radical than earlier epistemological challenges: "It is important not to confuse this view of religious assertions with the view that is adopted by atheists, or agnostics . . . our view that all utterances about the nature of God are nonsensical,

I

The extreme complexity of the problem is not difficult to show. Since the significant question about any statement is whether it is *true,* it seems evident that a statement is *meaningful* only if we can specify what experience or procedure, or sort of experience or procedure, would either verify or falsify it. The way in which the logical positivists developed this criterion of meaning is subject to many sorts of criticism,[2] but these do not concern us here, for we are interested primarily in the positive point being made: that meaning always involves reference to concrete experience, and unless the experiential referent can be located, the meaning of a term or sentence cannot be demonstrated; it is an empty abstraction.

Now many theological or religious sentences claim to be *speaking about* some reality (e.g., God), and thus have their meaning in reference to that reality. In so far as this is the case, all theories of theological meaning which tend to reduce it to ways in which a community speaks,[3] to the attitude or stance of the self,[4] to imperatives to act,[5] or to emotional feelings of well-being,[6] are inadequate to the problem at hand. If this is all that can be said about theological terms or statements, then clearly the views of most religious folk, and the explicit claims of most theologians, that they are speaking of the ultimate reality with which we have to do, are false. We must attempt to

---

so far from being identical with, or even lending any support to, either of these familiar contentions, is actually incompatible with them. For if the assertion that there is a god is nonsensical, then the atheist's assertion that there is no god is equally nonsensical, since it is only a significant proposition that can be significantly contradicted. . . . The point which we wish to establish is that there cannot be any transcendent truths of religion. For the sentences which the theist uses to express such 'truths' are not literally significant." (*Language, Truth and Logic,* 2nd ed. [London: Gollancz, 1946], 115, 117 f.)

[2] For some discussion of some of the problems see Ayer, *op. cit.,* preface to the 2nd ed.; Carl G. Hempel, "Problems and Changes in the Empiricist Criterion of Meaning," *Revue internationale de Philosophie,* IV (1950), 41–63; J. O. Urmson, *Philosophical Analysis, Its Development Between the Two World Wars* (Oxford: Clarendon, 1956); Geoffrey J. Warnock, *English Philosophy Since 1900* (London: Oxford University Press, 1958). Other discussion of these problems together with a useful summary of the history of the linguistic analysis of theological language in recent philosophy will be found in Frederick Ferré, *Language, Logic and God* (New York: Harper, 1961).

[3] E.g., Willem F. Zuurdeeg, *An Analytical Philosophy of Religion* (New York and Nashville: Abingdon, 1958).

[4] E.g., R. M. Hare, "Theology and Falsification," in Antony G. N. Flew and Alasdair MacIntyre, eds., *New Essays in Philosophical Theology* (London: S.C.M. Press, 1955), 99–103; and "Religion and Morals," in Basil Mitchell, ed., *Faith and Logic* (London: Allen & Unwin, 1957), 176–193.

[5] E.g., Richard B. Braithwaite, *An Empiricist's View of the Nature of Religious Belief* (Cambridge: Cambridge University Press, 1955).

[6] E.g., J. J. C. Smart, "The Existence of God," in Flew and MacIntyre, *op. cit.,* 28–46.

see, then, what, if any, experiential referent can be located for certain key theological terms.[7]

The character of the problem becomes evident as soon as one inspects closely such terms as "God" or "transcendence." For, in contrast to words like "chair" or "run," the experiential referents for which can easily be designated, God is not an object of experience. There is no place in experience to which we can point (literally or figuratively) and say this is what we mean by the word "God." On the contrary, God is defined as that being who *transcends* us and our world and whom we can never catch in a concept. God is known, we are told, only as he chooses to reveal himself; he is not accessible to us at our will, subject to our beck and call. We can experience all manner of finite beings and realities, and we develop linguistic symbols to designate them and bring them in some measure under our control. But God is the infinite reality, the ground of every experience, to be identified with none. Every other word can be given its meaning by pointing to some dimension or aspect or level or object of experience, but this is never possible with God. The new convert may refer the "warm feeling" in his heart to God, but God is not to be identified with this emotion; the biblicist may regard the words of the Bible as God's, but God himself is not paper and ink; the churchman may speak of God's presence among his people, but the religious community is not God; the moralist may be convinced that God speaks through conscience, but God is not simply a man's moral convictions. In each of these cases and all others the term God is used to indicate a reality that *transcends* the finite locus indicated; and one is theologically interested in this finite locus not for its own sake but only because of that reality which "transcends" it and "comes to us" through it.

It is theologically indispensable to distinguish God from every finite reality in this manner. As the Creator of the heavens and the earth—the source or ground or foundation of all that is—God cannot be identified with any particular reality which comes into being and passes away and is never its own ground; as the proper object of ultimate loyalty (faith) to which one can and

---

[7] Because theological statements claim to be *asserting* something to be *true,* it is doubtful that the problem of theological language can be resolved simply by recourse to the later Wittgensteinian view that the meaning of sentences is their *use* (see e.g., *The Blue and Brown Books* [Oxford: Blackwell, 1958], 4, 26, 65, 172 f.; *Philosophical Investigations,* trans. by G. E. M. Anscombe, 2nd ed. [Oxford: Blackwell, 1958], S 10–43). It is true, of course, that only *in their use* in actual theological or religious discourse will we be able to discover their proper meaning—and that whoever is not willing to make such an investigation has no right to discuss the problem of theological meaning—but inasmuch as these statements intend to refer to a reality beyond themselves their full meaning cannot simply be identified with their use.

should give one's whole being and whole life, God is to be distinguished from every proximate or penultimate value or ideal or being, for the latter are always related to certain *particular* interests or desires or needs of the self or society, and thus are only of relative and transitory interest and meaning. Indeed, to take such a finite and relative object as one's *god* is the very definition of idolatry: the whole Old Testament is the story of the struggle to overcome all such idolatries (both Hebrew and pagan) in the worship of the One High God, until at last Israel can see that to speak of God is to speak of the one who says: "I am the first and I am the last; besides me there is no god . . . I am the Lord, and there is no other" (Isa. 44:6; 45:5). The "radical monotheism" (H. R. Niebuhr) of Hebrew faith is significant precisely because it grasped the fact that every henotheism and idolatry fell short of genuine worship of God. God, to be God, must "transcend" everything finite.

The central problem of the meaning of theological language can now be summarized: (1) Referential terms or statements do not have their meaning simply in themselves: they gain meaning and content through their reference to something beyond themselves. Hence, the only way we can determine whether such a term or statement in fact has meaning is by locating its referent. If we can find nothing, that is, no item or locus in experience to which it refers, it must in fact be *empty of cognitive meaning* (and in this sense meaningless), however emotionally charged (and in this sense meaningful) it may be. (2) By definition the term "God" refers to that which transcends every finite experience and dimension of experience and can never be identified with any. By definition, therefore, "God" is not locatable in our world. "God is in heaven, and you upon earth" (Eccles. 5:2). (3) From these two premises it would seem to follow that the term "God" (and all cognate terms such as "transcendent," "revelation," "infinite," etc.) is in fact empty of cognitive meaning. *For how could any experiential evidence of any kind whatsoever bear on the question of the meaning of terms which refer to that which transcends all possible experience?* All statements using or implying such terms appear thus to be meaningless. Theology as a discipline claiming to speak of God would seem to be, then, an impossibility; either it in fact speaks of man and his world[8] or else it says nothing at all. *"Wovon man nicht sprechen kann, darüber muss man schweigen."*[9]

---

[8] Ludwig Feuerbach was the first to carry through this insight and to show in detail that all Christian theology could (and, as he believed, should) in fact be understood as misguided anthropology (see *The Essence of Christianity* [New York: Harper Torchbooks, 1957]).

[9] Ludwig Wittgenstein, *Tractatus Logico-Philosophicus* (London: Routledge & Kegan Paul, 1961), proposition 7.

II

It is evident that it will not be possible to show the meaning of theological terms in any ordinary way, for example, by indicating directly their experiential referent, for such a finite referent, as we have seen, is by definition ruled out. What, then, is to be done? We shall have to show that the meaning of words like "God" and "transcendence" is *similar* in some respects to certain types of ordinary meaning with referents in finite experience, and that these latter types of meaning can serve as *analogues* in terms of which the theological meanings can be apprehended. This means, of course, that even at best such theological meaning will always remain philosophically ambiguous and doubtful. For how can it be shown that the asserted analogy actually holds and is therefore justifiable? The skeptic on this point cannot be confuted. His position could be disproved only if one could in fact indicate the point or dimension of experience to which the word "God" necessarily applies, and this, by definition, cannot be done. What can be done is to show that this word, by analogy with certain other meanings, is at least intelligible, and that its meaningfulness, therefore, cannot be ruled out *a priori.*

It is clear that it is necessary to demonstrate this possibility of genuine (though only analogical) meaning if theology of any kind—confessional or biblical, systematic or philosophical—is to be possible, and if religious language is to be affirmed as actually saying something. If this cannot be done, the jig is up both with theology and faith. Inasmuch as this is a general *philosophical* task dealing with the very foundations of theology and faith, it can be regarded as the legitimate heir of natural theology for our time.[10] The old natural theology, which tried to prove the existence of God, has rightly been rejected by many from Hume and Kant to Barth on the grounds of the limitations of human knowledge and the transcendence and freedom of God. But precisely these limitations and this transcendence, we now can see, make it necessary to raise the question whether theological terms have any meaning at all. That question cannot be answered by the theological fiat that refers us to the self-authenticating character of revelation; it can be answered only through a careful philosophico-theological analysis which succeeds in showing that such words as "revelation" and "God" in fact are intelligible.

Our problem arises because in theology we seek to speak about that which

---

[10] Cf. I. M. Crombie: Natural theology's "function is, not to prove to us that God exists, but to provide us with a 'meaning' for the word 'God'. Without her we should not know whither statements concerning the word were to be referred; the subject in theological utterances would be unattached." ("Theology and Falsification," Flew and MacIntyre, *op. cit.,* 116.)

we cannot actually indicate, which transcends all possible experience. What sorts of analogies from within our experience could possibly be used to understand such language? What we need here is a *model* in terms of which the reality with which we are concerned can be imagined or thought. When we assert God's "transcendence" we are asserting *something specific* about God's relation to the world of our experience, but without a model in terms of which this can be grasped, there would be no way of distinguishing it from a bare "X." We need, then, a *model* of transcendence which is directly apparent in ordinary finite experience.

It is important that we understand just what is here being proposed. I am not going to attempt to show either that theological terms are in fact meaningful or what meaning they have. Such tasks as these, as we shall see, must be left to a positive theology which develops in a historical tradition. I shall simply try to indicate the place where theological terms fall on a logical map. All actual content or meaning must be otherwise supplied.[11] To accomplish our end it will be necessary to show that the concept of *transcendence* (of all possible experience) is intelligible. I will not seek to establish this by providing a *definition* of "transcendence" and then defending it, but rather by indicating points or dimensions of our ordinary finite experience which can appropriately be regarded as experiences of finite transcendence, and which, therefore, can be utilized as *models* for imagining, conceiving, and defining the transcendence in which theology is interested. (The word "God," we shall see, is a term which designates one particular concrete way of understanding this transcendence—a way which, incidentally, is especially congenial to Western, and, more specifically, Christian, theology.) Where, now, *within*

---

[11] It is to be noted that my proposal thus differs in important respects from Crombie's. For him "religious belief has two parents. . . . Its logical mother is what one might call *undifferentiated theism,* its logical father is particular events or occasions interpreted as theophanic. . . . Without the notion of God we could interpret nothing as divine, and without concrete events which we felt impelled to interpret as divine we could not know that the notion of divinity had any application to reality" (*op. cit.,* 111, 116). The difficulty with this (as can be clearly seen from the way Crombie develops the point) is that it suggests we know what God *is* apart from revelation, which only supplies predicates. As Barth has seen, this divides our knowledge of God into two pieces from two quite independent sources, and it is not at all clear how these two can be brought together. Even worse, a kind of "natural theology" really steals the show from "revelation" here, for the real meaning of the word "God" is supplied by Crombie's "undifferentiated theism." In the position I am trying to outline—a position rooted in what I call "the model of interpersonal transcendence" below—both of these difficulties are obviated, in that both subject and predicate of theological statements are derived from "revelation." All that our logical analysis can do is show the *possibility* that theological terms have meanings (analogically); but it would never have occurred to anyone to suggest this apart from the experienced meaning of a concrete revelation—in this respect Barth's view that with the knowledge of God actuality must precede possibility is certainly correct (e.g., *Church Dogmatics,* I, 1 [Edinburgh: Clark, 1936], § 2, 6).

concrete experience can we find a referent for the notion of "transcendence," that is, of that which *escapes* our experience and categories?

Our words, particularly nouns, generally are tools by means of which we control the various dimensions of our world. Each has its proper application to some aspect of that world, and its intelligibility, therefore, depends on our being able to locate at will its experiential referent. But this will be possible only if *our world*—at least that world about which we speak and think—*is directly or indirectly accessible to us.* For the world which science investigates, that is, the world of *objects of our sense perception,* this is of course the case, in principle at least. Such objects are known to us and thinkable by us only in so far as we are able in some measure to perceive them, and thus only in so far as they enter directly into our experience. Doubtless it is necessary for the scientist to postulate hypothetical realities (e.g., electrons) to account for all the subtleties of experience, but he is justified in doing so only if he can show that such hypotheses are required to give an adequate account of that which is in fact directly experienced. In this sense *all scientific objects,* though over against the knower, *are accessible* (*directly or indirectly*) *to the scientist through experience under his control.* If meaning, now, is understood according to a paradigm derived from this type of cognitive experience, some form of the verifiability criterion is to be expected, and all concepts referring to realities escaping our experience entirely will be excluded by definition as meaningless. It should occasion no surprise, therefore, that modern linguistic philosophy—heavily influenced by, and oriented toward, scientific knowledge as it is—should understand meaning in precisely these terms and therefore not be able to deal with the concept "transcendence."

However, a weighty assumption is being made when meaning is understood in this way, namely, that objective (scientific) experience is in fact the most important, or perhaps even the only, kind of genuinely cognitive experience, and that therefore it can appropriately provide the paradigm for all cognitive meaning. If it can be shown that there is another type of experience—equally common and inescapable and irreducible—in which cognitive meaning must necessarily be otherwise understood, then the universality of the scientific paradigm is undercut. Such experience in fact exists and is known to everyone, though, for certain historical reasons, it has not been given the philosophical attention afforded scientific experience. In the language dealing with the striving of the self for goals not presently accessible, and in that pertaining to the experience and knowledge of other persons, we are confronted with phenomena which cannot be adequately understood in terms of the (quasi-scientific) paradigm of meaning just outlined. It is these phenomena which provide concrete experiential loci, and thus *meanings,* for the concept of "transcendence."[12] Let us turn first to the peculiar character of our experience of other persons.

III

I do not intend here to enter into the contemporary discussion of whether genuine knowledge of "other minds"[13] is possible and if so how. Suffice it to say that that discussion is often based on the false premise that our knowledge of persons, like our knowledge of "things," is ordinarily or typically interpretation of and inference from sense data. But in fact, as a moment's reflection will show, though certain aspects of our knowledge of others are so rooted, the most important knowledge that we have of our friends (as well as our enemies)—that is, of persons as persons—is derived from *their acts of revealing or unveiling themselves to us when they communicate with us.* In this respect knowledge of persons is radically different from knowledge of objects. The latter knowledge depends exclusively on *what we do* to obtain the knowledge—perceive, infer, develop experimental testing procedures, etc. —and not at all on an act performed by the object known. But knowledge of persons depends quite as much on what *they* do—e.g., speak honestly and openly with us, or deliberately conceal from us how they feel—as on what we do.[14] Such knowledge arises out of the process of communication in which both knower and known actively participate, mutually revealing themselves to each other. Here another understanding subject provides us with, not mere sense data to interpret, but meaningful words and other gestures to understand, and it is through our understanding of his deliberate communication to us that we come to know him. This knowledge, then, arises out of a complicated *interpersonal* process involving the communicating, understanding, and

[12] To these two might be added the awareness that the "I" always transcends every given experience as its subject. However, precisely the elusiveness and unobservability of this "I" render all conceptions here highly problematical and therefore hardly suitable for the purpose of exemplifying and clarifying the already too obscure notion of transcendence.

[13] See, e.g., John Wisdom, *Other Minds* (Oxford: Blackwell, 1952).

[14] "All knowledge of persons is by revelation. My knowledge of you depends not merely on what I do, but upon what you do; and if you refuse to reveal yourself to me, I cannot know you, however much I may wish to do so. If in your relations with me, you consistently 'put on an act' or 'play a role', you hide yourself from me. I can never know you as you really are. In that case, generalization from the observed facts will be positively misleading. This puts the scientific form of knowledge out of court in this field. For scientific method is based on the assumption that things are what they appear to be; that their behavior necessarily expresses their nature. But a being who can pretend to be what he is not, to think what he does not think, and to feel what he does not feel, cannot be known by generalization from his observed behavior, but only as he genuinely reveals himself." (John Macmurray, *Persons in Relation* [London: Faber, 1961], 169.)

interpreting of meaningful symbols; its deepest root is not a (solipsistic) making of inferences from sense data, as much current epistemology portrays our knowledge of mere objects.

I cannot within the limits of this essay provide detailed analysis of this process of interpersonal knowledge. We are concerned here with observing only one point: that in so far as our knowledge of another self emerges within the process of communication, we are here encountering a reality which is, strictly speaking, beyond the reach and observation of our senses, which, therefore, must be understood in contrast with the ordinary objects of our (scientific and prescientific) experience. For interpersonal knowledge depends on the *other's act* and not simply my observation, that is, on something *intrinsically inaccessible* to me, something that I cannot at will make accessible. If we consider briefly what occurs in ordinary conversation, this will be clear. In speaking to someone, I *"throw" a meaning,* as it were, (I do not simply make a noise) out beyond the circle of my own world, to a personal center *transcending* my direct experience and not open to my view, but which I believe capable of apprehending my meaning. Only the other's body is visible to me, and thus within my world in the sense of being accessible to my experience, not the dynamic self with whom I am seeking to communicate, though I usually think of that self as somehow "in" the body confronting me. However, I put a question to the other precisely because the world accessible and open to me—and specifically, my direct experience of the other person—does *not* present me with the answer, and I must depend on the other self freely and honestly to respond to my query.

Our encounter with another self in the process of communication is thus an encounter with a reality *beyond* our reach and observation. We could not know this reality at all did he not choose to *reveal* himself to us from this beyond. For this reason the other self over against me is always *mystery* in some significant sense, always unknown (however well known), always transcendent of my world. The other self can, if he chooses, refuse to reveal himself to me at all, remaining almost completely out of my reach even though, of course, his *body* is directly at hand. Despite this inaccessibility, to speak of the other self as *real* and as experienced by me, in the moments he reveals himself, is certainly reasonable and proper.

The ordinary quasi-scientific sort of meaning cannot comprehend what is here involved: that I am related concretely and effectively to a reality which nevertheless escapes my experience and thus cannot properly be said to be a part of my world. (In this essay we are not concerned with understanding *ontologically* the peculiar character or structure of such "transcendent" realities, although that is a very important task indeed. Our interest must be confined to the mere locating of experiential referents in terms of which a concept of transcendence can be intelligibly developed.) In this experience-of-inaccessibility-except-in-moments-of-revelation we are provided with a model for the peculiar meaning of our word "transcendence."

IV

There is another dimension of the experience of selfhood to which the concept of transcendence can also be meaningfully referred. A self has the power to act. That is, a self is able to formulate objectives, to set them before himself as goals to be realized, and then to organize his life in such a way as to move toward and often to realize them. A large part—indeed, it could be contended, all—of our lives consists in just such teleological activity, directed and guided no doubt by a wide variety of values, goals, interests, and loyalties. In each case, however, the end sought clearly *transcends* the immediate present experience of the self as the goal or ideal toward which he is striving, but its significance for the self is none the less on that account. Indeed, it is precisely because the goal is not present, but is thus transcendent, that the self works toward it. This type of transcendence we can conveniently designate as "teleological" to distingiush it from the "interpersonal" transcendence which we have just considered.

Teleological transcendence is to be contrasted with interpersonal in a number of respects. For example, transcendence of the latter sort has a more absolute character than the former. The other self in certain respects forever escapes my grasp; even in moments in which he reveals himself to me, I am aware of a deep mystery beyond the revelation which I cannot penetrate. In goal-seeking activity, however, the transcendence is often only temporary. If I set myself the task of making a table, my objective transcends the *present* realities of my experience, but with the completion of the project the transcendence is overcome.

Of course, teleological transcendence can be much more enduring than this, as in the self's experience of striving toward the realization of ideal values like truth, justice, or beauty. Inasmuch as these objectives are never perfectly realized, they are experienced as always transcending the concrete world of our experience and thus eluding our grasp. This does not mean, however, that in its teleological activity the self sometimes experiences transcendence to be as "objective" as in interpersonal relations, although idealism has always supposed this to be the case. The goal of the self's striving, whether material or ideal, is always in some sense *posited* by the self as *his* goal. However much one might wish to maintain with the idealists that values "lure" us, the actual imagining or conceiving of the values, as well as the work involved in moving toward them, is entirely the activity of the self. In this sense the self's striving is always toward a reality contained *within* its world, at least its world of ideals.

In contrast, however, another *self* is over against me, not as a goal I project, but as a reality impinging on me. The other can and does speak and act toward me in ways completely out of my control and in no way dependent on my teleological activity. He reveals himself to me, or refuses, as he chooses. Doubtless my activity with reference to this other is often teleological—as when I deliberately seek to make another my friend—and thus teleological transcendence is involved here too, but the more fundamental transcendence here does not in this way depend on my activity; it depends rather on the fact that the other self is a reality forever outside my grasp, a reality with a life and activity of his own which becomes open to me only at his will. Precisely because the other self is himself an active power, he is *objective* to me in a way that my values and ideals—however significant they may be—can never be.

We have, then, two quite distinct models on which concepts of transcendence can be built, each rooted in living concrete experience, open and accessible to every man, each thus having "meaning."

V

Though I am not seeking in this essay to justify lifting either of these concepts out of its native habitat in order to use it analogically to speak of a reality transcending all possible human experience—that would be the task either of a natural theology (in the traditional sense) or of the positive exposition of some particular claim of revelation (i.e., dogmatic theology)—it is important to indicate here how diverse are the consequences for theology, depending on which model of transcendence one regards as the more fundamental.

If one makes teleological transcendence the model, one will come up with a theology of *being*. The ultimate reality will be that good "which moves [all other things but is] itself unmoved."[15] All finite reality will be viewed as necessarily grounded in this ultimate reality, and as, in turn, striving toward it. This final *telos* should not be viewed anthropomorphically any more than the objects of the self's striving are normally conceived as other selves: it can be viewed ethically as the ultimate good, aesthetically as perfect beauty, or

[15] Aristotle, *Metaphysics*, Bk. XII, 7

intellectually as being-itself or the ground of being or the absolute idea. Only when notions rooted in interpersonal transcendence are surreptitiously introduced is this ultimate reality conceived as personal, acting or loving, in short as "God" in anything like the Christian sense. "It is not that the Supreme reaches out to us seeking our communion: we reach towards the Supreme; it is we that become present."[16] Personalistic notions of ultimate reality, moreover, are usually viewed by theologians of this perspective as somewhat embarrassing anthropomorphisms, to be tolerated primarily because of man's "religious" needs (i.e., for subjective reasons) rather than because the understanding of reality requires it.[17]

On the other hand, if the theological model for the conception of the divine transcendence is rooted in interpersonal relations, a considerably different picture results. God's transcendence of our world and his independence of all our striving can be emphasized much more decisively, because here God is viewed as an independent agent capable of genuinely purposive and autonomous *acts* (not merely "activity"). Correspondingly, of course, the divine reality is viewed more anthropomorphically on this model, since in our finite experience only persons enjoy this kind of fully objective transcendence. Here, then, God, as a being who genuinely *acts* (in analogy with persons), is believed able to love and forgive, as well as punish and destroy, and knowledge of God results from his special act or acts of revealing himself; indeed, without such self-disclosing action no knowledge of him would be possible. Inasmuch as the term "God" carries precisely these personalistic connotations—rooted in religious experience and devotion—and is even used

---

[16] Plotinus, *The Enneads,* trans. by Stephen MacKenna, rev. ed. (London: Faber, 1956), VI, 9, par. 8.

[17] It will be observed that Paul Tillich's whole theological program rests on the model of teleological transcendence. Thus, the "method of correlation" with its view that human existence has a certain instability and thus inevitably poses certain questions driving us beyond the finite to its transcendent ground (*Systematic Theology* I [Chicago: University of Chicago Press, 1951], 61–66) is simply a reformulation of this model rooted in the self's striving. It should occasion no surprise, then, to find Tillich maintaining that the only literal statement which can be made about God is that he is "being-itself," all other statements, including specifically religious statements, being symbolic (*ibid.,* 238 ff.); nor is it surprising to discover that revelation for him is not so much the act of a personal being who transcends us, as an act in which the self transcends itself in "ecstasy" (111 ff.). Similarly, in the "traditional theism" of Eric L. Mascall, teleological transcendence is the determining model before which theological notions rooted in interpersonal transcendence must give way: "Certainly we must admit that, from the point of view of Christian devotion, the fact that God is Love is all-important. . . . But the attribute that is primary from the point of view of devotion may not necessarily be primary from the point of view of theology or of philosophy. For God has other attributes, such as power, wisdom and justice, and it does not seem possible to derive these from the fact of his love. Is there not something even more fundamental, from which love and all these other attributes can be deduced? . . . [This] formal constituent of deity is Being." (*He Who Is* [London: Longmans, Green, 1943], 11.)

as a kind of proper name, it seems to me it should be reserved for theological views developed on the basis of this model of interpersonal transcendence. "Being" is the much more appropriate central term for theologies grounded on the model of teleological transcendence.

The philosophical significance of the conflict between the positive-historical theologies of revelation and every form of "natural theology" can now be clarified. It is evident that the analogy of interpersonal transcendence can find no real place for a natural theology in the usual sense; no referent for the word "God" could possibly be located apart from his act of revelation (for the other person transcends my world in this sense absolutely, as we have seen). On this view, then, everything that is known about God—even the bare, formal meaning of the word "God"—develops in a concrete *history of revelation,*[18] just as my knowledge of other persons—indeed, even my knowledge that there are such realities as persons—develops only in and through their revelation of themselves to me. Moreover, just as in the history of my relations with another person I come to know him, as he and I mutually reveal ourselves—and that history then provides the context in which new encounters with the other occur and are understood—so our knowledge of God also develops historically, and this historical deposit provides the context for each new stage of religious awareness and theological understanding. Thus, Moses is the indispensable historical presupposition for Isaiah, and Isaiah for Jesus, just as Jesus is for Paul, Paul for Augustine, and Augustine for Luther and for us. For a philosophy or theology rooted in the model of interpersonal transcendence, the actual positive course of history is of philosophical importance since it is within this interpersonal history—and here alone—that the divine is apprehended.

There would seem to be no *prima facie* reason why a full-blown philosophy or theology might not be developed on the basis of this model. It would, however, be a kind of radical historicism quite unlike much traditional thinking about God (which has been rooted in the teleological model or in an uncritical mixture of the two models),[19] and it would be necessary to face much more seriously than anyone has yet done, certain difficulties arising out of the basic anthropomorphism of the view. Our experience of the transcendent reality of other persons is always mediated through their bodies—through the words they speak or write or the gestures and other motions they make. How, then, is God's reality mediated to us? through his "body," perhaps the

[18] The contrast here with Crombie's position (see n. 11 above) is sharp.

[19] The teleological model has been so much used in Christian theology that Heidegger, for example, takes it for granted that this is fully definitive of transcendence and that precisely this definition is peculiarly Christian (see *Sein und Zeit,* 7th ed. [Tübingen: Niemeyer, 1953], 49).

world? If so, what otherwise appear simply as ordinary physical events would have to be interpreted as linguistic symbols, and there seems little ground for that. Or is it possible, in developing the analogical meaning of interpersonal transcendence, to disregard the physical dimensions of interpersonal intercourse—dimensions which appear to be indispensable on the finite level? If this way is taken, then it must be shown both legitimate and possible to abstract the actual encounter with another in his transcendence from the sensory seeing, hearing, and touching through which such encounters appear always to be mediated in our finite experience. But this may prove exceedingly difficult, if not impossible.[20] However, these are problems to be faced in the actual working-out of a concept of God, a project beyond the scope of the present essay.

When the teleological model is followed, on the other hand, it is assumed there is an appropriateness or fitness of the Infinite Source and Goal to finite striving and needs, much as food proves to be an appropriate satisfaction for hunger. "Our hearts are restless till they find their rest in thee."[21] This structure becomes, then, the pattern in terms of which God's relation to the world is everywhere understood. History itself must transpire within the framework of this "cosmological idea."[22] Thus, it is in terms of this finite-Infinite relationship that the word "God" is given its root meaning, not in and through events of revelation. It is little wonder that for philosophers to whom this pattern appeared virtually self-evident, rather considerable claims could be made about the extent of our knowledge of God quite apart from his revelation, as in traditional "natural theology."

It is somewhat curious that the more anthropomorphic of the two models (and thus the one which seems to imply that God is most like us and presumably most easily knowable by us) is at the same time the model with which a more absolute kind of transcendence of God can be affirmed. For here he is the impenetrable mystery, known only in and through his revelation in concrete historical events. In contrast the model of transcendence that eschews anthropomorphisms of all sorts and regards God simply as *Being* turns out to be the one in which God is less hidden and less mysterious. For with teleological transcendence the fittingness or correspondence of the transcendent goal to the striving of the finite self is always implied, and with it a certain proportionality between the experienced finite order and the Infinite.

Of course, more recent thinkers operating with this model of transcend-

---

[20] These difficulties and others, involved in utilizing the experience of interpersonal encounter as a basis for speaking of God, have been made especially clear by Ronald W. Hepburn, *Christianity and Paradox* (London: Watts, 1958), chaps. 3, 4.

[21] Augustine, *Confessions,* Bk. I.

[22] The term is Austin Farrer's, *Finite and Infinite* (Westminster: Dacre, 1943), Pt. I.

ence, such as Paul Tillich and Austin Farrer, have been much more aware that if transcendence is, after all, real *transcendence* of our experience and knowledge, the pattern cannot be so clearly perceivable as earlier theologians had supposed. But this insight into the difficulties of "natural theology" has been purchased at a high price. For, taken together with the fact that teleological transcendence is really not easily reconcilable with a strong doctrine of revelation (which is, as we have seen, rooted in the other model), it means we have no real basis left for our alleged knowledge of God. We should not be surprised, then, that modern man has become increasingly dubious about the meaningfulness of all theological and religious language. When it became clear that teleological transcendence—far from making it possible to talk about God on the basis of our finite experience and knowledge—could be fully understood in terms of the imaginative and projective activities of the self (Feuerbach, Freud), it simply seemed no longer reasonable to try to speak of a radically transcendent reality, i.e., of God, at all.

It is, I suspect, partly the failure of theologians themselves to realize the significantly differing implications of the two models of transcendence that has led to the present serious questioning whether notions like "God" have any specifiable meaning. If the theologians had from the beginning taken the position that the model of transcendence appropriate for their work was interpersonal, it would have been clearer that the question of the reality of God—and, likewise, of the meaning of the word "God"—could not be answered by reference to an inspection of the finite experience directly open to everyone, but could be explored only within the context of a "history of revelation." This, of course, does not dissolve the problem, for the question now becomes, Can we in fact give any meaning to the claim that God has revealed and does reveal himself in history? Can the concept of God be adequately developed on a foundation of the model of interpersonal transcendence?—and that, as we have already noted, is difficult in the extreme to answer. But at least we would be conducting our philosophical investigation in an ontic realm where the mystery of the genuine transcendence and hiddenness of another is directly experienced. And this would seem more likely to provide us a basis for defining and understanding the word "God"—if that word indeed refers to a reality not readily accessible to us and disposable by us, but radically transcendent.

Analogy as a Principle of Theological Method Historically Considered

NIELS C. NIELSEN, JR.
Newton Rayzor Professor of Philosophy
Rice University
Houston, Texas

I. Analogy in Theological Theory

Analogy continues to be a principle of interpretation for a variety of theologies, Protestant and Roman Catholic. It is our thesis that its meaning is obscured when it is identified simply with scholastic natural theology. One particular interpretation, the *analogia entis,* has been developed from Aristotelian premises in Neo-Thomism. However, there are also Scotist and Molinist as well as Augustinian versions of this idea.[1] Among Protestants, Tillich and Barth acknowledge the positive role of analogy in their particular theologies.[2] General description of the idea usually asserts that it guards against uncritical anthropomorphism, the ascription of finite, distinctively human, or even physical characteristics to deity.[3] It is likewise a denial of "symbolism" and metaphysical agnosticism. God's transcendence requires that he should not be described in terms identical with those applied to man and the world. None the less, positive knowledge is presupposed in Christian affirmation of both creation and special revelation. Analogy makes it possible to speak of likeness and yet to preserve the mystery of the divine being. It is a way of distinguishing between immanence and transcendence while still relating them positively. As a principle of theological method, it makes explicit the theistic

[1] Erich Przywara, *Religionsphilosophie katholischer Theologie* (München: Oldenbourg, 1926), 67–82.

[2] Paul Tillich, *Systematic Theology* (Chicago: The University of Chicago Press, 1957), II, 115.

[3] A particularly important study, emphasizing these distinctions, is M. T. L. Penido, *Le Rôle de l'Analogie en Théologie Dogmatique* (Paris: Vrin, 1931).

presuppositions about the relation of God and the world. This concept distinguishes Christian interpretation from pantheism and also allows for a significant immanence of divine being without doing violence to the claim for God's transcendence.

It is clear that analogy belongs more characteristically to Western than to Eastern religion. Hinduism and Buddhism have attached less importance to it in their respective interpretations and practice. To be sure, the doctrines of such thinkers as Ramanuja and Shinran may support it implicitly; however, this is dubious because the idea of creation is absent from their theologies. By and large, the Hindu and Buddhist interpretations of man and the ultimate, assuredly conceived differently, do not allow sufficient discontinuity or self-identity for analogical description.[4] Hinduism in principle does not generally distinguish radically between humanity and deity. Buddhism, at least in its early form, denies any abiding essence. The ultimate, Nirvana, is finally beyond all conceptual or symbolic description.

Islam, standing at the opposite pole, has refused to modify its anthropomorphism by a doctrine of analogy. Insisting on the inscrutability of the divine will, it teaches that God truly sees, hears, and knows, but in a different manner than men. Islam refused Greek philosophical categories as well as the idea of incarnation. Christianity, by contrast, interpreted the relation between the Persons of the Trinity in a context of analogy. Protestants, in paricular, have questioned whether Platonic and Aristotelian perspectives used in such explanation are really compatible with the Christian kerygma. It is important to note that the idea of analogy continues even in theologies which claim to reject the Greek heritage, in such a way as to suggest that it is intrinsic to Christianity itself.

Analogy is not so much a method for gaining new knowledge as a means of making clear what is already implicit in a particular context. We maintain that it is more than an epistemological principle; it determines structure as well. Basically, the problem of theological knowledge turns on the relation of immanence and transcendence. Analogy is a principle of understanding which relates them positively at a wide variety of levels. It is a perspective for interpreting similarities and differences between God and the world, and a whole range of relationships in the world itself. The scope of analogical predication becomes clear when we acknowledge that immanence and transcendence are not exclusively religious categories, but implicit in a wide variety of types of knowledge.[5] Whereas judgments simply of identity or nonidentity

---

[4] Niels C. Nielsen, Jr., " 'Creation' East and West," *The Monist,* XLVII (1963), No. 3, 444–454.

[5] Msgr. de Solanges, *Dialogue sur l'Analogie* (Paris: Aubier, 1946).

would not be productive for knowledge, analogy yields an understanding in terms of likeness and difference. It allows for both individuality and process, presupposing a universe of ordered meanings rather than chaos. The fundamental problem in analogical description is the recognition of primary rather than incidental relationships. It raises the question of essence as well as existence. Invoked uncritically, it may lead to judgments of likeness where there is in fact only apparent similarity.

Christian theologians have applied a principle, assuredly useful in the evaluation of ordinary experience in the space-time context, to a reality which they understand to transcend the world. The grounds for doing so have been sometimes simply confessional; at other times, claims have been made from experience apart from faith. In the first case, analogy has been defined on exclusively dogmatic grounds. It is on such a premise that Barth develops his *analogia fidei.*[6] In the second case, it is legitimate not only to raise questions concerning nature as well as grace, but to investigate the possibility of an analogical relationship between immanence and transcendence at many different levels. Against a naturalism which asserts that the human person or the world in which he lives is self-complete, it may be argued that description is not exhaustive at the level of immanence. Both value and the dynamics of the personal life point analogically beyond themselves. Such an attempted explanation may be justified on Christian theological grounds from the doctrine of creation.[7] The unity of the finite world is not just in its own natural being, but from "beyond." Analogy is a way of identifying the asymmetrical relation between God and the universe he created.

Analogy, so conceived, joins philosophical and theological concerns. Indeed, its beginning may well have been with the prereflective belief in a higher realm whose perfection is mirrored in the world below.[8] The literal higher-lower distinction was in time abandoned in idealization and spiritualization. The methodological significance of analogy becomes clear only when it is appraised in terms of the relation of immanence and transcendence. The theological question is whether we should pass directly to confessional explanation or first attempt to understand existence in the world. Actually, there appears to be a dialectic between these two methods in Christian theological explanation of analogy. Aquinas attempted to begin from the world of creation, exploring the way in which nature is related to grace. Augustine began with "faith seeking understanding," but raised the question of knowl-

---

[6] Karl Barth, *Die kirchliche Dogmatik* (Zollikon-Zürich: Evangelischer Verlag, 1947–1959), I/1, 6, 11, 257–260, 460, 480.

[7] Austin Farrer, *Finite and Infinite* (Westminster: Dacre, 1943), 2 f.

[8] Hans Wagner, *Existenz, Analogie und Dialektik* (München: Reinhardt, 1953), 61.

edge. Barth, as a Protestant Augustinian, makes revelation his first premise, but must none the less treat the problem of creation. The attempt to appraise the idea of analogy apart from its role in both the history of philosophy and theology, leads to a restriction of its meaning. It is our thesis that analogy is a many-sided as well as a perennial principle of interpretation.

Some doctrines of analogy, namely, the Augustinian, have been oriented on the personal life of the self; others, notably the Thomistic, have been more cosmological. In terms of basic presuppositions, the setting of detail against detail is secondary. The primary question is whether the analogy pattern, particularly as it concerns God and the world, is still a valid one. An answer must survey the Platonic and Augustinian as well as the Aristotelian-Thomistic interpretations. We propose to treat the idea of analogy both historically and as an issue in contemporary theology. Our position is that it appears in a variety of philosophies and theologies as a principle of structure. It is a way of viewing reality which can be identified phenomenologically in the history of thought. The image-copy pattern is only one type of analogy.

II. The Place of Analogy in Greek Theology

Description of this idea simply in traditional terms has too often neglected if not obscured its contemporary relevance. G. F. Woods has attempted to rethink the question of theological explanation apart from scholastic metaphysics or the Neo-Kantianism and existentialism of modern Protestant theology.[9] He concludes that analogy is a necessary methodological reference in making explicit religious knowledge in a mode appropriate to our nature. It is a principle not only of analysis, but of positive description which makes plain what would otherwise be obscure.[10] Its knowledge value lies in the fact that it establishes a dialectic whereas there would otherwise be only negation. Our desire for comprehensive and unified explanation cannot be fulfilled apart from it.

Woods argues that a simple empiricism, even as an exclusive rationalism, stands opposed to analogy. Neither factual description nor rational deduction alone is adequate methodologically. Analogy looks for transcending objective factors which will relate the two, and it identifies such factors in historical and personal terms. It is a tool for exploring the meaning of our personal being as well as the world external to the self. Explanation is not primarily from mechanism or the world of sense, but the inner experience of reason, freedom, and value. Thus, analogy expands the field of explanation beyond

---

[9] George Frederick Woods, *Theological Explanation* (Welwyn: Nisbet, 1958), 3.
[10] *Ibid.*, 54.

any simple empiricism or rationalism; instead, there is a dialectic between the two in which both are probed in their widest bases. Put in traditional terms, the question is one of the relation of existence to essence.[11] Analogy premises that neither stands alone; they are related in a more comprehensive context of meaning and life.

Przywara has urged that the relation of immanence to transcendence is a primary problem of the *philosophia perennis*.[12] If Western philosophy is a series of footnotes on Plato as Whitehead believed, the wider outreach of our theme becomes clear.[13] The Platonic way of dealing with reality was basically analogical and included what are commonly identified as philosophical and theological interests. Moreover, the attempt to treat the problems it raises from the point of view of immanence alone restricts philosophical investigation. Heidegger's re-evaluation of Greek and Christian philosophy from this premise, for example, cannot avoid the problem of analogy. If, as he acknowledges, the transcendence of being has been a major concern of Western thought from Plato to Hegel, we may expect to find a variety of analogy doctrines relating existence to essence.[14] As a principle of structure, analogy sets the limits against exhaustive description of essence in simply immanent categories or a complete denial of structure from a "pure existentialism." So conceived, it is clear that analogy has had a variety of forms in the Western philosophical and theological traditions.

For both Greek and Christian philosophy, analogy is a principle which relates existence and essence in a self-transcending relation.[15] Being is beyond space-time in its ultimate fullness. Analogy is in effect a denial that man's existence is his essence. The human person realizes his nature only in part. Man, structured essentially, is not self-complete, but changing and developing. Not alone in his existence, but in his essence as well, he is finite. The traditional basis for analogical predication lies in the conviction that God, by contrast, is not only self-complete in his essence but is his own existence. Existence and essence are identical in his being, which is the fullness of actuality. By contrast, man and the world are constituted in the tension between the potential and the actual. Neither is self-complete; each depends on a cause beyond itself. Man, although constantly transcending his past existence, never finally reaches the fullness of actuality.

The idea of analogy is implicit in the Platonic-Aristotelian analysis of the tension between being and becoming. Parmenides understood that pure being

---

[11] Erich Przywara, *Analogia Entis* (München: Kösel & Pustet, 1932), 31.
[12] *Ibid.*, 149.
[13] Alfred North Whitehead, *Process and Reality* (New York: Humanities, 1959), 63.
[14] Martin Heidegger, *Zur Seinsfrage* (Frankfurt a. Main: Klostermann, 1956), 15–18.
[15] Przywara, *op. cit.*, 101–148.

has abiding meaning and unity and, on his view, must remain unchanging. His successors recognized that this rigorous self-identity could not allow for becoming or explain existence. If reality is identified with permanence alone, change is not allowed. If, on the other hand, we accept the view that all is flux and change, no rational explanation is possible. The antithesis between the Parmenidean and the Heraclitean views leads, historically, to the idea of analogy. The Platonic and Aristotelian epistemologies reject both extremes and premise analogy as the transcendent relation of essence to existence. Essence is not construed as Idea objectified, but as intrinsic to being. Analogical explanation presupposes the fullness of reality. It is premised ontologically on the plenitude of being, epistemologically on the principle of sufficient reason.[16] Becoming and change must have adequate explanation in reality to account for meaning and value.

Because being in its purity, immutability, and eternity cannot be reduced to our level of existence, our knowledge of it is analogical. For Plato, analogy is both a mode of relatedness and a principle of knowledge. His distinction between the eternal realm of Ideas and the world of change leads to an archetype-copy pattern. The lower is known from the higher, the particular in universal truth. Time is the moving image of eternity, but not identical with it! Although the forms do not exist primarily in space-time, they are none the less immanent to our experience, "mirrored" in the world of becoming. The doctrine of participation is an attempt to explain the relation of the lower to the higher. The searching critique to which Plato subjected his theory of knowledge in the later dialogues is the measure of his desire to express the analogical relationship with clarity. Analogy for Plato is not a static deductive formula. Rather, it is a principle which enables philosophical investigation to treat truth, goodness, and beauty universally and not simply in terms of isolated particularity. It joins likeness and unlikeness, immanence and transcendence, the many to the One.

According to Plato, our experience of reason in the world of space-time is not self-complete or self-explanatory, but rather directed beyond itself. Unlike the more immanentistic forms of nineteenth century idealism, he does not allow the human mind an exhaustive knowledge of essence. Rather, he presupposes the transcendence of the real which is conceived analogically in terms of value and soul. The eternal, as the fullness of reality, is the goal of the temporal. In turn, the higher gives pattern and direction to the lower. The analogical relation is a double one. On the one hand, order and the form of the Good impose themselves on the flux. There is a direction from above in

---

[16] Penido, *op. cit.*, 164.

all apprehension of meaning and truth by the human psyche. On the other hand, as is particularly clear in the Platonic doctrine of *eros,* there is an immanent teleology and ascent heavenward toward the fullness of reality and goodness in the apprehension of truth.

Paul Grenet distinguishes Platonic analogy from the earlier "anthropomorphic analogy" of popular Greek religion.[17] Homer and Hesiod, for example, tell how the gods were represented as supermen; the continuing life of the soul after death was envisaged in the pattern of bodily existence. Platonic analogy by contrast does not project the lower into the higher; instead, the fullness of being is reflected in space-time. Although the Platonic outlook represents elevated religious insight, its motivation is not primarily one of faith. Instead, it is an epistemological realism seeking insight about man and the world in which he lives.

Grenet finds the precursors of Platonic analogy in the Presocratic philosophers.[18] For example, Heraclitus in designating fire as a universal principle did not interpret it simply formally or empirically. Rather, he understood it as an irresistible power of renovation which belongs to the structures of existence. Similarly, he regarded conflict, even as Empedocles viewed love and hate, as a metaempirical concept. Anaxagoras, according to Grenet, was the first to describe the emerging analogical method by his phrase, repeated by Democritus: "Visible existences are a sight of the unseen."[19] Even as Anaxagoras continued to use the mechanical analogy of water in rotation, it was becoming clear that philosophy must look beyond the limits of body to intellect. Grenet argues that Anaxagoras made intelligence so inclusive that he was unable to distinguish it from any other aspect of reality.[20] Plato, by contrast, treated it as proportionate to the subject, human or divine, thus developing a valid analogical perspective.

The full scope of Plato's doctrine of analogy must be appraised from two dialogues, the *Republic* and the *Timaeus*. In the figure of the divided line, forms of knowledge are related analogically according to their degree of truth or reality. Hierarchies of knowledge correspond to hierarchies of being. In the *Timaeus,* Plato describes the four basic elements, fire, air, water, and earth, as related to each other in a series of mutually corresponding proportions.[21] Analogy is a unity of creating bond which makes for symmetry and harmony.

---

[17] Paul Grenet, *Let Origines de l'Analogie Philosophique dans les Dialogues de Platon* (Paris: Boivin & Cie, 1948), 41.

[18] *Ibid.,* 48.

[19] *Ibid.,* 51. Hermann Diels, *Fragmente der Vorsokratiker,* trans. by Kathleen Freeman (Oxford: Blackwell, 1942), 46b, fragment 21a.

[20] Grenet, *op. cit.,* 52.

[21] *Timaeus,* 31–32.

The elements correspond to different geometrical polyhedrons and are joined by the Demiurge to form an analogy. Inasmuch as the activities of the Demiurge are restricted by necessity, the analogy is not quite mathematically exact.[22] Plato explains further that the Demiurge made all things in the world analogous. He seems to mean that the realm of becoming is characterized not only by change, but by a rhythm of proportion. Grenet argues that Plato's idea of analogy is clarified from his claim that sound workmanship is not possible without a proper model.[23] The artist's work remains a copy; it is by nature not the same as the original from which it is taken.

Basic to Platonic analogy is a hypothesis concerning ground and causality; the latter is essentially of the order of intelligence. He describes the universe as made up of mixed living bodies governed by an intelligent cause.[24] It is the supreme and eternal cause, good and perfect, which gives essence and existence to all. In the *Philebus* and *Statesman* he uses the analogy of a king, in the *Statesman* of a pilot, in the *Philebus, Statesman,* and *Timaeus* of a father, educator, and artisan, to describe this cause. The universe follows the instructions of the intelligence which is its author and father. In the *Philebus, Timaeus,* and *Laws,* Plato uses the analogy of the soul of the body. Soul is living, reasonable, and characterized by spontaneous action.[25] Plato's method is a double one: comparison of empirically identified properties in a dialectical attempt to arrive at a convergence and their interpretation in terms of an intelligible universal cause. The identification of universal cause and the Good is progressive in the dialogues, the *Republic, Philebus,* and *Timaeus,* and is most clear in the last.[26]

Werner Jaeger has emphasized how much Aristotle was dependent on Plato. "His aim was to purge the philosophical consciousness of its mythical and metaphorical elements and to work out the strictly scientific foundations of a metaphysical view of the world that he took over in its main outlines from Plato."[27] Similarly, the background of the Aristotelian doctrine of analogy is in Plato's thought. Aristotle's criticism of Platonic symbol and myth led him to a greater emphasis on immanence in his understanding of the relation between the universal and the particular. Jaeger comments that his goal was "to elicit the ultimate grounds of experience from the facts themselves and from their inner laws."[28] The universal is known from the par-

---

[22] *Ibid.*, 53.
[23] Grenet, *op. cit.*, 183–186.
[24] *Timaeus,* 31–39.
[25] *Philebus,* 28, 30; *Timaeus,* 34; *Laws,* 904.
[26] *Timaeus,* 29.
[27] Werner Jaeger, *Aristotle* (Oxford: Clarendon, 1948), 377.
[28] *Ibid.*, 380.

ticular as the mind follows its own innate principles in the evaluation of sense data. Yet, even as he insisted on this *a posteriori* epistemological reference, Aristotle premised an analogical relationship between different particulars and the universal. His metaphysics, like that of Plato, is neither one of pure being nor of pure becoming, but rather presupposes both unity and plurality. Different centers of existence are related analogically in a dynamic order of being.

Aristotle used analogy as a biological as well as a mathematical category. It not only enabled him to relate animal species of the most remote types, but to identify organs performing similar functions in different animal genera. He used both arithmetical and geometrical analogy in treating such questions as virtue, friendship, and justice. Basically, it is not just a biological or ethical category for him, but logical and ontological, signifying likeness of relations. Book V of the *Metaphysics* differentiates between four kinds of units: numerical, specific, generic, and analogous. In each case, the wider classification comprises the narrower: analogy comprises the generic but the generic does not comprise the analogous. Book XII of the *Metaphysics* explains that the three fundamental metaphysical principles, form, privation, and matter, the four causes, as well as actuality and potentiality, are analogously common to all things. To be sure, Aristotle recognized that some causes can be expressed by a universal term while others cannot. Like Plato, he regarded the universe as an ordered whole and used analogy as a general concept to indicate common structure. Lyttkens concludes that analogy applies to a plurality of being ranging from prime matter to deity.[29]

Aristotle's philosophy is one of substance rather than Ideas, but not of substance without form. He began from the teleology which he believed to be immanent within the universe itself. The heavenly bodies derive their motions from formal or final causes—not from mere mechanical causation. Change requires an effective agent; the explanation of motion leads at last to a prime mover. The system of motions finds its explanation in an ultimate cause. Jaeger writes: "There must be form at the head of motion, and the highest form must be pure act, through and through determination and thought."[30] Teleology lays the basis for a doctrine of analogy. Aristotle does not envisage a Christian God who is the creator of the universe. God and the world are both eternal. The Platonic and Christian idea of the divine operation in the world is not emphasized. "God is one with the world not by penetrating it, nor by maintaining the totality of its forms as an intelligible world

---

[29] Hampus Lyttkens, *The Analogy Between God and the World* (Uppsala: Almquist & Wiksells Boktyckeri, 1952), 52.

[30] Jaeger, *op. cit.,* 385.

within himself, but because the world 'hangs' on him; he *is* its unity, although not in it. As each thing strives to realize its own form, it realizes for its part that infinite perfection which as a whole is God."[31] Less given to synoptic religious perspectives than Plato, Aristotle laid the basis for the syllogistic argument for God's existence.

III. Classical Uses of Analogy in Christian Thought

Augustinian analogy follows the Platonic tradition, distinguishing degrees of knowledge and being. It joins both philosophical and theological themes in a movement from faith to understanding to vision. The early Augustine shows clearly the influence of Neoplatonism in his concern for intellectual knowledge. As is well known, it was his reading of the *Enneads* which gave him a spiritual concept of deity as against Manichaean materialism and dualism. Augustine in his early works asked to know only God and the soul. The soul, he argued, must ascend away from sense to eternal wisdom. Yet he could not as a Christian regard the body as the prison house of the soul. Instead the relationship between soul and body was conceived positively. The Augustinian orientation is one of being drawn upward in ascent toward beatitude. Creature consciousness is in the end consciousness of God. Yet the soul never comprehends the deity fully or in the light of its own understanding. It remains separate from him while still related to him.

Augustine distinguished God's transcendent reality more completely from his immanent presence than either the earlier Platonism or Aristotelianism. The new positive as well as negative dimensions of his interpretation came not only from Neoplatonism, but increasingly and by contrast from the Christian doctrine of creation. It is the doctrine of creation, as Gilson points out, which brought a sense of radically transcendent being, fully separate from the world in its own self-completeness.[32] A new concept of absolute being is an essential insight in the Christian synthesis of Greek and Hebrew interpretations of deity. God creates *ex nihilo.* The analogical relation is one of full difference and likeness, as opposed to Platonic dualism.[33] The relationship between God and the world is asymmetrical. God is in no way dependent on the created order, but the universe is dependent on him for its sustenance and life.

Augustinian analogy has a voluntaristic character not typical of Platonism.

---

[31] *Ibid.,* 385.

[32] Etienne Gilson, *The Spirit of Mediaeval Philosophy,* trans. by A. H. C. Downes (New York: Scribner's, 1940), 47, 52, 95.

[33] Przywara, *Analogia Entis,* 105.

The creature is directed not just by intellect, but by will and love.[34] The soul's moral direction determines knowledge even more than in Plato. Finally, the way out of skepticism is for the soul to know its own true character. Confronted by its own functions of memory, intellect, and will, it at last cannot doubt that it is. The affirmation is not simply subjective, but leads to the recognition that the truth present to the soul is at the same time above it. Analogical knowledge is a knowing in a greater not-knowing, a middle way between reductionistic positivism and mystic illumination. Augustinian analogy is premised in the end on a Christian theistic doctrine of participation. Faith and grace, not just reason and nature, are necessary to authentic understanding. Commitment and insight are perennially linked with each other in growing existential apprehension of meaning. Faith seeks understanding. The analogical knowledge which proceeds from the dialectic between the two presuppose a logos. Yet mystery is only in part illumined by concept. An element of ineffability remains in all creaturely knowledge. According to Augustine, the soul knows itself in God. It does not apprehend meaning through its own light but by divine illumination. Platonic reminiscence is replaced by "remembering"; in the depths of the soul, true knowledge is to remember God.[35]

Augustine's remarkable introspective powers lead to a singularly penetrating analogical description of time.[36] God lives forever in eternity whereas the creature lives and dies after a few score years. Temporality is significantly the mark of man's finitude. Past, present, and future are together in a dynamic relationship: no one of the three is fully accessible to us. The past is known from memory and the future from expectation. The present is never self-complete, but apprehended only as a specious present. Time itself is measured in the soul. In introspection, we apprehend an elusive unity of immanent presence and transcendence. Knowledge is possible only because our finite, contingent experience has a self-transcending analogical relationship to the fullness of being in the deity. The order and structure of knowledge is from God himself and not autonomous.

The Augustinian perspective is not described fully apart from the image of the Trinity, which appears in memory, intellect, and will. It is not so much that the Trinity is to be explored from creation, as creation from deity. The temporal must look to the eternal for meaning. In short, there is not only movement from the world to God in quest of salvation and meaning. The

---

[34] Przywara, *Augustinus, Die Gestalt als Gefüge* (Leipzig: Hegner, 1934), 38–42. Przywara emphasizes the difference between Platonic *eros* and Christian *caritas*.

[35] Gilson, *Introduction à l'Étude de Saint Augustin* (Paris: Vrin, 1949), 94 f.

[36] *Confessions,* Book XI.

movement away from the world to God is met by that from God to the world. Thus, Augustinian analogy is singularly dynamic. The soul stands above sense, but not as its own ground. Its quest for happiness is a search for truth, the reality which can at last fulfill it. The soul moves restlessly beyond itself, still limited by its creaturely character. Augustine's abiding relevance arises from the fact that he joins existential insight with essential truth. The later Augustine shows a growing sense not only of the concreteness of God's manifestation in the Incarnation, but the mystery of his will.[37] God himself is the ground of all analogical explanation, the boundless being which is the source of likeness.

The idea of analogy, so often associated with Thomas Aquinas, plainly does not have its beginning in his thought. He was innovator to the extent that he gave it an Aristotelian rather than Platonic basis in the Christian tradition. The Thomistic criticism of Augustinian exemplarism parallels in part Aristotle's earlier treatment of the Platonic Ideas. However, Aquinas did not simply reformulate Aristotle's position in medieval terminology. Instead, he attempted to "convert" it to Christian truth.[38] Immanence and transcendence have their last unity in God himself as the fullness of actuality. Analogy is not at any level simply a rational, deductive principle. This is made doubly clear in that Aquinas employs both the analogy of proportion and the analogy of proportionality.[39] The latter, in particular, emphasizes the ineffability and mystery of God's being. Ultimately, the deity must be known from himself and not from a third apart from himself and the world. At no level is he fully disclosed. God, the transcendent ground and goal of all knowledge, remains veiled in mystery.

Aquinas' analogy has its first basis in philosophical knowledge; it is premised on the truth of nature rather than on supernatural revelation. Knowledge of God is from rational reflection based on common sense. Beginning in the world of the sensible, mind comes to understand its own principles and mode of action. God's existence is inferred and not apprehended directly.[40] The Thomistic proofs for God's existence presupposes that the creature's mode of knowledge parallels his mode of being. The creature is moved from potentiality to actuality, while God is the fullness of actuality. Aquinas believed that it is possible to distinguish philosophically between finite and

---

[37] Przywara, "Das Gnoseologische-Religiöse bei St. Augustin," *Augustinus* III (Madrid, 1958), No. 10–11, 269–280.

[38] Gilson, *The Spirit of Mediaeval Philosophy,* 75–77.

[39] Przywara, *Analogia Entis,* 95.

[40] Etienne Gilson, *The Philosophy of St. Thomas Aquinas,* trans. by Edward Bullough (London: Herder, 1939), 42, 49.

infinite being. This distinction makes clear the fundamental likeness and difference between God and the universe. God's being is necessary whereas that of the creature is finite and contingent. Aquinas' position as much as that of Augustine requires the principle of sufficient reason. Proof of God's existence presupposes necessary ontological judgments.

Aquinas' Aristotelianism, affirmed with courage, represented a new probing of the relation between faith and reason. Impressed by the science of his time, he proposed to begin not from the world of ideas, much less from mystical piety, but from the common experience of being in the world. On the other hand, he made analogy more of a Church principle than before. Analogy became a principle of ecclesiastical authority which guarantees the unity of the Word of the Church with itself as well as with Scripture.[41] Man can know his own end on earth by the natural light of reason. The acceptance of authority is necessary for knowledge of his supernatural end. The realms of nature and grace, although separated in the order of knowledge, are in the end united.[42] In practice, the way was opened for the domination of the former by the latter: criticism is taken up in synthesis. The Church is not set against the world but above it.

Przywara, arguing that both Augustinian and Thomistic analogy have a legitimate place in Christian theology, distinguishes them as follows:[43] for Augustine, God is Spirit and Personality, as it were the Absolute of these two, the summit of the stages of the cosmos; Aquinas regards God as superspiritual and superpersonal, beyond the self-contained tension of body-spirit and individual-community in creation. Augustine stresses the relative likeness between God and creation. A hierarchy of grades rises upward to God in the degrees of knowledge and being. Aquinas, while making the analogical relationship central, emphasizes the unlikeness of deity and creation. The hierarchy of grades in creation is a unity by itself which stands over against God as its creator. All created being remains at a distance from God.

Augustine describes the relation between creator and creation as one of participation in God. The image-copy analogy remains from Platonism, although developed in a many-sided way.[44] Attention centers on the "divine idea." To see creation as "hitherward from the creator" is most of all to see the being and activity of the creator. Augustine's Platonic vision sees all creation as if in a twinkling, dwelling in God, although to be sure the dif-

---

[41] Michael Schmaus, *Katholische Dogmatik* (München: Hueber, 1960), I, 301–308.

[42] Gilson, *The Philosophy of St. Thomas Aquinas,* 51.

[43] Przywara, *Religionsphilosophie katholischer Theologie,* 66–104.

[44] This tradition continues in Bonaventure. Cf. Etienne Gilson, *La Philosophie de Saint Bonaventure* (Paris: Vrin, 1924), 196–227.

ference between the two is preserved. In contrast, Aquinas approaches the spiritual finally only negatively. God's being is over against and above his creation. Understanding creation is to know it as positively other than the creator. He gives priority to individual reality and life in the world. The all-pervading truth, love, and light of the creator is the cause of the specifically creaturely "truth, love and light."

Augustinianism is, as it were, graduated upward. The subspiritual is the approach to the spiritual, and the spiritual is the approach to God. Humanity's endless striving is "seeking to find, and finding in order to seek." The true transcendence of God—not a self-evolution of divinity in the creature—is the meaning of immanence. Thomism, by contrast, envisages a convergence upward. The relation of creation to God resides in the totality of convergences of its different poles. Yet the separation between God and creation characteristic of Thomism does not imply the type of transcendence found in Deism, wherein God is a mere "Artificer of the Universe." God's all-pervading, all-effective immanence is the ground of the otherness between himself and creation. Creation not only strives toward its own proper essence, but out of unity with the universally active God.

We must be clear that it is not necessary to limit the idea of analogy to its pre-Reformation expression. Casserley's reinterpretation, although more from the point of view of philosophy than of theology, is an important one. He argues that the continuing Neo-Thomistic attempt to deduce the attributes of God from a concept of being does not take sufficient cognizance of the critical epistemology which has grown up with modern science.[45] Yet the basic mistake of scholastic analogy interpretation, on his view, was not so much one of cosmology as of a lack of a sense of history. Analogy does not necessarily require that the Aristotelian categories of form and substance as well as act are imposed on God. There are more dynamic personal, indeed more dialectical patterns of interpretation. Hans Wagner, one of the most discerning Roman Catholic interpreters among contemporary philosophers, has similarly criticized Thomistic analogy as weak in dialectic.[46] Casserley joins analogy with the Christian idea of the particular; it allows for the uniquely personal in relation to other persons. Understanding man's relation to the deity as created being, Christianity was able to make a new place for the individual in an open, dynamic interpretation of reality. Rather than subsuming the personal under the universal, analogy gives an existential basis for understanding its unique reality.

---

[45] J. V. Langmead Casserley, *The Christian in Philosophy* (New York: Scribner's, 1951), 216–218.

[46] Wagner, *Existenz, Analogie und Dialektik,* 168–171.

IV. Analogy in Protestant Theological Method

We may ask directly what meaning analogy can have as a principle of theological method in Protestantism. Karl Barth's resounding condemnation of the *analogia entis* first seemed a denial of any analogical description in the name of the Reformation. Declaring the *analogia entis* an illegitimate synthesis of nature and grace, Barth wrote: "Whereupon I at the same time allow myself to regard all other possible reasons for not becoming a Catholic as shortsighted and lacking in seriousness."[47] The early identification of analogy with natural theology has not been the last word for Barth himself. Roman Catholic theologians such as Erich Przywara and Hans Urs von Balthasar replied effectively that their church does not mean by nature what Barth at first supposed—a reality apart from grace.[48] Von Balthasar asserted further, in a book commended by Barth, that the Protestant had shifted from a negative dialectical appraisal of the relation between God and the world to a more positive analogical interpretation. Von Balthasar wrote:

> The substitution of analogy for the principle of dialectic does not occur abruptly. It cannot be grasped in a determined text; it is realized progressively and insensibly in the first volumes of the *Kirchliche Dogmatik*, and can be considered as finished in the third volume (*Die Lehre von Gott,* 1940) and in the works which are its contemporaries (*Credo,* 1935; *Gotteserkenntnis und Gottesdienst,* 1938). The second volume (1938) examines its principles without taking the occasion to develop them. The doctrine of analogy will unfold in an ever more manifest fashion from volume to volume in such a way as to become the central theme of the treatises devoted to creation (1945), to man (1948), and to predestination (1950). Whoever does not take this development into account will search in vain in the first volume of the *Kirchliche Dogmatik* (1932) for a precise formulation of this doctrine.[49]

Emil Brunner describes Barth as the first Protestant theologian to make the analogy of being the dividing line between the Roman Catholic and Protestant positions.[50] Barth was encouraged in this judgment by Przywara who interpreted the *analogia entis* as the formal principle of all major types of Roman Catholic theology.[51] Such a usage of the principle of analogy in the end may have obscured more than illuminated its meaning. Starting from

---

[47] Barth, *Die kirchliche Dogmatik,* I/1, viii–ix.

[48] Von Balthasar, *Karl Barth, Darstellung und Deutung seiner Theologie* (Köln: Hegner, 1951), 278–302.

[49] *Ibid.,* 116 f.

[50] Brunner, *The Christian Doctrine of Creation and Redemption, Dogmatics II,* trans. by Olive Wyon (Philadelphia: Westminster, 1952), 42–45.

[51] Przywara, *Religionsphilosophie katholischer Theologie,* 70–82.

nature, Barth argued, one can never reach grace.[52] Such an attempt underlies not only Roman Catholic sacramentalism, but its alleged synthesis of reason and faith. According to the Reformation, the Word of God cannot be known simply by human reason but only from God himself. We must speak for faith and not from any abiding relation in being. The latter signifies only a confused and unsuccessful approach from the side of sinful man. God says "No" to sinful man, standing over against man and defying all attempts to reach him through any natural immanence. Instead, whatever relation man has to God is from the divine sovereignty and action.

In evaluating earlier Protestant doctrines of analogy, Barth concluded that the position of the seventeenth century theologian, Quenstedt, was identical with that of Roman Catholicism.[53] Bouillard has pointed out correctly that this analysis is too simple.[54] Barth does not distinguish sufficiently between different schools of Catholic theology. Quenstedt's position is similar to that of Suarez rather than that of Cajetan who established the major tradition of later Thomistic interpretation.[55] The Protestant emphasized an intrinsic analogy of attribution rather than the analogy of proportionality as in Cajetan. According to Quenstedt, knowledge of God derives from recognition of the creature's dependence on him. The analogical relation is not a mutual one, such as is found between two species of a genus. Rather, it has its locus primarily in one pole and not the other, as between God and creation. Barth argues that Quenstedt's position is determined from the distinction between absolute and relative rather than from faith. Analogy is made a problem of diversity in unity and unity in diversity, in short, of a common being apart from grace. As against this position, Barth insists that Christian knowledge of God is from and through God. Analogy cannot be from the point of view of a spectator. God's Word to man determines his existence. This Word is a new possibility, an uncreated reality identical with God himself. If we are to speak of a relation between the Word of God and the word of man, it must be in actualistic terms.

Barth did not in the end propose to abandon the idea of analogy. In the place of the analogy of being, he developed instead his own interpretation of the analogy of faith.[56] God is not known from nature apart from grace, as Roman Catholic theology seemed to him to assert. God is known only through

---

[52] Barth, *Die kirchliche Dogmatik,* I/2, 324–356, is a description of his attitude toward natural religion.

[53] *Ibid.,* II/1, 267–275.

[54] Henri Bouillard, *Karl Barth* (Paris: Aubier, 1957), III, 194.

[55] The difference between these traditions is summarized in Hampus Lyttkens, *op. cit.,* 205–243.

[56] Edouard Burnier, *Bible et Théologie* (Lausanne: Roth, 1943), 173–181.

faith as the free Word of God is spoken in the divine act in history. This Word creates its own context apart from any general analogy structure of being. Barth defines analogy as a correspondence between the act of faith and the Word of God. He refers his readers to Romans 12:6 where Paul defines the analogy of faith as correspondence between the charisma of prophecy and the content of faith.[57] The analogy of faith requires no philosophical prolegomena. As used by Barth, it serves to exclude the concept of being from revelation and substitute one of act. Aristotelian substance and form are rejected; only act remains. Analogy is dynamic and not static because it has its basis in the freedom of God. We must use our words and language to express the truth and relation that we did not create and cannot control. Obedience and faith remake the context of analogical predication.

More important than Barth's brief exegesis of the analogy of faith is von Balthasar's claim that his entire methodology has passed from dialectic to analogy. Torrance agrees to the extent of finding a marked shift from his earlier to his later thought.[58] Barth's early writings, notably the *Commentary on the Epistle to the Romans,* were directed against the natural theology of nineteenth-century Protestantism as well as against Roman Catholicism. Both, in his judgment, attempted to establish a framework for theological reflection apart from the Word of God. Barth's early dialectical position is summarized by his following remark:

> If you ask me about *God,* and if I am ready to tell you about Him, dialectic is all that can be expected of *me*. Neither my affirmation nor my denial lays claim to being God's truth. Neither is more than a *witness* to that Truth which stands in the centre between every Yes and No.[59]

In time, Barth came to seek for a more positive position. Von Balthasar and Torrance agree that the decisive turning point came in his work on Anselm which led to the publication of *Fides Quaerens Intellectum* shortly before the beginning of the *Dogmatik*.[60]

Torrance also attaches importance to Barth's lectures, "Schicksal und Idee in der Theologie," delivered in Dortmund in March, 1929, as an exposition of Barth's opinions about philosophy.[61] Barth acknowledged that theology does not live in a room by itself, but operates with the same tools as philosophy, even though it fulfills its task of bearing witness to revelation in a dif-

---

[57] Barth, *Die kirchliche Dogmatik,* I/1, 257.

[58] Thomas F. Torrance, *Karl Barth, An Introduction to His Early Theology, 1910–1931* (London: S.C.M. Press, 1962).

[59] *Ibid.,* 87.

[60] Von Balthasar, *op. cit.,* 93, 148.

[61] Barth, *Theologische Fragen und Antworten. Gesammelte Vorträge* (Zollikon: Evangelischer Verlag, 1957), 54–92.

ferent way. Barth's evaluation of both realism and idealism in the end has implications for the major forms of analogy in the Christian tradition, particularly for the claim that one form complements the other. The danger of realism on his view is that it too often judges actuality simply from within the limits of one's own experience. Religious realism in general means that God is ontologically and noetically man's unavoidable fate. This, according to Barth, is the implication of Aquinas' position. But God's Word in revelation is both different and new.[62] God lets himself be known as the one who comes to the sinner. Only if we understand that God's knowability arises from his freedom, will we know what it means for him to be actual.

Although Barth is not prepared to abandon theological realism based on this premise, he acknowledges that no serious theology can escape idealism. Unpurified by idealism, theology cannot be anything more than a pagan monstrosity given over to demonology. Raising the question of truth, idealism emphasizes the transcendence of God over the given. But idealism, too, carries a danger of its own, namely, ideology. Philosophical idealism has too often exchanged a human logos for the divine one, denying that truth comes from God's act rather than our own.[63]

The basis of Barth's *analogia fidei* is not nominalism or existentialism, but the *fides quaerens intellectum* of Anselm. The analogical method of the *Dogmatik,* as von Balthasar has described it, must be understood against the background of Barth's earlier criticism of nineteenth-century Neo-Protestantism. Operating from the double presupposition of pietism and the Enlightenment, Neo-Protestantism did not regard religious knowledge as rational in its own right. The theologian sought to develop a coherent and meaningful interpretation of religious experience by the use of concepts taken from ethics and philosophy. Barth committed himself to analogy when he took the opposite position, describing the Word of God itself as rational event. Theology is rational in its own right because of the rationality of its proper object.[64] The Word of God is, so to speak, a concrete universal. Barth's criticism of medieval theology, realist or idealist, is that it did not achieve a proper subordination of its thought forms to its proper object. Nominalism is to be regarded as a protest against an inadequate theology, rather than an adequate positive position. Nominalism was in fact already latent in the later scholastic doctrine of the attributes of God based on a false separation between the being and action of God. Barth interprets Anselm in terms of a dynamic

---

[62] *Ibid.,* 69.
[63] Torrance, *op. cit.,* 171.
[64] Barth, *Anselm: Fides Quaerens Intellectum,* trans. by Ian W. Robertson (Richmond: Knox, 1960), 49–52.

rationality which presupposes the active self-communication of the divine truth. The utter objectivity of God prescribes the manner and limits of our knowledge, while it is at the same time the basis of analogical predication.

> Thus along with Anselm's notion of dynamic rationality there goes a notion of dynamic analogy carrying a relationship of adequacy and inadequacy, or partial likeness and partial unlikeness, between the knowledge of faith and its proper object. . . . the inadequacy of theological statements does not mean that they are false, but on the contrary reflects the *truth* of their relation to their object.
>
> . . . Barth links so closely together the analogical relationship set up between the knowing creature and the God known and the ontological relationship between the creation and God as it is revealed and finally made good in Jesus Christ. . . . It is only in Jesus Christ, who is both the image and reality of God, that we can think and speak of God in such a realist way that our human forms are not an empty shell but are filled from above with the Truth of God.[65]

Barth's theology sets the idea of analogy in an Augustinian context; however, this is without the epistemological structures of Augustine himself. Barth's tendency to equate epistemological and soteriological concerns appears in his *analogia fidei*. Bouillard has criticized him with some justification for confusing analogy with a representation of God's essence, charging that on occasion he even tends to speak of God in spatial terms.[66] It is clear that Barth does not intend to subject his views to all the distinctions of Roman Catholic theology! His return to actualistic, even personalistic language in developing his analogical description reflects the vitality of his theology. Thomism gave analogy the double form of affirmation and negation. Aquinas was explicit in holding that God is not known in his essence. Torrance remarks that Aquinas made the distinction between the givenness of God and all other beings so vast and fundamental that the being of God was treated as a nongiven and nonbeing.[67] Barth's position is more positive, based on revelation: there is sure and certain knowledge of God. It is interesting that in replying to Barth, von Balthasar and Bouillard do not propose to defend the entire Roman Catholic tradition of natural theology. Von Balthasar argues primarily for a theological doctrine of nature as corollary to belief in creation. Bouillard distinguishes carefully between Aquinas' ideas and those of his later interpreters.[68] Whereas Aquinas treated analogy as a mode of judgment appropriate to human experience, later interpreters, Cajetan and Suarez, made

---

[65] Torrance, *op. cit.*, 189 f., 193 f.

[66] Bouillard, *op. cit.*, III, 207.

[67] Torrance, *op. cit.*, 148–180, treats the problem of the relation of philosophy to theology.

[68] Bouillard, *op. cit.*, III, 199.

it the property of a concept and defined it as a particular mode of abstraction.

The contemporary problem is not just whether theology can proceed from nature, which Barth denies, but whether analogy can be limited exclusively to theology as much as he supposes. Bultmann and his followers have begun from philosophical inquiry as well as from exegesis, as they have drawn on the ideas of Martin Heidegger. The continuing relevance of Bultmann's thought suggests that Barth's *"Nein"* against natural theology did not settle as much as he supposed. In short, a variety of problems arise from outside dogmatics and are yet relevant to it. The history of religion as well as philosophy in general continues to develop important perspectives in their own ways. Barth, in placing them outside the scope of analogy proper, has limited the range of his ideas. Not the least significant are the varieties of existential philosophy which have one source not too different from that of Barth initially, namely, Kierkegaard. Bultmann spoke briefly of analogy on one occasion, but apparently in the reverse of the traditional manner.[69] Rather than considering his position in detail, we turn to the ideas of Heidegger on which he has drawn.

V. Heidegger and the Method of Analogy

A major critique of theological analogy is implied clearly in Heidegger's philosophy. To be sure, religious as well as philosophical questions are at stake in his analysis, even as in the case of Plato. Heidegger, in criticism of the naturalism, formalism, and rationalism of so much of modern philosophy, has again raised the problem of being. However, he explicitly denies any knowledge of reality beyond space-time. Although he claims that his premises do not require him to decide between pantheism, atheism, and theism, he is clear that being as such is not God.[70] Indeed, he charges that acceptance of the Christian logos had dulled Western man's concern for being. Only as we grasp that the question of being is not one of deity, can we understand why it remains of continuing importance. Heidegger proposes to show how the question of transcendence developed and has now come to an end in the Western tradition. He abandons not only the Christian logos, which in his judgment substitutes a dogmatic faith for philosophical concern about being, but the entire Western tradition of metaphysics from Plato to Hegel.[71]

Heidegger urges that earlier thinkers have missed the fundamental meaning

[69] John Macquarrie, *The Scope of Demythologizing* (London: S.C.M. Press, 1960), 202–206.

[70] Heidegger, *Platons Lehre von der Wahrheit: Mit einem Brief über den "Humanismus"* (Berne: Francke, 1954), 84, 96.

[71] *Ibid.*, 49–52.

of being by looking for it beyond the world. We must turn instead to the being of concrete things-that-are. Nietzsche unmasked once and for all the theistic claims in philosophy by announcing the death of God. Heidegger's position is the reverse of an analogical interpretation which attempts to explain the things-that-are from "God, Idea, or the Absolute Ego."[72] He proposes instead to reopen the question of being by an existential phenomenology which acknowledges no atemporal or eternal reality. Langan argues that Heidegger substitutes phenomenology for metaphysics on the premise that philosophy is always preparatory to being's own finite progressive revelation of itself.[73] Being (*Sein*) never truly manifests itself as an evident, simple penetrable essence. Heidegger speaks rather of *Seiende*. As finite, it reveals itself through finite *Dasein*.

Heidegger proposes to explain both the revealing and dissimulation of being. In his own unique language, he speaks of an eschatological "gathering together of being" which makes possible surpassing of both tradition and metaphysics.[74] Heidegger asks us to return to the Pre-Socratics to understand what has happened subsequently. It is clear that his analysis is not simply historical. He wishes to emphasize themes which he regards as primary. Anaximander, Heraclitus, and Parmenides did not think of *Seiende* as lying beyond the sum total of physical things. Rather, for them all was one in the primordial presence of what-is-present. Being was conceived as unveiledness itself. Heidegger uses the term *"Anwesen,"* in his own peculiar way.

It was Plato and Aristotle who thought in terms of the "one," the "Good," "Idea," "the thought of thought," and *actus purus*. They looked for diviner things beyond the totality of material things for explanation. The last possible form, the thingliest of things, appeared in Hegel's affirmation of absolute spirit. According to Heidegger, Hegel was the only Western thinker to experience the history of thought by thinking it.[75] With him, the metaphysical tradition came to its *"Vollendung in der Neuzeit."* Thought could go only one way, namely, toward the affirmation of nonabsolute subjective will and the denial of system. Hegel achieved the ultimate subjective *Weltbild,* even absorbing temporality itself into his system. With Nietzsche, the *"Abendland kommt nach Abend."* Understanding its outermost possibility, Nietzsche destroyed the grounds for any future metaphysics.

Nietzsche discredited once and for all the idea of a supersensory world as a source of value. How then can we rescue being, thus "left in the lurch" his-

---

[72] Heidegger, *Sein und Zeit* (Tübingen: Niemeyer, 1953), 2–15, 207–211.

[73] Thomas Langan, *The Meaning of Heidegger* (New York: Columbia University Press, 1959), 13.

[74] Heidegger, *Holzwege* (Frankfurt a.Main: Klostermann, 1952), 301.

[75] *Ibid.*, 298 f.

torically? Heidegger proposes to treat it phenomenologically, from its own internal structure, the relation of *Dasein* to itself, rather than conformity to transcendent meaning or value. At this point, the self-contained temporality of *Dasein* is fundamental to his analysis. His reflection seeks recognition of one's own essential finitude. The freedom of *Dasein* has no limits, either imposed from without or built from within; in this sense, it is absolute. Meaning is grounded only in its free projection. There is no causal ground. Instead, man is thrown into the world. We do not see or know beyond temporality. Death is the ultimate limit of our being. Acceptance of this fact gives authenticity to personal existence.

Heidegger's philosophy is of relevance for theology. He seeks to come to terms with *Dasein*—unlike much post-Kantian epistemological inquiry, and thus to raise again the question of being. His intent is to develop a perspective which goes beyond the idealism-realism antithesis. The idea of analogy similarly seeks to combine and go beyond these two. However, by contrast, Heidegger's analysis approaches a pure dialectic; he offers a phenomenology and not metaphysics. His thought does have value presuppositions, largely negative, in spite of his efforts to disassociate himself from nihilism. Langan writes:

> Each time we have penetrated to the depth of notions such as mystery, the *Heilige,* the grace of Being, *aletheia* itself, we have been unable to retain our initial excitement, for we came to suspect that they were high flown words hiding the real emptiness of an existence for which there is no "other." "Mystery" turns out to hide no incomprehensibly rich other, but only our own limits; the *Heilige* turns out to hold no real gift, but is rather an expression of our finite "not yet"; the "grace of Being" turns out to be no real gift, for it is drawn inexplicably from our own resources.[76]

Our thesis is that analogy as a principle of theological knowledge is premised on a realism which is more inclusive than that of Heidegger. Langan seems justified in the charge that he is not careful enough about the given, nowhere offering a description of what it means to "let the thing be as it is."[77] His phenomenological analysis does not speak clearly enough to the critical point: "the precise nature of the fusion of ecstatic, intentional transcendental horizon with the thing as it is in its brute reality."[78] To say that man is thrown into the world is to offer a negative answer to the question of meaning which limits further reflection about essence if not existence. Heidegger's view of death conditions his thought from the outset. Our position is that a more

[76] Langan, *op. cit.,* 231.
[77] *Ibid.,* 229.
[78] *Ibid.,* 229.

positive religious outlook would necessarily alter his doctrine of *Dasein.* It was the willingness to speak of "essence in-over existence" which made possible the Western tradition of philosophy and theology.

We have concluded this study with a reference to Heidegger because of his present influence on Protestant theology. The many-sidedness of his thought seems to us to have been understated in Bultmann's use of *Sein und Zeit* as an anthropological description of the human condition apart from faith. Our question is whether the problems which Heidegger treats phenomenologically, at times with such great brilliance, do not really demand a doctrine of analogy. We began our analysis with the claim that the idea of analogy does not belong exclusively to any one school of Christian theology. Our description of the tradition from Plato to Aquinas was an attempt to show its many-sidedness. We have treated Barth and Heidegger among contemporary thinkers because they seem to raise fundamental questions about the continuing relevance of this concept. It is our position that no single interpretation exhausts the meaning of the idea. Outlined by Plato and enriched by Augustine, it has yet been developed first in one direction and then in another by later thinkers. It remains of continuing relevance because the fundamental problem, the relation of immanence and transcendence, continues to be of concern to both philosophers and theologians.

Analogy cannot be exclusively theological, as Barth supposes. In a sense, it remains confessional for Christian theologians, but not self-enclosed. To be sure, it can be used irresponsibly as a principle of eclectic synthesis and unity rather than of criticism. Finally, however, its meaning must be considered in the broadest possible terms: it has relevance for the philosopher as well as the theologian. This is the case because the question of transcendence is not simply one of soteriology. Analogy must be approached at a variety of different levels. As a way of relating existence and essence, it is intrinsic to Christian theology itself. An inclusive view of the history of Western philosophy and religion shows how perennial it has been; we have not treated all possible interpretations. No one single idea of analogy ought to be made exhaustive. Because it is grounded in the structures of experience, explaining them in part, it is relevant in many different concerns and circumstances.

Modern Papal Social Teachings

R. PAUL RAMSEY
Harrington Spear Paine Professor of Religion
Princeton University
Princeton, New Jersey

When Leo XIII issued the encyclical *Rerum Novarum* on May 15, 1891, his aim was to point a way between the then existing economic liberalism and an extreme collectivism, believed by many to be the only remedy. Forty years later when, on May 15, 1931, the anniversary encyclical *Quadragesimo Anno* was issued by Pius XI, the context was the great depression, social legislation already enacted in most countries, and a moderate but still "materialistic" socialism. Neither of these pioneering documents undertook analysis of social and economic problems as *world* problems that could be solved only through international action by nations looking decisively beyond their own borders. However, the importance of the Papal documents was that they proved the relevance of more "organic" notions of social legislation and "associations" within a nation's economy. By a revision and extension of ancient and medieval insights into social responsibility, a relevant message was offered for the reconstruction of the disorders of free enterprise capitalism. In the two earlier encyclicals the controlling idea was the *national* common good. On July 15, 1961, two months to the day later than the seventieth and the thirtieth anniversary of those older encyclicals, John XXIII moved to repair a deficiency in Roman Catholic social teachings.

We may never know the exact reason *Mater et Magistra* ("Mother and Teacher of all nations . . .") was delayed beyond the anniversary date. But it is important to realize that bishops all over the world made criticisms and suggestions that were reflected in the final draft. Thus does the Pope propose to speak in encyclical letters not only to the whole church but for the whole church. This is a process not altogether unlike the way in which the National and World Council of Churches make pronouncements and issue position papers, except that, in the latter, laymen share directly in speaking to and for the churches. In this, we may as well admit, there are some disadvantages as well as advantages, if the aim is not simply immediate relevance but the continuous development of Christian social ethics upon a sound and well-articulated theological foundation.

In any case, these three social encyclicals are now a significant part of the intellectual history of the modern period. They deserve the same careful conceptual analysis—tracing the movement of ideas from one to another—which many of us learned from Robert Lowry Calhoun was the first and highest respect to be paid to any great theological document. To undertake this is the purpose of this chapter. John XXIII's last great encyclical, *Pacem in Terris,* is another story that must be told elsewhere.[1]

To exhibit the growth of Catholic social principles up to and into *Mater et Magistra* requires us to turn first to Pope John's review of Catholic social principles in the first half of his encyclical, to the references to his predecessors' earlier encyclicals, and directly to the 1891 and the 1931 encyclicals themselves. Only then will we have the proper background for understanding the late Pontiff's statement of "new aspects of the social question," which he submits to analysis in terms of the "*universal* common good."

Leo XIII

Rerum Novarum (1891): The Condition of the Working Class

The three cardinal teachings of this so-called "Magna Charta of the economic-social reconstruction of the modern era" were (1) its defense of the right of private property, (2) its appeal mainly to "charity" to insure the social use of private property, and (3) its pronouncement upon the right of industrial workers to join "associations" or unions.

1. At the very outset, and at great length, this encyclical defended the inalienable right of private ownership: "Every man has by nature the right to possess property as his own. This is one of the chief points of distinction between man and the animal creation." Because of the work of "the mind," "which renders a human being human" in exercising dominion over physical nature, a man rightfully should possess not only "things that perish in the use of them," but stable and permanent possessions which "remain his own for further use." Because man looks to the future and has recurring needs, and has children with their own future needs, he rightfully should possess things "for his advantage in time yet to come." To affirm, on the basis of

[1] Paul Ramsey, *"Pacem in Terris," Religion in Life,* XXXIII (Winter 1963–1964), 116–135.

Genesis, "that God has given the earth for the use and enjoyment of the whole human race, is not to deny that private property is lawful." That only means that specific portions of the earth were not as yet assigned, and this can offer no comfort even for a moderate or Christian Socialism.

Man's industry renders some portion of the earth his own. By "expending upon it his solicitude and skill . . . he makes his own that portion of nature's field which he cultivates—that portion on which he leaves, as it were, the impress of his individuality." The imprint of his personality upon things, the mixing of the unique powers of his very being with inert nature, makes improvements in things that are "indistinguishable and inseparable" from the things themselves. To alienate these things from him would be to alienate a man from that proper part of himself he has put into them. Therefore, for the state to extinguish private property would be "emphatically unjust, because [this] would rob the lawful possessor, bring State action into a sphere not within its competence, and create utter confusion in the community." This, of course, is the classical argument for the natural right of private property, which prevailed in the West from Aristotle through Thomas Aquinas to John Locke. By a curious twist, it also undergirded Karl Marx's "labor theory of value" and supplied the moral justification for communism as the only means of restoring to workers their alienated humanity, correcting the robbery of what is their *own* by the profit system.

To this, the encyclical adds its own special derivation of private property as belonging "to a man in his capacity of head of a family." This would be in danger of extinction if the state presumed to limit possession to those things which perish in the use of them. *Rerum Novarum,* therefore, declares without qualification that *"the first and most fundamental principle* . . . , if one would undertake to alleviate the condition of the masses, must be the *inviolability of private property."* This principle, as we shall see, has undergone displacement, and, as it were, has been "refuted by a thousand qualifications" in subsequent Catholic thought. This is a chief point to note in coming to understand the significance of *Mater et Magistra.*

2. The right to *own* possessions is one thing; the right to *use* them as one pleases is quite another. By means of Aristotle's ancient distinction between ownership (which should be private) and use (which should be common), we come to a second major principle in Catholic social theory and to an elucidation, however primitive at this stage, of the manner in which common use should be insured. Aristotle's "among friends all things are common" was, by Catholicism, only Christianized into "charity." To the question, How must one's possessions be used? this encyclical answers in the words of Thomas

Aquinas, "Man should not consider his outward possessions as his own, but as common to all, *so as to share them without hesitation when others are in need.*" Just as surely as it was said to be "emphatically unjust" for the state to trespass on the right of private property, so also it is emphatically stated that the direction and utilization of property to the end of common use "is a duty not of justice (save in extreme cases), but of Christian charity."

The Church's task is to "arouse everywhere the heroism of charity." Upon the state, of course, there devolves some part in "the work of remedy and relief." But the basic business of the state is "to make sure that the laws and institutions, the general character and administration of the commonwealth, shall be such as *of themselves to realize public well-being and private prosperity.*" The ruling category for the duty of states in this encyclical is, therefore, emphatically not common use (that is left to charity) but *distributive justice.* The "first and chief" duty of rulers is "to act with strict justice—with that justice which is called by the schoolmen *distributive*—toward each and every class alike." And "the chief thing to be realized is the safe-guarding of private property by legal enactment and public policy."

It may be sufficient to say that the social teaching of Leo's encyclical advances only a little beyond the viewpoint of such conservative Roman Catholics as still edit the *National Review* and who endorse policies of public well-being and private prosperity. By contrast, the main current of Protestant social thought, at the end of the nineteenth century, was laying down far more advanced Magna Chartas for the reconstruction of the social order.

3. It is true that Leo XIII rejected the notion that wages are to be fixed only by the free consent of individuals or that the state should intervene only to enforce such labor contracts. He wrote, "a man's labor bears two notes or characters." First of all, labor is personal; and "were we to consider labor so far as it is *personal* merely, doubtless it would be within the workman's right to accept any rate of wages whatsoever." But labor, as exercise of personal freedom, is "a mere abstract supposition." Accordingly, then, and secondly, it must be considered that "man's labor is *necessary.*" It is necessary for him to live, and live a truly human life, by his labor. Therefore, beneath all contractual relations "there underlies a dictate of natural justice more imperious and ancient than any bargain between man and man, namely, that remuneration ought to be sufficient to support a frugal and well-behaved wage-earner."

On moral grounds, therefore, Leo XIII rejected the idea that a contract to labor, freely made in an open labor market, will automatically be productive of justice and the common good. But Papal teaching was not yet ready to conclude from this a substantive notion of the common good to be sought directly by positive action of the state. Instead, Leo wrote, *"in order to supersede undue interference on the part of the State,* . . . it is advisable that recourse be had to societies or boards. . . ." Such "associations" may be of various sorts and for a number of purposes; but the most important of all are "workingmen's unions." As models he offered "the artificers' guilds of olden times" and affirmed that "such unions should be suited to the requirements of this our age." Such a union may strengthen workingmen in contracting their labor. This will supersede undue interference on the part of the state, or forestall the necessity of securing justice by state intervention. And furthermore to "enter into a 'society' of this kind is the natural right of man." It is as natural a right as private property, and both these rights seem to possess one main benefit, that by them state action is kept at minimum.

Subsequent Catholic social teaching extends the meaning of labor's right to organize. It significantly changes the legitimate purposes of union by mixing the "contract of labor" with the "contract of partnership." At the same time, later social encyclicals have substantially revised the pre-eminence given by *Rerum Novarum* to the right of private ownership together with its large reliance on charity to secure utilization of private property for the common good.

While alert to the fact that "the condition of the working classes is the pressing question of the hour," *Rerum Novarum* applied rather inadequate social principles to the solution of that urgent question. H. Richard Niebuhr once discerningly remarked that, when Leonine encyclicals "address themselves to the 'Gentiles' they do not take common ground with them, arguing on the basis of a common philosophy, but recommend to them the philosophy of Thomas' day." Niebuhr continues:

> Leo writes in the patriarchial spirit of a feudal society, not as one who participates in the modern political movement as Thomas shared in the medieval. What is sought here is not the synthesis of Christ with present culture, but the re-establishment of the philosophy and the institutions of another culture.[2]

It is, however, a cultural fact that this more organic conception of society had considerable viability in contrast to economic liberalism or extreme collectivism. Nevertheless, the future and widespread relevance of these teachings depended on their revision in the course of interpreting them. That was the work of Pius XI and John XXIII.

---

[2] H. Richard Niebuhr, *Christ and Culture* (New York: Harper, 1951), 138 f.

Pius XI

Quadragesimo Anno (1931): On Reconstructing the Social Order

This encyclical more than any other deserves to be regarded as the charter of modern Roman Catholic social teaching. Its principles are taken up without substantial change in the encyclical of John XXIII. To understand *Quadragesimo Anno,* we have to dismiss as rhetoric several of its exuberant comments upon *Rerum Novarum,* to the effect that after 1891 "Catholic principles of sociology gradually became part of the intellectual heritage of the whole human race." Of equal dubiety was the claim that the earlier encyclical "completely overthrew those tottering tenets of Liberalism which had long hampered effective interference by the government." If Leo XXIII overthrew anything even that was tottering, it was by virtue of his subsequent interpreters, who undertook "to defend from calumny the Leonine doctrine" of private property, charity, and limited state action.

Quadragesimo Anno marks off a "twofold aspect of ownership, which is individual or social according as it regards individuals or concerns the common good." Thus, while affirming the right of private property, Pius XI equally affirmed the intrinsic social character of property. While affirming, with Leo, a distinction between ownership and use, Pius made common use inhere in the nature of property itself rather than in the duty of charity. It may be that the direction of property to common use does not come under the norm of distributive justice in which roots the inherent right of ownership. Nevertheless, these principles are derived from the nature of property itself and not alone from charity. Thus, they come under the common good which it is the business of the state to pursue. Therefore, it is affirmed that "the public authority, in view of the common good, may specify more accurately what is licit and what is illicit for property owners in the use of their possessions." It is asserted, of course, that "when civil authority adjusts ownership to meet the needs of the public good it acts not as an enemy, but as the friend of private owners." It ought also to be asserted, however, that, on the principles established by this encyclical, civil authority acts *positively* as a friend of the public good, and not only remedially or as a referee.

Rerum Novarum had stated that "the earth even though apportioned amongst private owners, ceases not thereby to minister to the needs of all; *for there is no one who does not live on what the land brings forth." Quadragesimo Anno* cited this statement, but significantly omitted the final clause. That clause had left largely to chance, to charity, or to the effectuality of "associations" the ministration of private property to the needs of all. The social use of property had now been accepted as an integral part of the inherent nature of property and, at the same time, an integral part of the common good which positive intervention by the state must insure. Therefore, despite this encyclical's repetition of the traditional argument for the right of private ownership and despite its many warnings that the state ought never abolish private property, a long step forward was taken in Catholic social theory and in the principles governing the practices of governments.

The next step was to be taken by *Mater et Magistra* (1961), where, as we shall see, the individual and social character of *the person,* personal *initiative* and *work,* takes the place of the personal and social character *of property,* which had been the basic concept in the 1931 encyclical. Pius XI had, it is true, also spoken of "the individual and social character of *labor.*" In the latest encyclical this becomes more central and emphatic. And, now, John XXIII has joined with this "the principle of subsidiarity" (drawn from Pius XI's encyclical) in making the best social arrangement of the various sources of initiative in a society. We shall see that John XXIII had only to extend this view of the common good into his crucial concept of the "universal common good."

Meanwhile, another thing to be noted in *Quadragesimo Anno* is its introduction of the joint concept of "social justice and social charity." Along with the "universal common good," this notion of "social justice and social charity" was to play a decisive role in *Mater et Magistra;* but we can best understand its meaning here at the point of its first emergence in social encyclical teachings. The reconstruction of the social order upon the basis of the common good requires that all social institutions "be imbued with the spirit of justice." Social justice must "pervade all economic activity." In order for this to be so, "social charity" must pervade and its spirit be imbued into "social justice." "Social charity," Pius wrote, "should be, as it were, the soul of this order and the duty of the state will be to protect and defend it effectively." Thus, as social justice is the soul of the common good and of a proper economic order, so social charity is the soul of social justice. Thus also, in the development of encyclical teaching, at the very moment when social justice became a positive concept for shaping the social order and state intervention, charity ceased to be remedial alone and became a social agent, actively intervening in the task of social justice.

This seems to me a most important instance of "Christ transforming the justices of men." It alone is sufficient to refute the ordinary Roman apologetic contention (when speaking to the "Gentiles" or when condemning Protestantism for its "fideism" and for its ethics of ambiguity or contextual decision) that natural reason and natural justice uninspired by social charity are competent to derive all the necessary principles of social justice. In the development of Papal teachings, plainly, it seems not to have happened that way. Instead, a positive notion of social justice and the duty of the state to intervene actively in economic affairs were twins born of "social justice and social charity," or of Christ illuminating, transforming, and elevating the justice and the reason of men.

It should, moreover, be noted that this concept that joins social justice and social charity was introduced precisely at the point in the encyclical where recognition is given to economic facts which indicate that minimal state action will not suffice: "The economic supremacy which within recent times has taken the place of free competition," the Pope wrote, "needs to be curbed strongly and ruled with prudence." And later in the encyclical: "Free competition is dead; economic dictatorship has taken its place. Unbridled ambition for domination has succeeded the desire for gain; the whole economic life has become hard, cruel and relentless in a ghastly measure." Neither Leo's state nor his fundamental social principles were equal to mastering "that type of social rulership."

Of *Quadragesimo Anno* there remains to be mentioned a significant extension of the right of labor organization, as compared with *Rerum Novarum* (1891), and its extension and modification of the "contract of labor." It is stated that the liberty to form associations extends "beyond the limits of a single trade," for example, to industrial unions such as the C.I.O. But the most significant advance over Leonine teaching was Pius' statement that "in the present state of human society . . . we deem it advisable that the wage contract should, when possible, be modified somewhat by a contract of partnership." Such a contract of partnership meant, at first, profit sharing and some form of joint ownership. But this idea of partnership of persons in a common enterprise, when applied more to its *direction* than to its *ownership,* made it possible for John XXIII—in combination with other principles—to displace the issue of either private or joint *ownership* of property from the central position it had long occupied in Catholic social teaching.

JOHN XXIII: *Mater et Magistra (1961)*

Part One of the new social encyclical summarizes the teachings of *Rerum Novarum* and "opportune developments" in the 1931 document of Pius XI and the teachings of Pius XII. It repeats the condemnation of economic liberalism, contained in the 1891 encyclical letter, with its "law of the strongest"—now termed a "naturalistic" viewpoint that denies "any relation between economic activity and morality." It is stated that "both competition in the liberal sense and the class struggle in the Marxist sense are contrary to nature and the Christian conception of life."

In his summary of the two foregoing social encyclicals, John XXIII of course made provision for the right of private property. "Private property, including that of productive goods, is a natural right which the state cannot suppress." *Rerum Novarum* did *not* affirm the right of private property, as did *Quadragesimo Anno,* that "embedded *within it is a social function,* and it is, thus, a right that is exercised for one's personal benefit and for the good of others." This was a *use* of possessions extrinsically added to private property by charity and a "social nature" was not yet "embedded in" property itself. Thus, *Quadragesimo Anno,* far the greater encyclical, alone should be regarded as a true progenitor of the present one. John XXIII mentioned property again in passing reference to this feature of the 1931 encyclical's teaching: "Concerning private property, our predecessor reaffirms its natural law character and emphasizes its social aspect with its corresponding function." That was first affirmed in 1931. This is important to note, because it is only on the basis of a social function embedded in property itself that there can be derived a *positive* function *of the state* in directing the uses of privately owned property to the common good.

John XXIII also singled out from *Quadragesimo Anno* the suggestion that "the contract of work be modified by elements taken from the contract of partnership, in such a way that 'the wage earners are made sharers in some sort in the ownership, or the management, or the profits.' " He further employs the governing concept of that encyclical which requires that the social order be tested by the standard of "social justice and social charity." Indeed, these ideas are made controlling in *Mater et Magistra* and are extended in their application. Thus, the more recent encyclical may be regarded as a footnote to *Quadragesimo Anno* (1931), but not to *Rerum Novarum* (1891).

Between the 1931 and the 1961 encyclical, there was also the Radio Message of Pius XII on Pentecost of 1941 commemorating the fiftieth anniversary of *Rerum Novarum.* The Roman Pontiff followed *Quadragesimo Anno* in going quite beyond the Leonine encyclical and in adopting a much more positive idea of the common good in relation to property. Therefore *Mater et Magistra* had only to summarize Pius XII's teachings, and advance them thus:

> In the objective order established by God, the right to property should be so arranged that it is not an obstacle to the satisfaction of "the unquestionable need that the goods, which were created by God for all men, should flow equally to all, according to the principles of justice and charity."

Of Part Two of John's social encyclical, entitled "Explanation and Development of the Teaching in *Rerum Novarum,*" the thing clearly to be noted is that this section contains far more "development" than "explanation." The reader of encyclicals simply has to grow accustomed to the proclivity of Pontiffs to say of tradition, "it is our present teaching, only applied more exactly."

Be that as it may, the first thing to notice is that, unlike the previous social encyclicals and John's own summaries of them, this section of constructive "explanation and development" conspicuously delays to take up the subject of private property. It does not premise discussion on the right of private property; but, following Pius XI and Pius XII, but not Leo, it proceeds to elaborate more and more the intrinsic social function and import of property, and the state's positive role in securing social justice, and to articulate more fully a notion of the common good through common use. Private property is treated extensively only toward the end of this section—and, seemingly, to allay doubt that this traditional teaching is reconfirmed, or that it might no longer be needed.

The prominence formerly given to the treatment of private property is now accorded (and this serves the same purpose) to the view that "the economic order is the creation of *personal initiative.*" At the same time, "the principle of subsidiarity" now displaces property in insuring that personal initiative by individuals and associations of individuals will not be extinguished by the state.

In the line of social encyclicals, the principle of subsidiarity was first used in *Rerum Novarum* (1891), where its formulation was quite negative. It acknowledged that the state is required to stand ready to restrain gross social evils. So it held that in invoking "the aid and authority of the law," our principle should be that "the law must not undertake more, nor proceed further, than is required for the remedy of the evil or the removal of the mischief." By contrast, in the 1931 encyclical—and in connection with the more positive function of the state in directing the economy toward the common good—this warning or limit becomes a principle protecting personal initiative and the initiative of associations of persons in their subsidiarity, or independence in subordination to state initiative. It was from the later and not the earlier encyclical that John XXIII quoted, endorsing this "principle of social philosophy, unshaken and unchangeable." He wrote as follows:

> Just as it is wrong to withdraw from the individual and commit to the community at large what private enterprise and industry can accomplish, so too it is an injustice, a grave evil and a disturbance of right order for a larger and higher organization to arrogate to itself functions which can be performed efficiently by smaller and lower bodies. Of its very nature, the true aim of all social activity should be to help individual members of the social body, but never to destroy or absorb them.

So *Mater et Magistra* observes that public authorities, impelled as they are "to exercise in the field of economics a multiform action, at once more vast, more profound and more organic," still ought not "reduce evermore the sphere of freedom of the personal initiative of individual citizens," or of "lesser corporations" within society.

Clearly it is now the principle of subsidiarity that is appealed to for the preservation of personal and group initiative below the state level, and not merely private property, as in the 1891 encyclical.

Moreover, John XXIII did not follow the 1931 encyclical in simply reasoning to a social function of property more basic to its nature than derives to it through charity. It is *the person* who is both private and social in nature, not first of all his property. Personal initiative has first of all both the end of perfecting the individual and contributing to social justice. For this reason the statesman should direct initiative at all levels to the supreme temporal end of social justice and the common good in accord with the principle of subsidiarity among diverse agencies of economic initiative. These would include associations or "intermediary bodies" within the state. It is because of the central importance of this revised version of the principle of subsidiarity that the latest encyclical can accept degrees of "socialization" in modern life (which means "the progressive multiplication of relations in society") that doubtless would have been condemned by Leo XIII as invasions of private property and "emphatically unjust" threats to the independence of the individual.

Therefore Pope John referred to "an *innate exigency* in human nature," not in order to argue as did Leo XIII for the natural right of mere ownership, but to argue that this "demands that when men are engaged in productive activity, they have the opportunity of employing their own responsibility and perfecting their own being." This innate exigency in human nature also provided the ground for John's acceptance and more extended application of Pius XI's suggestion that elements of the "contract of partnership" be used to modify the "contract of labor." It is some form of *par-*

ticipation as partners in economic enterprise in which they are engaged, and not in mere ownership of things, that will enable workers to perfect themselves and express fully their initiative and their humanity. Men can in this way be enabled to "unfold their proper activity" in the economic order.

Of course this means that, especially in a rapidly expanding economy where companies are enlarging their productive endeavors "by means of self-financing," that workers who also have helped to make this possible will be deprived of something of their "own" unless they acquire shares in such companies. Doubtless this entails the natural justice of a man's owning some part of the enterprise which, by his labor, he has helped to build and upon which he has impressed his individuality. As the way of unfolding man's proper personality, the emphasis is placed upon partnership in the *direction* of enterprises rather than upon mere ownership.

This weighty shift of emphasis has equal relevance to public enterprises. Without specifying just how this should be accomplished, it is suggested that elements from the "contract of partnership" need to be appropriated. Likewise it is declared that "the problem of the participation of the workers is an ever present one, whether the enterprise is private or public." And, further, it is said that "every effort should be made that the enterprise become *a community of persons* in the dealings, activities and standing of all its members." It will be a more "humane environment that encourages the working classes to assume greater responsibility within enterprises."

With this end in view, *Mater et Magistra* calls attention to the fact that "it is not the decisions made within the individual productive units which are those that have the greatest bearing" upon human fulfillment and responsibility. *Mater et Magistra* goes further and makes its most extensive application of the principle of partnership in the following words:

> Instead it is those made by public authorities or by institutions that act on a world-wide, regional or national scale in regard to some economic sector or category of production. Hence the appropriateness or imperativeness that among such authorities or institutions, besides the holders of capital or the representatives of their interests, the workers also or those who represent their rights, demands and aspiration should have their say.

We have now come to the latest development of Catholic social thought. It has moved from the simple right of labor unions and a slight but necessary modification of "the contract of labor" all the way to the participation of working men in the policy decisions that affect the "universal common good." If this is economy, it is political economy; and the possibility of accomplishing these goals is, one would suppose, the problem of democratic participation in state decisions that take positive initiative, in accord with the subsidiarity of lesser initiatives, to direct the economy toward both the national and the universal common good.

And now we must observe that, only after all the foregoing had been established, did John XXIII take up the matter of private property in his construction of Christian social principles. Not only the location of the discussion of this "natural right" but also the substance of what is said about it make evident the radical change that has taken place in Catholic social teachings. We are told: "Today, men strive to acquire professional training rather than to become owners of property," and "they have greater confidence in income derived from work or rights founded on work than in income derived from capital or rights founded on capital." Moreover, "this is in conformity with the preëminent position of work, as the immediate expression of the individual against capital, a good by nature instrumental." Not only capital, we might add, but also property in other forms is an instrumental good further removed from the person than his daily work. We must, however, remind ourselves that in the "tradition," the right of ownership was argued on the premise that *things* most immediately received the impress of a man's industry and personality, and so become his own. Pope John's finding as to the moral law and his finding as to economic facts in the present day seem now to have diminished or subordinated man's dominion over nature in coming to possess some portion of it.

The person within the common good, the person and his work or economic activity, now occupy the center of the stage; and, as we have seen, the principles governing a good economic order are social justice, subsidiarity of personal and group initiatives, and manifold attempts at partnership in the *direction* or determination of economic affairs. To be sure, John XXIII pointed out that the facets of the present economic world (doubtless including the "managerial revolution" which rendered *direction* more fundamental than *ownership*) "have certainly contributed to spreading doubt that a principle of economic and social order consistently taught by our predecessors has diminished or lost its importance, namely the principle of the natural right of private ownership, inclusive of productive goods." Thus, as it were, crabwise, the late Pope backed into a discussion of private property as a right of man and strove to reformulate Catholic social teachings while not seeming so to do. Thus, as Lord Acton once observed, tradition is constrained to produce what it never had to preserve.

"There is no reason for such a doubt to persist," the Pope affirmed. Despite the protest, what the present encyclical declares strongly supports the conclusion that such a departure has in fact been made. "The right of private ownership of goods . . . has a permanent validity precisely because it is a natural right founded on the ontological and finalistic priority of individual human beings as compared with society." But plainly this too locates property within the social context of the person and the common good. Quite plainly, also, the older argument for the right of private property was based on the ontological and finalistic priority of the individual as compared with physical nature, into which each individual by his industry puts a part of himself and so makes it his own. To be sure, in this view common use was effected first by charity and then by the cautious development of concepts of social justice and eventually by more positive state action. But there is altogether a different context for the treatment of property when the priority of individual human beings in societal context is stressed. Then, it is a question of the freedom of personal initiative in comparison with social initiative, as in the principle of subsidiarity. It is a question of a person unfolding himself by means of his initiative and work involving, again, the principle of partnership and participation in the *direction* of enterprises. Therewith, it is a question of the person sharing in the common good in such a way that the common good flows back upon each of its members. This is to be not only in material benefits and by sharing ownership but also by sharing in a community of persons engaged in its own self-direction toward temporal ends.

Within this context, it is true, a right of private property may be *derived.* So it is said, "It would be useless to insist on free and personal initiative in the economic field if the same initiative were not permitted to dispose freely of the means indispensable to its achievement." But this is a *derivation,* it would seem, of a right of private ownership. It is not a social theory initially based upon an ontological argument for the inherent and natural right of private property. Moreover, *what* is really derived is the natural justice of a man's sharing in the *direction* of things (which may or may not require ownership) and freedom in the disposal of his person and work and its fruits. In the classical argument, private appropriation and possession were prior and fundamental. The root problem, then, was to bring about common use on the basis of private right. Now, both in theory and fact, it seems to be recognized that the *use* of property, whether we like it or not, is incurably social or common. And now the "trick" is to bring about equitable private or personal participation in that common use. This now gives content to the norm of social justice, and defines a *good* common good.

The way in which this can be achieved is not, in the main, by keeping the state from extinguishing private ownership, although that follows too. It is by keeping the state from extinguishing personal initiative in the *direction* of things and by urging it, in accord with the principle of subsidiarity, to nurture such initiative and partnership in the (now incurably) political and fully socialized economy. We must, therefore, accept only *cum grano salis* the Pope's statement reaffirming the natural right of private ownership:

> It is incomprehensible how the innate character of a right can be called into question when it has as its main source the fruitfulness of work and is continually fomented by the same thing, when it is a right that constitutes an apt means to assert one's personality and to exercise responsibility in every field and an element of solidarity and of security for family life and of the peaceful and orderly development of society.

Concerning the first of the reasons here adduced for the innateness of this right, it may be observed that, in classical Catholic economic theory, while private property was the *fruit* of work, it did not have its main source in the *fruitfulness* of work nor did it have to be continually fomented. Concerning the second reason adduced, it must be said that the right of property was never so much an apt means to assert one's personality as it was an apt result of having asserted it in gaining dominion over nature. Catholic social teachings have thus now achieved more dynamic and realistic formulation by giving primacy, not to the innate natural right of ownership, but to the principles we have exhibited in the analysis of the common good in *Mater et Magistra.* These principles root in the relation of the person and his work to the common good, to the universal common good, and to God above him rather than in the relation of the person and his work to physical nature beneath him. In the Pope's own excellent summary:

> The fundamental principle . . . is, as is seen from what has thus far been said, that individual human beings are and should be the foundation, the end, and the subjects of all the institutions in which social life is carried on, that is, individual human souls *considered insofar as they are and should be* by their *nature intrinsically social* and insofar as they exist in the plan of Providence, and by their elevation to the supernatural order.

Not without this teleology, it may be said in conclusion, that is, not without viewing man as elevated by grace, can "social charity" become the soul of "social justice." Not without it can it be necessary always and everywhere to affirm that the common good should flow back and include all persons, or the national common good find sufficient reason for extension into the "universal common good" for serving the solidarity of all mankind.

A Protestant Response to the Authority of Encyclicals for Catholic Action

Two points remain to be noted in *Mater et Magistra,* namely, the authority of an encyclical and the Pope's remarks aimed at eliciting concrete response in action to its teachings: When "the Christianization of the economic and social sectors of the temporal order" is at stake, Catholics are warned that, after the instruction given them by the encyclical, "they should not exhaust themselves in interminable discussion and, under pretext of the better or the best, omit to do the good that is possible and is thus obligatory." These teachings are to be disseminated through every available instrumentality. Catholics everywhere are to be taught to "look, judge, act" in these terms; and moreover their "education is also carried on through action." The "Apostolate of the Laity" has special responsibility in addressing itself to social questions along Christian lines. These teachings are "not merely abstract ideas" but "something to be translated into deeds," and "reduced to action."

Here precisely, in its bearing on lay action, the authority of the encyclical is clearly stated:

> When the Hierarchy has made a decision on the point at issue, Catholics are bound to obey their directives, because the Church has the right and obligation not merely to guard ethical and religious principles, but also to intervene authoritatively in the temporal sphere when it is a matter of judging the application of these principles to concrete cases.

While laymen are to exercise their own professionally qualified judgments in spheres where they are expert,

> it is equally necessary, however, that they act within the framework of the principles and directives of Christian social teaching and in an attitude of loyal trust and filial obedience to ecclesiastical authority. Let them remember that when, in the execution of temporal affairs, they do not follow the principles and directives of Christian social teaching, not only do they fail in their obligations and often violate the rights of their brethren, but they can even cast into discredit that very doctrine which, in spite of its intrinsic value, seems to be lacking in a truly directive power.

Clearly, the "directive power" of these teachings for the laity "in the formation of institutions that in their finality are temporal" flows not only from their "intrinsic value" but also from the extrinsic authority of the Church that teaches them in the name of Truth.

It is fashionable to say that an encyclical is "not infallible" or "not necessarily infallible" and to conclude from this that after an encyclical has been issued Catholic opinion and action can properly vary as widely as before. This is often claimed to be the difference between an encyclical and the pronouncement of dogma. The latter is infallible and absolutely binding for the Catholic conscience. But Catholic thought is nothing if not exact in the expression of its meaning. "Not infallible" does not mean any the less authoritative. A dogma is unreformable; the truth it states always was true and will always remain true. In contrast, through encyclicals on the social question, directed to that area of coincidence between public questions and matters of faith and morals, the Church teaches not infallibly but no less authoritatively.

These teachings are, of course, reformable. They may and do develop and change, as we have seen, in the course of time. They are refined in meaning and extended in application. But this does not diminish their authority for Roman Catholic conscience. As said the *Catholic Encyclopaedia* concerning the *Syllabus of Errors* (an encyclical):

> Even should the condemnation of many propositions not possess that unchangeableness peculiar to infallible decisions, nevertheless the binding force of the condemnation in regard to all propositions is beyond doubt. . . . All Catholics, therefore, are bound to accept the Syllabus. Exteriorly, they may neither in word nor in writing oppose its contents; they must also assent to it interiorly.

And Pius XII turned aside in his encyclical *Humani Generis* (August 21, 1950) to reflect on the authority of an encyclical letter as follows:

> Nor must it be thought that what is expounded in encyclical letters does not itself demand consent, on the pretext that in writing such letters the Popes do not exercise the supreme power of their teaching authority. . . . If the supreme Pontiffs in their official documents purposely pass judgment on a matter up to that time under dispute, it is obvious that the matter according to the mind and will of the same Pontiffs, cannot be any longer considered a question open to discussion among theologians.

We need not pause to comment on the circularity of statements in an encyclical letter which must be given interior and exterior assent before it follows that Catholics must assent interiorly and exteriorly to all its propositions. In addition to the foregoing explanation of the meaning of "not infallible," it ought also to be understood that by the expression "not *necessarily* infallible" an additional degree of authority is, in fact, secured. For this means that even in encyclicals the Pontiff *may* be uttering not only authoritative changeable teaching but unchanging truth as well.

That aspects of the social question fall within the area of authoritative teaching on "faith and morals" ("republishing" the law of nature or the rational moral law) was long ago made plain in *Quadragesimo Anno* (1931):

> It is Our right and Our duty to deal authoritatively with social and economic questions. . . . [The Church] never can relinquish her God-given task of interposing her authority, *not indeed in technical matters,* for which she has neither the equipment nor the mission, but in *all those*

> *that have a bearing on moral conduct.* For the deposit of truth entrusted to Us by God, and Our weighty office of propagating, interpreting and urging in season and out of season *the entire moral law,* demand that *both social and economic questions* be brought within Our supreme jurisdiction, *in so far as they refer to moral issues.*

In claiming this jurisdiction the supreme Pontiffs must necessarily be the ones who determine *whether* and *what* economic and social questions are closely enough related to moral issues that they may rule authoritatively upon them.

Mater et Magistra takes long steps forward in defining Roman Catholic social doctrine. We may henceforth regard the category of the "universal common good," and the specific principles for the direction of action to this grand end, contained in the present encyclical, as authoritatively binding Catholic thought and action. This is involved when the Pope speaks to and for the whole Roman church. This is involved in "the review" which John XXIII "in union with you . . . has been able to make of the various problems of modern social life," with its statements and resolves "for the direction of Catholic action." The most astonishing thing is not the act of claiming to speak to mankind with such authority, but the act which John XXIII, a humble Christian man, had to perform the next moment, namely, his act of believing, as an obedient son and servant of the Church, that he had just uttered "not necessarily infallible" statements fully binding on his own conscience.

Protestants are bound to have mixed feelings toward the extrinsic authority now placed behind social teachings many of which they heartily applaud—which, indeed, they themselves have been enunciating for quite some time. No matter how much we admire the political theory of Jacques Maritain, for example, and despite the fact that we have learned much and shall continue to learn from him, puzzlement and doubt cannot but be cast over the whole of his "liberal" Catholic thought by the fact that it all sprang from a re-examination of the errors of a right-wing movement with which he was associated as a young man. To such a re-examination he was driven simply by giving interior assent, as Maritain declares, to "the liberating intervention of the Church which, in 1926, exposed the errors of Action Française, following which," he says, "I finally examined Maurras' doctrines and saw what they were worth."[3] What would Maritain have been had his church intervened in the temporal order on the other side?

A similar question pertains to the whole course of modern Roman Catholic

---

[3] Joseph W. Evans and Leo R. Ward, eds., *The Social and Political Philosophy of Jacques Maritain* (New York: Scribner's, 1955), ix, quoting from his diary in the Foreword.

social teachings. When appropriate tribute to the intrinsic greatness of these teachings has been made, one can only greet with a certain sadness the liberal thought and action of fellow Christians whose minds have been formed and their wise action directed by an unearthly earthly authority. It is rather like social morality by permission, certainly by authoritative interpretation! Nevertheless, we should be thankful for blessings even when mixed. New strength and wisdom may now be infused into the policies of nations, for the stormy years ahead, by the bold lead given them by John XXIII. We may regret (as did the Jesuit weekly *America*) the fact that *Mater et Magistra* contained no reference to the problem of race relations, since this is certainly a domestic issue that has also ominous international implications. We may also regret that the encyclical departed so far from the two foregoing social encyclicals in not carrying forward Catholic teaching with regard to the *present* condition of the *industrial* working class.

If, however, the teaching of *Mater et Magistra* is spread abroad in this land, and "reduced to action," may not Protestants also hope for a recession of the do-it-yourself McCarthyism that is widespread and still virulent in its attack on local, state, and national Councils of Churches for the leadership they have given toward the formation of national policy in the light of the universal common good and the solidarity of all mankind? This do-it-yourself McCarthyism continues potent if somewhat disconnected; and it cannot be denied that it has often persisted with the complicity of clerical silence and the silence of the Catholic press. While none should adopt wrong means to some good end, it may be that God Himself can bring many good things to pass out of an intrinsically deplorable obeisance to ecclesiastical positivism; and the lordship of Christ alone over the consciences of men may even be exerted where it is most clearly denied.

A Select Bibliography of Robert Lowry Calhoun's Writings

Compiled by RAYMOND P. MORRIS
Librarian, Professor of Religious Literature
and Jane E. McFarland, *Reference Librarian*
The Divinity School, Yale University
New Haven, Connecticut

Books and Brochures

God and the Common Life. New York: Charles Scribner's Sons, 1935, pp. 303. (Reissued as a reprint, with added foreword by the author, Hamden, Conn.: The Shoe String Press [1954], pp. xxiv, 303.)
"First prepared for delivery as the Nathaniel W. Taylor lectures at Yale University, in April, 1934."

God and the Day's Work; Christian Vocation in an Unchristian World. New York: Association Press, 1943, pp. 74. (Reissued as an Association Press Reflection Book [1957], pp. 128.)

The Good News of God. Pamphlet prepared for a special Commission on Evangelism, National Council of Churches, presented to the General Board Meeting in the Spring of 1957, and to the Biennial Meeting of the Council in December, 1957. National Council of Churches, 1957, pp. 23.

What is Man? New York: Association Press (Hazen Books on Religion), 1939, 1947, pp. 76. (Reissued as a reprint in *God, Jesus, and Man.* New York: Association Press [1953].)
The reprint forms part of a work comprising these Hazen book classics: *God,* by Walter M. Horton; *Jesus,* by Mary Ely Lyman; *What is Man?* by Robert Lowry Calhoun.

Contributions to Edited Works

"Christ and the Church," *The Nature of the Unity We Seek,* ed. Paul S. Minear. St. Louis: Bethany Press, 1958, pp. 52–78.
"Official Report of the North American Conference on Faith and Order, September 3–10, 1957, Oberlin, Ohio."

"Church, State and Human Devotion," *Church and State in the Modern World.* New York: Harper, 1937, pp. 43–82.
Contains the lectures for 1937 of the Rauschenbusch Lectureship Foundation of the Colgate-Rochester Divinity School, Rochester, N.Y.

"The Dilemma of Humanitarian Modernism," *The Christian Understanding of Man,* by T. E. Jessop, R. L. Calhoun, N. Alexeiev [and others]. London: G. Allen & Unwin [1938], pp. 45–81.

"The Gospel for This World," *Making the Gospel Effective,* ed. William K. Anderson. Nashville: Commission on Ministerial Training, The Methodist Church [c1945], pp. 25–34.

"The Historical Relations Between Religion and Intellectual Freedom," *Religion and Freedom of Thought,* by Perry Miller [and others]. Garden City, N.Y.: Doubleday, 1954, pp. 24–45.

"History of Philosophy," *College Reading and Religion; A Survey of College Reading Materials,* sponsored by the Edward W. Hazen Foundation and the Committee on Religion and Education of the American Council on Education. New Haven: Yale University Press, 1948, pp. 1–27.

"The Language of Religion," *The Unity of Knowledge,* by Lewis Leary. Garden City, N.Y.: Doubleday, 1955 (Columbia University Bicentennial Conference Series, 1), pp. 248–262.

"A Liberal Bandaged but Unbowed," *The Christian Century Reader, Representative Articles, Editorials, and Poems Selected from More Than Fifty Years of the Christian Century,* by Harold E. Fey and Margaret Frakes. New York: Association Press [1962], pp. 113–122.

"The Place of Language in Religion," *Philosophy of Religion, A Book of Readings,* ed. George Abernethy and Thomas A. Langford. New York: Macmillan [1962], pp. 296–318.

"From Robert L. Calhoun, 'The Language of Religion,'" *The Unity of Knowledge,* ed. Lewis Leary . . . pp. 252–262."

"The Place of Religion in Higher Education," *Religion and the Modern World,* by Jacques Maritain, Joseph L. Hromadka, William J. McGarry [and others] . . . Philadelphia: University of Pennsylvania Press, 1941, pp. 63–71.

University of Pennsylvania Bicentennial Conference.

"Plato as Religious Realist," *Religious Realism,* ed. Douglas Clyde Macintosh . . . New York: Macmillan, 1931, pp. 193–251.

"The Semi-Detached Knower," *The Nature of Religious Experience, Essays in Honor of Douglas Clyde Macintosh,* ed. Eugene Garrett Bewkes, Julius Seelye Bixler, R. L. Calhoun [and others]. New York: Harper, 1937, pp. 156–183.

"Theology and the Humanities," *The Meaning of the Humanities: Five Essays,* by Ralph Barton Perry, August Charles Krey, Erwin Panofsky, Robert Lowry Calhoun, Gilbert Chinard, [and] introd. by Theodore Meyer Greene. Princeton: Princeton University Press; London: H. Milford, Oxford University Press, 1938, pp. 119–150.

Contains the Spencer Trask Lectures for 1937–38.

"Work and Vocation in Christian History," *Work and Vocation: A Christian Discussion,* ed. John Oliver Nelson. New York: Harper [1954], pp. 82–115.

"Work as Christian Vocation Today," *Work and Vocation: A Christian Discussion,* ed. John Oliver Nelson. New York: Harper [1954], pp. 159–185.

"Worship and the Roots of Living," *Contemporary Religious Thought,* comp. Thomas S. Kepler. New York and Nashville: Abingdon [c1941], pp. 279–283.
"From *God and the Common Life,"* New York, 1935, pp. 237–250.
"Worship and Work," *Interpreting Religion,* by Donald Walhout. Englewood Cliffs, N.J.: Prentice-Hall, 1963, pp. 287–291.
"From . . . *God and the Day's Work,"* Reflection Books edition. New York: Association Press, 1957, pp. 98–108, 113–114.

Contributions to Periodicals

"Atomic War and the Christian Faith," *Social Action,* Supplement Issue (April, 1946), pp. 24.
Federal Council of the Churches of Christ in America. Commission on the Relation of the Church to the War in the Light of the Christian Faith.
"Building for the Future," *Social Action,* VII:9 (1941), pp. [5]–6.
"Christ and the Church," *Brethren Life and Thought,* III (1958), pp. [39]–63.
"This was a major address at Oberlin" (Oberlin Faith and Order Conference, The Nature of the Unity We Seek).
"Christ-the Hope of the World," *The Ecumenical Review,* VII:2 (1955), pp. 140–150.
"Christ the Hope of the World: Issues Confronting the 1954 World Council Assembly—V," *The Christian Century,* LXX:49 (1953), pp. 1418–1420.
"Christ—the Hope of the World; Opening Addresses at the Second Assembly of the World Council of Churches, Northwestern University, Evanston, Illinois, August 15, 1954," *The Christian Century,* LXXI:34 (1953), pp. 1005–7, 1011.
"Christian Conscience and the State" (with Roland Herbert Bainton), *Social Action,* VI:8 (1940), pp. 4-41.
"Christian Faith and World Order" (with John C. Bennett and Theodore C. Hume), *Social Action,* VIII:6 (1942), pp. 12–37.
"Churches and the Church," *The Intercollegian,* XLV:8 (1928), pp. 221, 222, 232.
"Cristo a Experança do Munde," *Testimonium,* II (1954), pp. 63–68.
"The Day's Work as Christian Vocation," *Social Action,* XV:13 (1949), pp. 13–20.
"Democracy and Natural Law," *Natural Law Forum,* V (1960), pp. 31–69.
"Evanston—an American Evaluation," *The Christian Century,* LXXII:1 (1955), pp. 14–15.
"A Final Statement," *Christendom,* II:2 (1937), pp. 215–218.
"God as More than Mind," *Christendom,* I:2 (1936), pp. 333–349.
"God in a Growing World," *The Intercollegian,* XLV:5 (1928), pp. 132–133, 136.
"Historical Signposts Point the Way," *Social Action,* IX:5 (1943), pp. 5–6.
"How Far Beyond Humanism?" *Christendom,* III:4 (1938), pp. 554–565.
"How Shall We Think of God?" *Christendom,* I:4 (1936), pp. 593–611.

"International Prayer Meeting," *The Christian Century,* LIX:10 (1942), pp. 319.

"Long Step Forward; First and Second Interpretation" (with Robert S. Bilheimer), *Christianity and Crisis,* XII (1952), pp. 130–133.

"Moral Obligation and Religious Conviction," *Confluence,* IV (1955), pp. 174–193.

"The Place of Religion in Higher Education," *Yale Divinity News,* XXXVII:4 (1941), pp. 1–3.

"This contains excerpts from an address given at the University of Pennsylvania Bicentennial Conference."

"The Power of God and the Wisdom of God," *Christendom,* II:1 (1937), pp. 36–49.

"Reason and Revelation in Religious Knowledge," *Harvard Divinity School Bulletin,* XXIII (1957–58), pp. [27]–46.

"The Dudleian lecture for the academic year 1957–58, Harvard University—Delivered at Andover Chapel, January 31, 1957."

"The Redemption of Time," *Yale Divinity News* (May, 1959), pp. 3–10.

"An article by Professor Calhoun based on his talks in Marquand Chapel, Yale Divinity School."

"The Relation of the Church to the War in the Light of the Christian Faith," *Social Action,* X:10 (1944), pp. 5–79.

This is a Report of the Council for Social Action of the Congregational Christian Churches of which Robert Lowry Calhoun was chairman and a member of the committee making the final revision of the written report.

"Religion and Marxism: a Conflict?" *The Modern Monthly,* IX (1935), pp. 23–27.

"Religion: Prose or Poetry," *The Intercollegian,* XLV:2 (1927), pp. 25–26, 34, 37.

"Revelation through Jesus Christ," *The Intercollegian,* XLV:4 (1928), pp. 93–94, 102.

"Role of Historical Theology," *The Journal of Religion,* XXI:4 (1941), pp. 444–454.

"Science and Religion," *Yale Divinity News* (January, 1960), pp. 3–21.

A Dialogue between scientists and theologians as it took place at a Yale Divinity School Convocation. Telescoped version.

"Sin, Pain, and Healing," *The Intercollegian,* XLV:6 (1928), pp. 157–158, 164.

"Taking Evolution Seriously," *The Intercollegian,* XLV:3 (1927), pp. 61–62, 66.

"A Task for Protestantism:—a Christian Doctrine of World Order," *Social Action,* VIII:6 (1942), pp. [5]–12.

"Theology in Strenuous Days," *The Intercollegian,* XLV:1 (1927), pp. 4–6.

"Thought and Action in Religious Living," *The Journal of Religion,* XXII:2 (1942), pp. 125–136.

"Torches of the Spirit," *The Intercollegian,* XLV:7 (1928), pp. 192–193, 197.

"The Way toward Religion," *The Intercollegian,* XLV:9 (1928), pp. 255–256, 258.

"Upon Dean Weigle's Retirement," *Yale Divinity News,* XLIV:[3] (1949), pp. 1–3.
"What Sort of Unity Do We Want?" *The Student World,* XXXI:1 (1938), pp. 15–26.

Unpublished Manuscripts by Robert Lowry Calhoun

An Introduction to the Philosophy of Thomas Davidson. Ph.D. dissertation, Yale University, 1923.
Lectures on the History of Christian Doctrine. New Haven: Printed Privately for Private Circulation, 1947.
There have been other printings of this in 1949 and 1957, the first and third occurring in 3 volumes, the other in one volume.
Lectures on the History of Philosophy. New Haven: Printed Privately for Private Circulation [c1958].
Reproduction made by Carl Nelson from lectures at Yale Divinity School, 1950–1951.
Lewis French Stearns Lectures in Theology, at Bangor Theological Seminary, 1956; Dudleian Lecture, Harvard Divinity School, 1957; Ayer Lectures in Theology, at Colgate-Rochester Divinity School, 1958; Danforth Lectures in Theology, at Cornell University, 1958.

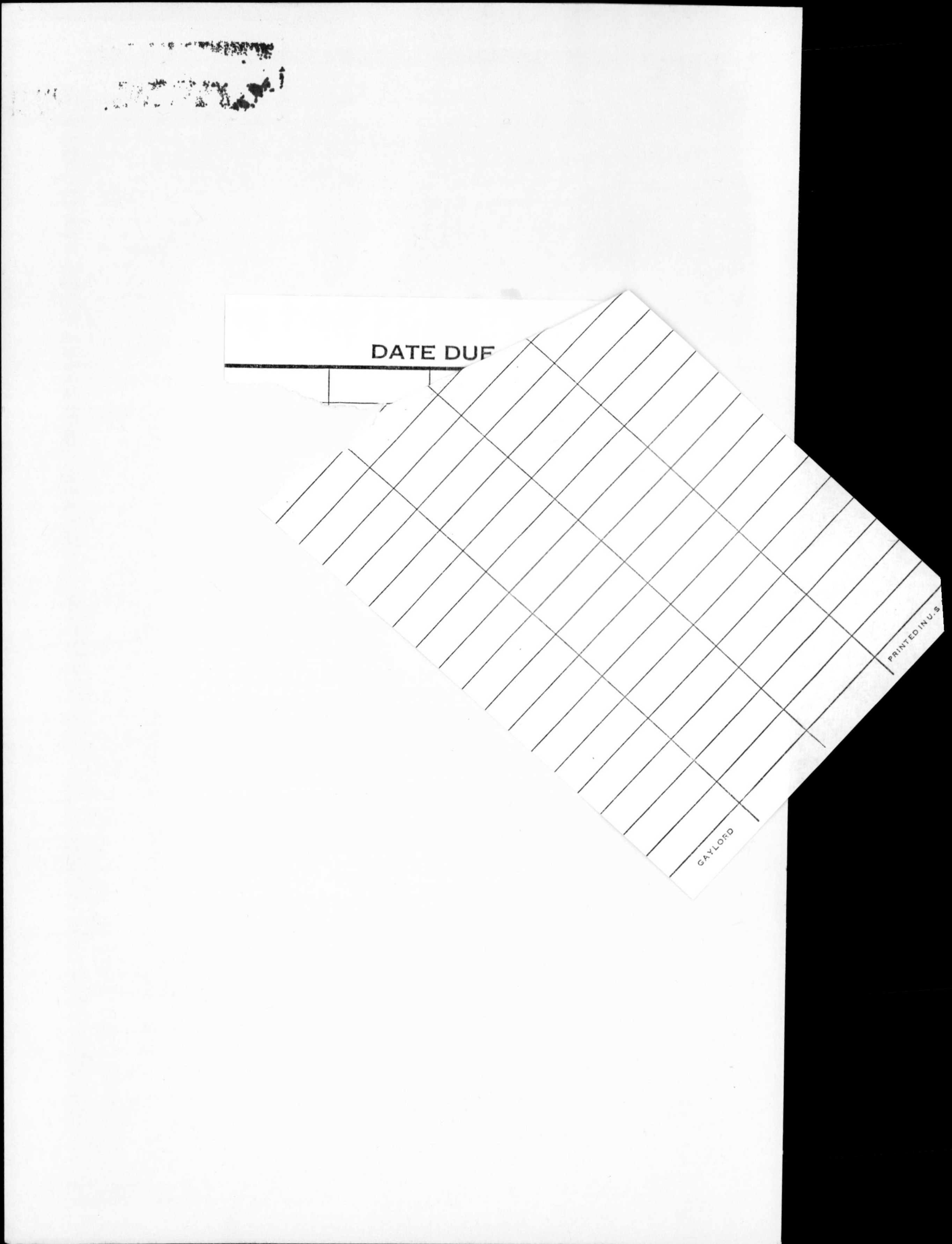